Reader's Guide
to
SAMUEL JOHNSON

Reader's Guide to SAMUEL JOHNSON

S. Dorsch

CENTRUM PRESS
NEW DELHI-110002 (INDIA)

CENTRUM PRESS
H.O.: 4360/4, Ansari Road, Daryaganj,
New Delhi-110 002 (India)
Ph.: 23278000, 23261597

B.O.: No. 1015, Ist Main Road, BSK IIIrd Stage
IIIrd Phase, IIIrd Block,
Bangalore - 560 085 (India)
Tel.: 080-41723429
Visit us at: www.centrumpress.com

Reader's Guide to Samuel Johnson

First Edition, 2009

ISBN 978-93-80106-87-8

PRINTED IN INDIA

Printed at Balaji Offset, Delhi.

Contents

Preface

Johnson, born in Lichfield, England, on September 18, 1709; was not a healthy infant, and there was considerable question as to whether he would survive: he was baptized almost immediately. Johnson was scarred from scrofula, and suffered a loss of hearing and was blind in one eye, thanks largely to nursing from a tubercular nursemaid. During his toddler years, he had an open "issue" in his arm, to drain fluids. Stop for a moment, and think about a small child being singled out in this way, and what it must have meant. In spite of these infirmities, there are early tales of his independence.

Once, when his babysitter failed to pick him up on time from nursery school, Johnson decided he would get home on his own, crawling on all fours in order to see the gutter and avoid falling in. The babysitter followed at some distance, but when Johnson saw her watching, protested against her following him, vehemently. The availability of the books in his father's shop, and his natural proclivity for learning, contributed to his having extensive knowledge at an early age. When Johnson spent time with an elder cousin, he was exposed to a broad range of thinking and cultivation, of the sort he wouldn't have ordinarily seen in Lichfield. He later attended Oxford for about a year, but left for financial reasons.

His poverty at Oxford was noticed by another student, who left a pair of new shoes outside Johnson's door during the night; while Johnson's poverty was itself humiliating, the fact that another would notice and make Johnson a beneficiary of charity enraged him. So Johnson had to leave Oxford; it must have been a horrible disappointment to someone who was so learned, to leave for financial reasons, and see his academic inferiors succeed in an arena where he couldn't. During this period he went into a severe depression; his friend Edmund Hector helped him remain productive, in spite of the depression. In 1735, Johnson married Elizabeth "Tetty" Porter, a woman several years older than him: she was 46, and he 25.

As a young man, Johnson tried his hand at a career as a schoolmaster, and was unsuccessful— largely because he didn't have a degree. To some extent, his ungainly appearance, twitches, and mannerisms made it difficult to maintain the respect of his students. He eventually (1737) went to London to seek his fortune, and found employment as a writer for various periodicals. In addition to writing book reviews and derivative biographies, at one point he was assigned the task of writing thinly disguised reports of the debates in Parliament. (Censorship ruled out actual reportage, so Johnson had to write from surreptitiously-taken notes, filling them out in much the same way as a TV movie made today might embellish a skeleton of fact into a drama. The identities of the speakers were thinly disguised; readers could tell who was who, and the government was unwilling to admit to the underlying truth.)

Chapter 1

Introduction

Samuel Johnson (often referred to as Dr Johnson) (18 September 1709 [O.S. 7 September] – 13 December 1784) was an English author. Beginning as a Grub Street journalist, he made lasting contributions to English literature as a poet, essayist, moralist, novelist, literary critic, biographer, editor and lexicographer. Johnson was a devout Anglican and political conservative, and has been described as "arguably the most distinguished man of letters in English history". He is also the subject of "the most famous single work of biographical art in the whole of literature": James Boswell's *Life of Samuel Johnson*.

Johnson was born in Lichfield, Staffordshire, and attended Pembroke College, Oxford for a year, before his lack of funds forced him to leave. After working as a teacher he moved to London, where he began to write essays for *The Gentleman's Magazine*. His early works include the biography *The Life of Richard Savage*, the poems *London* and *The Vanity of Human Wishes*, and the play *Irene*. After nine years of work, Johnson's *Dictionary of the English Language* was published in 1755; it had a far-reaching impact on Modern English and has been described as "one of the greatest single achievements of scholarship". The *Dictionary* brought Johnson popularity and success; until the completion of the *Oxford English Dictionary*, 150 years later, Johnson's was viewed as the pre-eminent British dictionary.

His later works included essays, an influential annotated edition of William Shakespeare's plays, and the widely read novel *Rasselas*. In 1763, he befriended James Boswell, with whom he later travelled to Scotland; Johnson described their travels in *A Journey to the Western Islands of Scotland*. Towards the end of his life, he produced the massive and influential *Lives of the Most Eminent English Poets*, a collection of biographies and evaluations of 17th- and 18th-century poets. Johnson had a tall and robust figure, but his odd gestures and tics were confusing to some on their first encounter with him. Boswell's *Life*, along with other biographies, documented Johnson's behaviour and mannerisms in such detail that they have informed the posthumous diagnosis of Tourette syndrome (TS), a condition unknown in the 18th century. After a series of illnesses he died on the evening of 13 December 1784, and was buried in Westminster Abbey. In the years following his death, Johnson began to be recognised as having had a lasting effect on literary criticism, and even as the only great critic of English literature.

Born on 18 September 1709 to Michael Johnson, a bookseller, and his wife, Sarah Ford, Samuel Johnson often claimed that he grew up in poverty. Since both families had money, it is uncertain what happened between Michael and Sarah's marriage and the birth of Samuel just three years later to provoke such a change in fortune. Johnson was born in the family home above his father's bookshop in Lichfield, Staffordshire and, because his mother Sarah was 40 when she gave birth, a "man-midwife" and surgeon of "great reputation" named George Hector was brought in to assist. He did not cry and, with doubts surrounding the newborn's health, his aunt claimed "that she would not have picked such a poor creature up in the street". As it was feared the baby might die, the vicar of St Mary's was summoned to perform a baptism. Two godfathers were chosen: Samuel Swynfen, a physician and graduate of Pembroke College, Oxford, and Richard Wakefield, a lawyer, coroner, and Lichfield town clerk.

Johnson's health improved and he was put to wet-nurse with Joan Marklew. He soon contracted scrofula, known at that time as the "King's Evil" because it was thought royalty could cure it. Sir John Floyer, former physician to Charles II, recommended that the young Johnson should receive the "royal touch", which he received from Queen Anne on 30 March 1712. However, the ritual was ineffective, and an operation was performed that left him with permanent scars across his face and body. With the birth of Johnson's brother, Nathaniel, a few months later, Michael was unable to keep on top of the debts he had accumulated over the years, and his family was no longer able to live in the style to which it had been accustomed.

"When he was a child in petticoats, and had learned to read, Mrs Johnson one morning put the common prayer-book into his hands, pointed to the collect for the day, and said, 'Sam, you must get this by heart.' She went up stairs, leaving him to study it: But by the time she had reached the second floor, she heard him following her. 'What's the matter?' said she. 'I can say it,' he replied; and repeated it distinctly, though he could not have read it over more than twice."

– Boswell's *Life of Samuel Johnson*

Johnson demonstrated signs of great intelligence as a child, and his parents, to his later disgust, would show off his "newly acquired accomplishments". His education began at the age of three, and came from his mother who had him memorise and recite passages from the Book of Common Prayer. When Johnson turned four, he was sent to a nearby school, and, when he reached the age of six, he was sent to a retired shoemaker to continue his education. A year later, Johnson was sent to Lichfield Grammar School, where he excelled in Latin. During this time, Johnson started to exhibit the tics that would influence how people viewed him in his later years, and which formed the basis for the posthumous diagnosis of Tourette syndrome. He excelled at his studies and was promoted to the upper school at the age of nine. During this time, he befriended Edmund Hector, nephew of his "man-midwife" George Hector, and John Taylor, with whom he remained in contact for the rest of his life.

At the age of 16, Johnson was given the opportunity to stay with his cousins, the Fords, at Pedmore, Worcestershire. There he became a close friend of Cornelius Ford, who employed his knowledge of the classics to tutor Johnson while he was not attending school. Ford was a successful, well-connected academic, but was also a notorious alcoholic whose excesses contributed to his death six years after Johnson's visit. Having spent six months with his cousins, Johnson returned to Lichfield, but Mr. Hunter, the headmaster, "angered by the impertinence of this long absence", refused to allow him to continue at the grammar school.

Unable to return to Lichfield Grammar School, Johnson was enrolled into the King Edward VI grammar school at Stourbridge. Because the school was located near Pedmore, Johnson was able to spend more time with the Fords, and he began to write poems and verse translations. However, he spent only six months at Stourbridge before returning once again to his parents' home in Lichfield.

During this time, Johnson's future was uncertain as his father was deeply in debt. To earn money, Johnson began to stitch books for his father, and it is possible that Johnson spent most of his time in his father's bookshop reading various works and building his literary knowledge. They remained in poverty until Sarah Johnson's cousin, Elizabeth Harriotts, died in February 1728 and left enough money to send Johnson to college. On 31 October 1728, a few weeks after he turned 19, Johnson entered Pembroke College, Oxford. The inheritance did not cover all of his expenses at Pembroke, but Andrew Corbet, a friend and fellow student at Pembroke, offered to make up the deficit.

Johnson made friends at Pembroke and read much. In later life, he told stories of his idleness. He was later asked by his tutor to produce a Latin translation of Alexander Pope's *Messiah* as a Christmas exercise. Johnson completed half of the translation in one afternoon and the rest the following morning. Although the poem brought him praise, it did not bring the material benefit he had hoped for. The poem later appeared in *Miscellany of Poems* (1731), edited by John Husbands, a Pembroke tutor, and is the earliest surviving publication of any of Johnson's writings. Johnson spent the rest of his time studying, even over the Christmas vacation. He drafted a "plan of study" called "Adversaria", which was left unfinished, and used his time to learn French while working on his knowledge of Greek.

After thirteen months, poverty forced Johnson to leave Oxford without a degree, and he returned to Lichfield. Towards the end of Johnson's stay at Oxford his tutor, Jorden, left Pembroke and was replaced by William Adams. He enjoyed Adams as a tutor, but by December, Johnson was already a quarter behind in his student fees, and he was forced to return home. He left behind many books that he had borrowed from his father because he could not afford to transport them and as a symbolic gesture in that he hoped to return to the school soon.

He eventually received a degree: just before the publication of his *Dictionary* in 1755, Oxford University awarded Johnson the degree of Master of Arts. He was awarded an honorary doctorate in 1765 by Trinity College Dublin and in 1775 by Oxford University. In 1776, he returned to Pembroke with Boswell and toured the college with his previous tutor Adams, who was then its Master. He used that visit to recount his time at the college, his early career, and to express his later fondness for Jorden.

Little is known about Johnson's life between the end of 1729 and 1731; it is likely that he lived with his parents. He experienced bouts of mental anguish and physical pain during years of illness; his tics and gesticulations associated with Tourette syndrome became more noticeable and were often commented upon. By 1731 Johnson's father was deeply in debt and had lost much of his standing in Lichfield. Johnson hoped to get an usher's position which became available at Stourbridge Grammar School, but as he did not have a degree his application was passed over on 6 September 1731. At about this time, Johnson's father became ill and developed an "inflammatory fever" which led to his death in December 1731. Johnson eventually found employment as undermaster at a school in Market Bosworth, run by Sir Wolstan Dixie, 4th Baronet who allowed Johnson to teach without a degree. Although Johnson was treated as a servant, he found pleasure in teaching despite thinking it boring. After an argument with

Dixie he quit the school, and by June 1732 he had returned home.

Johnson continued to look for a position at a Lichfield school. After being turned down for a position in Ashbourne, he spent his time with his friend Edmund Hector, who was living in the home of the publisher Thomas Warren. At the time Warren was starting his *Birmingham Journal*, and he enlisted Johnson's help. This connection with Warren grew, and Johnson proposed a translation of Jeronimo Lobo's account of the Abyssinians. Johnson read Abbé Joachim Le Grand's French translations, and thought that a shorter version might be "useful and profitable". Instead of writing the whole work himself, he dictated to Hector, who then took the copy to the printer and made any corrections. Johnson's *A Voyage to Abyssinia* was published a year later. He returned to Lichfield in February 1734, and began an annotated edition of Poliziano's Latin poems, along with a history of Latin poetry from Petrarch to Poliziano; a *Proposal* was soon printed, but a lack of funds halted the project.

Johnson remained with his close friend Harry Porter during a terminal illness, which culminated when Porter died on 3 September 1734, leaving his wife Elizabeth Jervis Porter (otherwise known as "Tetty") widowed at the age of 41, with three children. Some months later, Johnson began to court her. The Reverend William Shaw claims that "the first advances probably proceeded from her, as her attachment to Johnson was in opposition to the advice and desire of all her relations". Johnson was inexperienced in such relationships, but the well-to-do widow encouraged him and promised to provide for him with her substantial savings. They married on 9 July 1735, at St. Werburgh's Church in Derby. The Porter family did not approve of the match, partly because Johnson was 25 and Elizabeth was 21 years his elder, and Elizabeth's marriage to Johnson so disgusted her son Jervis that he severed relations with her. However, her daughter Lucy had accepted Johnson from the start, and her other son, Joseph, accepted the marriage later.

In June 1735, while working as a tutor for Thomas

Whitby's children, Johnson had applied for the position of headmaster at Solihull School. Although Walmesley gave his support, Johnson was passed over because the school's directors thought he was "a very haughty, ill-natured gent., and that he has such a way of distorting his face (which though he can't help) the gent[s] think it may affect some lads". With Walmesley's encouragement, Johnson decided that he could be a successful teacher if he ran his own school. In the autumn of 1735, Johnson opened Edial Hall School as a private academy at Edial, near Lichfield. He had only three pupils: Lawrence Offley, George Garrick, and the 18-year-old David Garrick, who later became one of the most famous actors of his day. The venture was unsuccessful and cost Tetty a substantial portion of her fortune. Instead of trying to keep the failing school going, Johnson began to write his first major work, the historical tragedy *Irene*.

Biographer Robert DeMaria believed that Tourette syndrome likely made public occupations like schoolmaster or tutor almost impossible for Johnson to hold; this may have led Johnson to "the invisible occupation of authorship". Johnson left for London with his former pupil David Garrick on 2 March 1737, the day Johnson's brother had died. He was penniless and pessimistic about their travel, but fortunately for them, Garrick had connections in London, and the two were able to stay with his distant relative, Richard Norris. Johnson soon moved to Greenwich near the Golden Hart Tavern to finish *Irene*.

On 12 July 1737 he wrote to Edward Cave with a proposal for a translation of Paolo Sarpi's *The History of the Council of Trent* (1619), which Cave did not accept until months later. In October 1737 Johnson brought his wife to London, and he found employment with Cave as a writer for *The Gentleman's Magazine*. His assignments for the magazine and other publishers during this time were "almost unparalleled in range and variety", and "so numerous, so varied and scattered" that "Johnson himself could not make a complete list". In May 1738 his first major work, the poem *London*, was published anonymously. Based on Juvenal's Satire III, it describes the character Thales leaving for Wales to escape the problems of London, which it portrays as a place of crime, corruption, and neglect of the poor.

Johnson could not bring himself to regard the poem as earning him any merit as a poet. Alexander Pope claimed that the author "will soon be déterré" (brought to light, become well known), but this would not happen until 15 years later. In August, Johnson's lack of an MA degree from Oxford or Cambridge led to his being denied a position as master of the Appleby Grammar School. In an effort to end such rejections, Pope asked Lord Gower to use his influence to have a degree awarded to Johnson. Gower petitioned Oxford for an honorary degree to be awarded to Johnson, but was told that it was "too much to be asked". Gower then asked a friend of Jonathan Swift to plead with Swift to use his influence at the University of Dublin to have a Masters degree awarded to Johnson, in the hope that this could then be used to justify an MA from Oxford, but Swift refused to act on Johnson's behalf.

Between 1737 and 1739, Johnson befriended Richard Savage. Feeling guilty about living on Tetty's money, Johnson stopped living with her and spent his time with Savage. They were poor and would stay in taverns or sleep in "night-cellars" except for nights that they would roam the streets because they lacked the necessary funds. Savage's friends tried to help him by attempting to persuade him to move to Wales, but Savage ended up in Bristol and again fell into debt. He was committed to debtors' prison and died in 1743. A year later, Johnson wrote *Life of Mr Richard Savage* (1744), a "moving" work which, in the words of the biographer and critic Walter Jackson Bate, "remains one of the innovative works in the history of biography".

In 1746, a group of publishers approached Johnson about creating an authoritative dictionary of the English language; a contract with William Strahan and associates, worth 1,500 guineas, was signed on the morning of 18 June 1746. Johnson claimed that he could finish the project in three years. In comparison, the Académie Française had forty scholars spending forty years to complete its dictionary, which prompted Johnson to claim, "This is the proportion. Let me see; forty times forty is sixteen hundred. As three to sixteen hundred, so is the proportion of an Englishman to a Frenchman". Although he did not succeed in completing the work in three years, he did manage to finish it in nine, justifying his boast. According to Bate, the *Dictionary* "easily ranks as one of the greatest single achievements of scholarship, and probably the greatest ever performed by one individual who labored under anything like the disadvantages in a comparable length of time".

Johnson's dictionary was not the first, nor was it unique. It was, however, the most commonly used and imitated for the 150 years between its first publication and the appearance of the *Oxford English Dictionary* in 1928. Other dictionaries, such as Nathan Bailey's *Dictionarium Britannicum,* included more words, and in the 150 years preceding Johnson's dictionary about twenty other "English" dictionaries had been produced. However, there was open dissatisfaction with the dictionaries of the period. In 1741, David Hume claimed: "The Elegance and Propriety of Stile have been very much neglected among us. We have no Dictionary of our Language, and scarce a tolerable Grammar". Johnson's *Dictionary* offers insights into the 18th century and "a faithful record of the language people used". It is more than a reference book; it is a work of literature.

For a decade, Johnson's constant work on the *Dictionary* disrupted his and Tetty's living conditions. He had to employ numerous assistants for the copying and mechanical work, which filled the house with incessant noise and clutter. He was always busy with his work, and kept hundreds of books around. John Hawkins described the scene: "The books he used for this purpose were what he had in his own collection, a copious but a miserably ragged one, and all such as he could borrow; which latter, if ever they came back to those that lent them, were so defaced as to be scarce worth owning". Johnson was also distracted by Tetty's health, as she started to show signs of a terminal illness. To accommodate both his wife and his work, he moved to Gough Square near his printer, William Strahan.

In preparation for the work, Johnson wrote a *Plan* for the *Dictionary*. This *Plan* was patronised by Philip Stanhope, 4th Earl of Chesterfield, to Johnson's displeasure. Chesterfield did not care about praise, but was interested by Johnson's abilities. Seven years after first meeting Johnson to go over the work, Chesterfield wrote two anonymous essays in *The World* recommending the *Dictionary*. He complained that the English language lacked structure and argued in support of the dictionary. Johnson did not like the tone of the essay, and he felt that Chesterfield had not fulfilled his obligations as the work's patron. Johnson wrote a letter expressing this view and harshly criticising Chesterfield, saying "Is not a patron, my lord, one who looks with unconcern on a man struggling for life in the water, and when he has reached ground, encumbers him with help? The notice which you have been pleased to take of my labours, had it been early, had been kind: but it has been delayed till I am indifferent and cannot enjoy it; till I am solitary and cannot impart it; till I am known and do not want it." However, Chesterfield accepted this without any ill will and, impressed by the language, kept the letter displayed on a table for anyone to read.

During his work on the dictionary, Johnson made many appeals for financial help in the form of subscriptions: patrons would get a copy of the first edition as soon as it was printed in compensation for their support during its compilation. The appeals ran until 1752. The *Dictionary* was finally published in April 1755, with the title page acknowledging that Oxford had awarded Johnson a Master of Arts degree in anticipation of the work. The published dictionary was a huge book. Its pages were nearly 18 inches (46 cm) tall, and the book was 20 inches (51 cm) wide when opened; it contained 42,773 entries, to which only a few more were added in subsequent editions, and sold for the extravagant price of £4 10s, the equivalent of about £350 today. An important innovation in English lexicography was to illustrate the meanings of his words by literary quotation, of which there are around 114,000. The authors most frequently cited include Shakespeare, Milton and Dryden. It was years before

"Johnson's Dictionary", as it came to be known, turned a profit. Author's royalties were unknown at that time, and Johnson, once his contract to deliver the book was fulfilled, received no further monies from its sale. Years later, many of its quotations would be repeated by various editions of the *Webster's Dictionary* and the *New English Dictionary*.

Besides working on the *Dictionary*, Johnson also wrote various essays, sermons, and poems during these nine years. He decided to produce a series of essays under the title *The Rambler* that would run every Tuesday and Saturday for twopence each. Explaining the title years later, he told his friend, the painter Joshua Reynolds: "I was at a loss how to name it. I sat down at night upon my bedside, and resolved that I would not go to sleep till I had fixed its title. *The Rambler* seemed the best that occurred, and I took it". These essays, often on moral and religious topics, tended to be more grave than the title of the series would suggest; his first comments in *The Rambler* were to ask "that in this undertaking thy Holy Spirit may not be withheld from me, but that I may promote thy glory, and the salvation of myself and others". The popularity of *The Rambler* took off once the issues were collected as a volume; they were reprinted nine times during Johnson's life. Writer and printer Samuel Richardson, enjoying the essays greatly, questioned the publisher as to who wrote the works; only he and a few of Johnson's friends were told of Johnson's authorship. One friend, the novelist Charlotte Lennox, includes a defence of *The Rambler* in her novel *The Female Quixote* (1752). In particular, the character Mr. Glanville says, "you may sit in Judgment upon the Productions of a *Young*, a *Richardson*, or a *Johnson*. Rail with premeditated Malice at the *Rambler*; and for the want of Faults, turn even its inimitable Beauties into Ridicule" (Book VI, Chapter XI). Later, she claims Johnson as "the greatest Genius in the present Age".

"His necessary attendance while his play was in rehearsal, and during its performance, brought him acquainted with many of the performers of both sexes, which produced a more favourable opinion of their profession than he had harshly expressed in his Life of Savage ... He for considerable time used to frequent the Green Room, and seemed to take delight in dissipating his gloom, by mixing in the sprightly chit-chat of the motley circle than to be found there. Mr David Hume related to me from Mr Garrick, that Johnson at last denied himself this amusement, from considerations of rigid virtue; saying, "I'll come no more behind your scenes, David; for the silk stockings and white bosoms of your actresses excite my amorous propensities"."

– Boswell's *Life of Samuel Johnson*

However, not all of his work was confined to *The Rambler*. One such work, *The Vanity of Human Wishes*, was written with such "extraordinary speed" that Boswell claimed Johnson "might have been perpetually a poet". The poem is an imitation of Juvenal's *Satire X* and claims that "the antidote to vain human wishes is non-vain spiritual wishes". In particular, Johnson emphasises "the helpless vulnerability of the individual before the social context" and the "inevitable self-deception by which human beings are led astray". The poem was critically celebrated but it failed to become popular, and sold less than *London*. In 1749, Garrick made good on his promise that he would produce *Irene*, but its title was altered to *Mahomet and Irene* to make it "fit for the stage". The show eventually ran for nine nights.

Tetty Johnson spent most of her time in London ill, and in 1752 she decided to return to the countryside while Johnson was busy working on his *Dictionary*. She died on 17 March 1752, and, at word of her death, Johnson wrote a letter to his old friend Taylor, which according to Taylor "expressed grief in the strongest manner he had ever read".

He wrote a sermon in her honour, to be read at her funeral, but Taylor refused to read it, for reasons which are unknown. This only exacerbated Johnson's feelings of being lost, and his despair after the death of his wife, and John Hawkesworth had to take over organising the funeral.

Johnson felt guilty about the poverty in which he believed he had forced Tetty to live, and blamed himself for neglecting her. He became outwardly discontent, and his diary was filled with prayers and laments over her death until his own. She was his primary motivation, and her death hindered his ability to complete his work.

On 16 March 1756, Johnson was arrested for an outstanding debt of £5 18s. Unable to contact anyone else, he wrote to the writer and publisher Samuel Richardson. Richardson, who had previously lent Johnson money, sent him six guineas to show his good will, and the two became friends. Soon after, Johnson met and befriended the painter Joshua Reynolds, who so impressed Johnson that he declared him "almost the only man whom I call a friend". Reynolds' younger sister Frances observed during their time together "that men, women and children gathered around him [Johnson], laughing" at his gestures and gesticulations. In addition to Reynolds, Johnson was close to Bennet Langton and Arthur Murphy. Langton was a scholar and an admirer of Johnson who persuaded his way into a meeting with Johnson which led to a long friendship. Johnson met Murphy during the summer of 1754 after Murphy came to Johnson about the accidental republishing of the *Rambler* No. 190, and the two became friends. Around this time, Anna Williams began boarding with Johnson. She was a minor poet who was poor and becoming blind, two conditions that Johnson attempted to change by providing room for her and paying for a failed cataract surgery. Williams, in turn, became Johnson's housekeeper.

To occupy himself, Johnson began to work on *The Literary Magazine, or Universal Review*, the first issue of which was printed on 19 March 1756. Philosophical disagreements erupted over the purpose of the publication when the Seven Years' War began and Johnson started to write polemical essays attacking the war. After the war began, the *Magazine* included many reviews, at least 34 of which were written by Johnson. When not working on the *Magazine*, Johnson wrote a series of prefaces for other writers, such as Giuseppe Baretti, William Payne and Charlotte Lennox. Johnson's relationship with Lennox and her works was particularly close during these years, and she in turn relied so heavily upon Johnson that he was "the most important single fact in Mrs Lennox's literary life". He later attempted to produce a new edition of her works, but even with his support they were unable to find enough interest to follow through with its publication. To help with domestic duties while Johnson was busy with his various projects, Richard Bathurst, a physician and a member of Johnson's Club, pressured him to take on a free slave, Francis Barber, as his servant.

These efforts, however, consumed only a small portion of his time; his work on *Edition of Shakespeare* took up the rest. On 8 June 1756, Johnson published his *Proposals for Printing, by Subscription, the Dramatick Works of William Shakespeare,* which argued that previous editions of Shakespeare were edited incorrectly and needed to be corrected. However, Johnson's progress on the work slowed as the months passed, and he told music historian Charles Burney in December 1757 that it would take him until the following March to complete it. Before that could happen, he was arrested again, for a debt of £40, in February 1758. The debt was soon repaid by Jacob Tonson, who had contracted Johnson to publish *Shakespeare,* and this encouraged Johnson to finish his edition to repay the favour. Although it took him another seven years to finish, Johnson completed a few volumes of his *Shakespeare* to prove his commitment to the project.

In 1758, Johnson began to write a weekly series, *The Idler,* which ran from 15 April 1758 to 5 April 1760, as a way to avoid finishing his *Shakespeare.* This series was shorter and lacked many features of *The Rambler*. Unlike his independent publication of *The Rambler, The Idler* was published in a weekly news journal *The Universal Chronicle,* a publication supported by John Payne, John Newbery, Robert Stevens and William Faden. Since *The Idler* did not occupy all Johnson's time, he was able to publish his philosophical novella *Rasselas* on 19 April 1759. The "little story book", as Johnson described it, describes the life of Prince Rasselas and Nekayah, his sister, who are kept in a place called the Happy Valley in the land of Abyssinia.

The Valley is a place free of problems, where any desire is quickly satisfied. The constant pleasure does not, however, lead to satisfaction; and, with the help of a philosopher named Imlac, Rasselas escapes and explores the world to witness how all aspects of society and life in the outside world are filled with suffering. They return to Abyssinia, but do not wish to return to the state of constantly fulfilled pleasures found in the Happy Valley. *Rasselas* was written in one week to pay for his mother's funeral and settle her debts; it became so popular that there was a new English edition of the work almost every year. References to it appear in many later works of fiction, including *Jane Eyre, Cranford* and *The House of the Seven Gables.* Its fame was not limited to English-speaking nations: *Rasselas* was immediately translated into five languages (French, Dutch, German, Russian and Italian), and later into nine others.

By 1762, however, Johnson had gained notoriety for his dilatoriness in writing; the contemporary poet Churchill teased Johnson for the delay in producing his long-promised edition of Shakespeare: "He for subscribers baits his hook / and takes your cash, but where's the book?" The comments soon motivated Johnson to finish his *Shakespeare,* and, after receiving the first payment from a government pension on 20 July 1762, he was able to dedicate most of his time towards this goal. Earlier that July, the 24-year-old King George III granted Johnson an annual pension of £300 in appreciation for the *Dictionary.* While the pension did not make Johnson wealthy, it did allow him a modest yet comfortable independence for the remaining 22 years of his life. The award came largely through the efforts of Sheridan and the Earl of Bute. When Johnson questioned if the pension would force him to promote a political agenda or support various officials, he was told by Bute that the pension "is not given you for anything you are to do, but for what you have done".

On 16 May 1763, Johnson first met 22-year-old James Boswell—who would later become Johnson's first major biographer—in the bookshop of Johnson's friend, Tom Davies. They quickly became friends, although Boswell would return to his home in Scotland or travel abroad for months at a time. Around the spring of 1763, Johnson formed "The Club", a social group that included his friends Reynolds, Burke,

Garrick, Goldsmith and others (the membership later expanded to include Adam Smith and Edward Gibbon). They decided to meet every Monday at 7:00 pm at the Turk's Head in Gerrard Street, Soho, and these meetings continued until long after the deaths of the original members.

"During the whole of the interview, Johnson talked to his Majesty with profound respect, but still in his firm manly manner, with a sonorous voice, and never in that subdued tone which is commonly used at the levee and in the drawing-room. After the King withdrew, Johnson shewed himself highly pleased with his Majesty's conversation and gracious behaviour. He said to Mr Barnard, 'Sir, they may talk of the King as they will; but he is the finest gentleman I have ever seen.'"

– Boswell's *Life of Samuel Johnson*

On 9 January 1765, Murphy introduced Johnson to Henry Thrale, a wealthy brewer and MP, and his wife Hester. They struck up an instant friendship; Johnson was treated as a member of the family, and was once more motivated to continue working on his *Shakespeare*. Afterwards, Johnson stayed with the Thrales for 17 years until Henry's death in 1781, sometimes staying in rooms at Thrale's Anchor Brewery in Southwark. Hester Thrale's documentation of Johnson's life during this time, in her correspondence and her diary (*Thraliana*), became an important source of biographical information on Johnson after his death.

Johnson's edition of *Shakespeare* was finally published on 10 October 1765 as *The Plays of William Shakespeare, in Eight Volumes ... To which are added Notes by Sam. Johnson* in a printing of one thousand copies. The first edition quickly sold out, and a second was soon printed.

The plays themselves were in a version that Johnson felt most true to the original based on his analysis of the manuscript editions. Johnson's revolutionary innovation was to create a set of corresponding notes that allow readers to identify the meaning behind many of Shakespeare's more complicated passages or ones that may have been transcribed incorrectly over time. Included within the notes are occasional attacks upon rival editors of Shakespeare's works and their editions.

Years later, Edmond Malone, an important Shakespearean scholar and friend of Johnson's, stated that Johnson's "vigorous and comprehensive understanding threw more light on his authour than all his predecessors had done". In February 1767 Johnson was granted a special meeting with King George III. This took place at the library of the Queen's house, and it was organised by Barnard, the King's librarian. The King, hearing that Johnson would visit the library, commanded Barnard to introduce him to Johnson. After a short meeting, Johnson was impressed with both the King himself and their conversation.

On 6 August 1773, eleven years after first meeting Boswell, Johnson set out to visit his friend in Scotland, to begin "a journey to the western islands of Scotland", as Johnson's 1775 account of their travels would put it. The work was intended to discuss the social problems and struggles that affected the Scottish people, but it also praised many of the unique facets of Scottish society, such as a school in Edinburgh for the deaf and mute. Also, Johnson used the work to enter into the dispute over the authenticity of James Macpherson's Ossian poems, claiming they could not have been translations of ancient Scottish literature on the grounds that "in those times nothing had been written in the Earse [i.e. Gaelic] language". There were heated exchanges between the two, and according to one of Johnson's letters, MacPherson threatened physical violence. Boswell's account, *The Journal of a Tour to the Hebrides* (1786), was a preliminary attempt at a biography before his *Life of Johnson*. Included were various quotes and descriptions of events, including anecdotes such as Johnson swinging around a broadsword while wearing Scottish garb, or dancing a Highland jig.

In the 1770s, Johnson, who had tended to be an opponent of the government early in life, published a series of pamphlets in favour of various government policies. In 1770 he produced *The False Alarm*, a political pamphlet attacking John Wilkes. In 1771, his *Thoughts on the Late Transactions Respecting Falkland's Islands* cautioned against war with Spain. In 1774 he printed *The Patriot,* a critique of what he viewed as false patriotism. On the evening of 7 April 1775, he made the famous statement, "Patriotism is the last refuge of the scoundrel." This line was not, as widely believed, about patriotism in general, but the false use of the term "patriotism" by John Stuart, 3rd Earl of Bute (the patriot-minister) and his supporters; Johnson opposed "self-professed Patriots" in general, but valued what he considered "true" patriotism.

The last of these pamphlets, *Taxation No Tyranny* (1775), was a defence of the Coercive Acts and a response to the Declaration of Rights of the First Continental Congress of America, which protested against taxation without representation. Johnson argued that in emigrating to America, colonists had "voluntarily resigned the power of voting", but they still had "virtual representation" in Parliament. In a parody of the Declaration of Rights, Johnson suggested that the Americans had no more right to govern themselves than the Cornish people. If the Americans wanted to participate in Parliament, said Johnson, they could move to England and purchase an estate. Johnson denounced English supporters of American separatists as "traitors to this country", and hoped that the matter would be settled without bloodshed, but that it would end with "English superiority and American obedience". Years before, Johnson had advocated that the English and the French were just "two robbers" who were stealing land from the natives, and that neither deserved to live there. After the signing of the 1783 Peace of Paris treaties, marking the colonists' defeat of the British, Johnson was "deeply disturbed" with the "state of this kingdom".

"Mr Thrale's death was a very essential loss to Johnson, who, although he did not foresee all that afterwards happened, was sufficiently convinced that the comforts which Mr Thrale's family afforded him, would now in great measure cease."

– Boswell's *Life of Samuel Johnson*

On 3 May 1777, while Johnson was trying to save Reverend William Dodd from execution, he wrote to Boswell that he was busy preparing a "little Lives" and "little Prefaces, to a little edition of the English Poets". Tom Davies, William

Strahan and Thomas Cadell had asked Johnson to create this final major work, the *Lives of the English Poets*, for which he asked 200 guineas, an amount significantly less than the price he could have demanded. The *Lives*, which were critical as well as biographical studies, appeared as prefaces to selections of each poet's work, and they were quite larger than originally expected. The work was finished in March 1781 and the whole collection was published in six volumes. As Johnson justified in the advertisement for the work, "my purpose was only to have allotted to every Poet an Advertisement, like those which we find in the French Miscellanies, containing a few dates and a general character."

Johnson was unable to enjoy this success because Henry Thrale, the dear friend with whom he lived, died on 4 April 1781. Life changed quickly for Johnson, and Hester Thrale became interested in the Italian singing teacher Gabriel Mario Piozzi, which forced Johnson to move on from his previous lifestyle. After returning home and then travelling for a short period, Johnson received word that his friend and tenant Robert Levet, had died on 17 January 1782. Johnson was shocked by the death of Levet, who had resided at Johnson's London home since 1762. Shortly afterwards Johnson caught a cold which turned into bronchitis, lasting for several months, and his health was further complicated by "feeling forlorn and lonely" by Levet's death being accompanied by that of Johnson's friend Thomas Lawrence and his housekeeper Williams.

Although he had recovered his health by August, he experienced emotional trauma when he was given word that Hester Thrale would sell the residence that Johnson shared with the family. What hurt Johnson the most was the possibility that he would be left without her constant company. Months later, on 6 October 1782, Johnson attended church for the final time in his life, to say goodbye to his former residence and life. The walk to the church strained him, but he managed the journey unaccompanied. While there, he wrote a prayer for the Thrale family:

To thy fatherly protection, O Lord, I commend this family.

Bless, guide, and defend them, that they may pass through this world, as finally to enjoy in thy presence everlasting happiness, for Jesus Christ's sake. Amen.

Hester Thrale did not completely abandon Johnson, and asked him to accompany the family on a trip to Brighton. He agreed, and was with them from 7 October until 20 November 1782. On his return, his health began to fail him, and he was left alone following Boswell's visit on 29 May 1783 until he travelled to Scotland. On 17 June 1783, Johnson's poor circulation resulted in a stroke and he wrote to his neighbour, Edmund Allen, that he had lost the ability to speak. Two doctors were brought in to aid Johnson; he regained his ability to speak two days later. Johnson feared that he was dying, and wrote:

The black dog I hope always to resist, and in time to drive, though I am deprived of almost all those that used to help me. The neighbourhood is impoverished. I had once Richardson and Lawrence in my reach. Mrs. Allen is dead. My house has lost Levet, a man who took interest in everything, and therefore ready at conversation. Mrs. Williams is so weak that she can be a companion no longer. When I rise my breakfast is solitary, the black dog waits to share it, from breakfast to dinner he continues barking, except that Dr. Brocklesby for a little keeps him at a distance. Dinner with a sick woman you may venture to suppose not much better than solitary. After dinner, what remains but to count the clock, and hope for that sleep which I can scarce expect. Night comes at last, and some hours of restlessness and confusion bring me again to a day of solitude. What shall exclude the black dog from an habitation like this?

By this time he was sick and gout-ridden. He had surgery for gout, and his remaining friends, including novelist Fanny Burney (the daughter of Charles Burney), came to keep him company. He was confined to his room from 14 December 1783 to 21 April 1784. His health had begun to improve by May 1784, and he travelled to Oxford with Boswell on 5 May 1784. By July, many of Johnson's friends were either dead or gone; Boswell had left for Scotland and Hester Thrale had become engaged to Piozzi. With nobody to visit, Johnson expressed a desire to die in London and arrived there on 16 November 1784. On 25 November 1784, he allowed Burney to visit him and expressed an interest to her that he should leave London; he soon left for Islington, to George Strahan's home. His final moments were filled with mental anguish and delusions; when his physician, Thomas Warren, visited and asked him if he were feeling better, Johnson burst out with: "No, Sir; you cannot conceive with what acceleration I advance towards death."

"A few days before his death, he had asked Sir John Hawkins, as one of his executors, where he should be buried; and on being answered, "Doubtless, in Westminster Abbey," seemed to feel a satisfaction, very natural to a Poet."

– Boswell's *Life of Samuel Johnson*

Many visitors came to see Johnson as he lay sick in bed, but he preferred only Langton's company. Burney waited for word of Johnson's condition, along with Windham, Strahan, Hoole, Cruikshank, Des Moulins and Barber. On 13 December 1784, Johnson met with two others: a young woman, Miss Morris, whom Johnson blessed, and Francesco Sastres, an Italian teacher, who was given some of Johnson's final words: "*Iam Moriturus*" ("I who am about to die"). Shortly afterwards he fell into a coma, and died at 7:00 pm.

Langton waited until 11:00 pm to tell the others, which led to John Hawkins' becoming pale and overcome with "an agony of mind", along with Seward and Hoole describing Johnson's death as "the most awful sight". Boswell remarked, "My feeling was just one large expanse of Stupor ... I could not believe it. My imagination was not convinced." William Gerard Hamilton joined in and stated, "He has made a chasm, which not only nothing can fill up, but which *nothing has a tendency to fill up*. -Johnson is dead.- Let us go to the next best: There is nobody; *-no man can be said to put you in mind of Johnson.*"

Johnson's works, especially his *Lives of the Poets* series, describe various features of excellent writing. He believed that the best poetry relied on contemporary language, and he disliked the use of decorative or purposefully archaic language. In particular, he was suspicious of the poetic language used by Milton, whose blank verse he believed would inspire many bad imitations. Also, Johnson opposed the poetic language of his contemporary Thomas Gray. His greatest complaint was that obscure allusions found in works like Milton's *Lycidas* were overused; he preferred poetry that could be easily read and understood. In addition to his views on language, Johnson believed that a good poem incorporated new and unique imagery.

In his smaller poetic works, Johnson relied on short lines and filled his work with a feeling of empathy, which possibly influenced Housman's poetic style. In *London*, his first imitation of Juvenal, Johnson uses the poetic form to express his political opinion and, as befits a young writer, approaches the topic in a playful and almost joyous manner. However, his second imitation, *The Vanity of Human Wishes*, is completely different; the language remains simple, but the poem is more complicated and difficult to read because Johnson is trying to describe complex Christian ethics. These Christian values are not unique to the poem, but contain views expressed in most of Johnson's works. In particular, Johnson emphasises God's infinite love and shows that happiness can be attained through virtuous action.

When it came to biography, Johnson disagreed with Plutarch's use of biography to praise and to teach morality. Instead, Johnson believed in portraying the biographical subjects accurately and including any negative aspects of their lives. Because his insistence on accuracy in biography was little short of revolutionary, Johnson had to struggle against a society that was unwilling to accept biographical details that could be viewed as tarnishing a reputation; this became the subject of *Rambler* 60. Furthermore, Johnson believed that biography should not be limited to the most famous and that the lives of lesser individuals, too, were significant; thus in his *Lives of the Poets* he chose both great and lesser poets. In all his biographies he insisted on including what others would have considered trivial details to fully describe the lives of his subjects. Johnson considered the genre of autobiography and diaries, including his own, as one having the most significance; in *Idler* 84 he explains how a writer of an autobiography would be the least likely to distort his own life.

Johnson's thoughts on biography and on poetry coalesced in his understanding of what would make a good critic. His works were dominated with his intent to use them for literary criticism. This was especially true of his *Dictionary* of which he wrote: "I lately published a Dictionary like those compiled by the academies of Italy and France, *for the use of such as aspire to exactness of criticism, or elegance of style*". Although a smaller edition of his *Dictionary* became the standard household dictionary, Johnson's original *Dictionary* was an academic tool that examined how words were used, especially in literary works. To achieve this purpose, Johnson included quotations from Bacon, Hooker, Milton, Shakespeare, Spenser, and many others from what he considered to be the most important literary fields: natural science, philosophy, poetry, and theology. These quotations and usages were all compared and carefully studied in the *Dictionary* so that a reader could understand what words in literary works meant in context.

Not being a theorist, Johnson did not attempt to create schools of theories to analyse the aesthetics of literature. Instead, he used his criticism for the practical purpose of helping others to better read and understand literature. When it came to Shakespeare's plays, Johnson emphasised the role of the reader in understanding language: "If Shakespeare has difficulties above other writers, it is to be imputed to the nature of his work, which required the use of common colloquial language, and consequently admitted many phrases allusive, elliptical, and proverbial, such as we speak and hear every hour without observing them".

His works on Shakespeare were devoted not merely to Shakespeare, but to understanding literature as a whole; in his *Preface* to Shakespeare, Johnson rejects the previous dogma of the classical unities and argues that drama should be faithful to life. However, Johnson did not only defend Shakespeare; he discussed Shakespeare's faults, including his lack of morality, his vulgarity, his carelessness in crafting plots, and his occasional inattentiveness when choosing words or word order. As well as direct literary criticism, Johnson emphasised the need to establish a text that accurately reflects what an author wrote. Shakespeare's plays, in particular, had multiple editions, each of which contained errors caused by the printing process. This problem was compounded by careless editors who deemed difficult words incorrect, and changed them in later editions. Johnson believed that an editor should not alter the text in such a way.

"After we came out of the church, we stood talking for some time together of Bishop Berkeley's ingenious sophistry to prove the non-existence of matter, and that every thing in the universe is merely ideal. I observed, that though we are satisfied his doctrine is not true, it is impossible to refute it. I never shall forget the alacrity with which Johnson answered, striking his foot with mighty force against a large stone, till he rebounded from it, 'I refute it *thus*.'"

– Boswell's *Life of Samuel Johnson*

Johnson's tall and robust figure combined with his odd gestures were confusing to some; when William Hogarth first saw Johnson standing near a window in Samuel Richardson's house, "shaking his head and rolling himself about in a strange ridiculous manner", Hogarth thought Johnson an "ideot, whom his relations had put under the care of Mr. Richardson". Hogarth was quite surprised when "this figure stalked forwards to where he and Mr. Richardson were sitting and all at once took up the argument ... [with] such a power of eloquence, that Hogarth looked at him with astonishment, and actually imagined that this ideot had been at the moment inspired". Not everyone was misled by Johnson's appearance; Adam Smith claimed that "Johnson knew more books than any man alive", while Edmund Burke thought that if Johnson were to join Parliament, he "certainly would have been the greatest speaker that ever was there". Johnson relied on a unique form of rhetoric, and he is well known for his "refutation" of Bishop Berkeley's immaterialism and his claim that matter did not actually exist but only seemed to exist:

during a conversation with Boswell, Johnson powerfully stomped a nearby stone and proclaimed of Berkeley's theory, "I refute it *thus*!"

Johnson was a devout, conservative Anglican and a compassionate man who supported a number of poor friends under his own roof, even when unable to fully provide for himself. Johnson's Christian morality permeated his works, and he would write on moral topics with such authority and in such a trusting manner that, Walter Jackson Bate claims, "no other moralist in history excels or even begins to rival him". However, Johnson's moral writings do not contain, as Donald Greene points out, "a predetermined and authorized pattern of 'good behavior'", even though Johnson does emphasise certain kinds of conduct. He did not let his own faith prejudice him against others, and had respect for those of other denominations who demonstrated a commitment to Christ's teachings. Although Johnson respected John Milton's poetry, he could not tolerate Milton's Puritan and Republican beliefs, feeling that they were contrary to England and Christianity. He was an opponent of slavery on moral grounds, and once proposed a toast to the "next rebellion of the negroes in the West Indies". Beside his beliefs concerning humanity, Johnson is also known for his love of cats, especially his own two cats, Hodge and Lily. Boswell wrote, "I never shall forget the indulgence with which he treated Hodge, his cat."

Although Johnson was also known as a staunch Tory, he admitted to sympathies for the Jacobite cause during his younger years but, by the reign of George III, he came to accept the Hanoverian Succession. It was Boswell who gave people the impression that Johnson was an "arch-conservative", and it was Boswell, more than anyone else, who determined how Johnson would be seen by people years later. However, Boswell was not around for two of Johnson's most politically active periods: during Walpole's control over British Parliament and during the Seven Years' War. Although Boswell was present with Johnson during the 1770s and describes four major pamphlets written by Johnson, he neglects to discuss them because he is more interested in their travels to Scotland. This is compounded by the fact that Boswell held an opinion contradictory to two of these pamphlets, *The False Alarm* and *Taxation No Tyranny*, and so attacks Johnson's views in his biography.

In his *Life of Samuel Johnson* Boswell referred to Johnson as Dr Johnson so often that he would always be known as Dr Johnson, even though he hated being called such. Boswell's emphasis on Johnson's later years depicted him only as an old man who involved himself in taverns, but this depiction is appealing. Although Boswell, a Scotsman, was a close companion and friend to Johnson during many important times of his life, like many of his fellow Englishmen Johnson had a reputation for despising Scotland and its people. Even during their journey together through Scotland, Johnson "exhibited prejudice and a narrow nationalism". Hester Thrale, in summarising Johnson's nationalistic views and his anti-Scottish prejudice, said: "We all know how well he loved to abuse the Scotch, & indeed to be abused by them in return."

Johnson had several health problems, including childhood tuberculous scrofula, gout, testicular cancer, and a stroke in his final year that left him unable to speak; his autopsy indicated that he had pulmonary fibrosis along with cardiac failure probably due to hypertension, a condition then unknown. Although Johnson overall was probably as healthy as others of his generation, he displayed signs consistent with several diagnoses, including depression and Tourette syndrome (TS).

There are many accounts of Johnson suffering from bouts of depression and what Johnson thought might be madness. As Walter Jackson Bate puts it, "one of the ironies of literary history is that its most compelling and authoritative symbol of common sense—of the strong, imaginative grasp of concrete reality—should have begun his adult life, at the age of twenty, in a state of such intense anxiety and bewildered despair that, at least from his own point of view, it seemed the onset of actual insanity". To overcome these feelings, Johnson tried to constantly involve himself with various activities, but this did not seem to help. Taylor said that Johnson "at one time strongly entertained thoughts of Suicide". Boswell claimed that Johnson "felt himself overwhelmed with an horrible melancholia, with perpetual irritation, fretfulness, and impatience; and with a dejection, gloom, and despair, which made existence misery".

Early on, when Johnson was unable to pay off his debts, he began to work with professional writers and identified his own situation with theirs. During this time, Johnson witnessed Christopher Smart's decline into "penury and the madhouse", and feared that he might share the same fate. Hester Thrale Piozzi claimed, in a discussion on Smart's mental state, that Johnson was her "friend who feared an apple should intoxicate him". To Hester Thrale, what separated Johnson from others who were placed in asylums for madness—like Christopher Smart—was his ability to keep his concerns and emotions to himself.

Two hundred years after Johnson's death, the posthumous diagnosis of Tourette syndrome became widely accepted. The condition was unknown during Johnson's lifetime, but Boswell describes Johnson displaying signs of TS including tics and other involuntary movements.

According to Boswell "he commonly held his head to one side ... moving his body backwards and forwards, and rubbing his left knee in the same direction, with the palm of his hand ... [H]e made various sounds" like "a half whistle" or "as if clucking like a hen", and "... all this accompanied sometimes with a thoughtful look, but more frequently with a smile. Generally when he had concluded a period, in the course of a dispute, by which time he was a good deal exhausted by violence and vociferation, he used to blow out his breath like a Whale."

There are many similar accounts; in particular, Johnson was said to "perform his gesticulations" at the threshold of house or in doorways.

When asked by a little girl why he made such noises and acted in that way, Johnson responded: "From bad habit." The diagnosis of the syndrome was first made in a 1967 report, and TS researcher Arthur K. Shapiro described Johnson as "the most notable example of a successful adaptation to life despite the liability of Tourette syndrome". Details provided by the writings of Boswell, Hester Thrale, and others reinforce the diagnosis, with one paper concluding:

[Johnson] also displayed many of the obsessional-compulsive traits and rituals which are associated with this syndrome ... It may be thought that without this illness Dr Johnson's remarkable literary achievements, the great dictionary, his philosophical deliberations and his conversations may never have happened; and Boswell, the author of the greatest of biographies would have been unknown.

—JMS Pearce, Journal of the Royal Society of Medicine, July 1994.

POETRY

Johnson's literature, especially his *Lives of the Poets* series, is marked by various opinions on what would make a poetic work excellent. He believed that the best poetry relied on contemporary language, and he disliked the use of decorative or purposefully archaic language. In particular, he was suspicious of John Milton's language, whose blank verse would mislead later poets, and could not stand the poetic language of Thomas Gray. On Gray, Johnson wrote, "Gray thought his language more poetical as it was more remote from common use". Johnson would sometimes write parodies of poetry that he felt was poorly done; one such example is his translation of Euripides's play, *Medea* in a parody of one poet's style along side of his version of how the play should be translated. His greatest complaint was the overuse of obscure allusion found in works like Milton's *Lycidas,* and he preferred poetry that could be easily read. In addition to his views on language, Johnson believed that a good poem would incorporate new and unique imagery.

In his shorter works, Johnson preferred shorter lines and to fill his work with a feeling of empathy, which possibly influenced Alfred Edward Housman's poetry. In *London,* his first imitation of Juvenal, Johnson uses the form to express his political opinion. It is a poem of his youth and deals with the topic in a playful and almost joyous manner. As Donald Greene claims, "its charm comes from youthful exuberance and violence with which the witty invective comes tumbling out" in lines like:

Here malice, rapine, accident conspire,
And now a rabble rages, now a fire;
Their ambush here relentless ruffians lay,
And here the fell attorney prowls for prey;
Here falling houses thunder on your head,
And here a female atheist talks you dead.

However, his second imitation, *The Vanity of Human Wishes,* is completely different; the language remains simple, but the poem is more complicated and difficult to read because Johnson is trying to describe Christian ethics. These Christian values are not unique to the poem, but are part of Johnson's works as a whole. In particular, Johnson emphasizes God's infinite love and that happiness can be attained through virtuous action.

In terms of biography, Johnson did not agree with Plutarch's model of using biographies to teach morals and compliment the subjects. Instead, Johnson believed in portraying the subjects accurately, including any negative aspects of an individual's life. Although revolutionary and more accurate as a biographer, Johnson had to struggle with his beliefs against a society that was unwilling to hear of details that may be viewed as tarnishing a reputation. In *Rambler* 60, Johnson put forth why he thought society could not be comfortable with hearing the negative truth of individuals that they admire:

All joy or sorrow for the happiness or calamities of others is produced by an act of imagination that realizes the event, however fictitious, or approximates it, however remote, by placing us, for a time, in the condition of him whose fortune we contemplate, so that we feel, while the deception lasts, whatever motions would be excited by the same good or evil happening to ourselves... Our passions are therefore more strongly moved, in proportion as we can more readily adopt the pains or pleasure proposed to our minds, by recognizing them as once our own. Also, Johnson did not feel that biography should be limited to the most important people, but felt that the lives of lesser individuals could be deemed the most significant.

In his *Lives of the Poets,* he chose great and lesser poets, and throughout all of his biographies, he always insisted on included what others may consider as trivial details in order to fully describe the lives of his subjects. When it came to autobiography, and diaries including his own, Johnson considered that genre of work as one having the most significance; he explains this in *Idler* 84, when he described how a writer of an autobiography would be the least likely to distort their own life.

Johnson's thoughts on biography and on poetry found their union in his understanding of what would make a good critic. His works were dominated with his intent to used them for literary criticism, including his *Dictionary* to which he wrote: "I lately published a Dictionary like those compiled by the academies of Italy and France, *for the use of such as aspire to exactness of criticism, or elegance of style*". Although the smaller dictionary was written for the masses and become the common household dictionary, Johnson's original dictionary was an academic tool that examined how words were used, especially those uses that were found in literary works. To achieve this purpose, Johnson included quotations from Bacon, Hooker, Milton, Shakespeare, Spenser, and many others from the literary fields that Johnson thought were most important: natural science, philosophy, poetry, and theology. These quotes and usages were all compared and carefully studied, so that others could understand what words meant in literature.

Johnson felt that words, in and of themselves, were meaningless, but that meaning comes from context. The only way to understand the word is to examine its usage, and a critic must understand lexicography before they can understand what people are saying. Later critics would attempt to create theories to analyse the aesthetics of literature, but Johnson was not a theorist and he used his ideas only for the practical purpose in order to better read the works. When it came to Shakspeare's plays, Johnson emphasized the role of a reader in understanding language when he wrote, "If Shakespeare has difficulties above other writers, it is to be imputed to the nature of his work, which required the use of common colloquial language, and consequently admitted many phrases allusive, elliptical, and proverbial, such as we speak and hear every hour without observing them".

His works on Shakespeare were not devoted just to Shakespeare, but to critical theory as a whole, and, in his *Preface* to Shakespeare, Johnson rejects the previous belief of the classical unities and establishes a more natural theory on what makes drama work: drama should be faithful to life. In particular, Johnson claimed that "Among [Shakespeare's] other excellences it out to be remarked, because it has hitherto been unnoticed, that his *heroes are men*, that the love and hatred, the hopes and fears, of his chief personages are such as common to other human beings. Shakespeare's excellence is not the fiction of a tale, but the representation of life: and his reputation is therefore safe, till human nature shall be changed." Besides defending Shakespeare, Johnson was willing to discuss Shakespeare's faults, especially his lacking of morality, his vulgarity, and carelessness in crafting plots.

Besides direct literary criticism, Johnson emphasized the need to establish a text that accurately reflects what an author wrote. In his *Preface*, Johnson analyzed the various versions of Shakespeare's plays and argued how an editor should work on them. Shakespeare's plays, in particular, had multiple editions that each contained errors from the printing process. This problem was compounded by careless editors deeming difficult words as incorrect and changing them in later editions. Johnson believed that an editor should not alter the text in such a way, and, when creating his own edition of Shakespeare's plays, he relied on the thousands of quotations and notes that he used in crafting his *Dictionary* in order to restore, to the best of his knowledge, the original text.

Johnson was, in the words of Steven Lynn, "more than a well-known writer and scholar"; he was a celebrity. His activities and the state of his health in his later years were constantly reported in various journals and newspapers, and when there was nothing to report, something was invented. According to Bate, "Johnson loved biography," and he "changed the whole course of biography for the modern world. One by-product was the most famous single work of biographical art in the whole of literature, Boswell's *Life of Johnson,* and there were many other memoirs and biographies of a similar kind written on Johnson after his death." These accounts of his life include Thomas Tyers's *A Biographical Sketch of Dr Samuel Johnson* (1784); Boswell's *The Journal of a Tour to the Hebrides* (1785); Hester Thrale's *Anecdotes of the Late Samuel Johnson,* which drew on entries from her diary and other notes; John Hawkins's *Life of Samuel Johnson (1787),* the first full-length biography of Johnson; and, in 1792, Arthur Murphy's *An Essay on the Life and Genius of Samuel Johnson,* which replaced Hawkins's biography as the introduction to a collection of Johnson's *Works.*

Another important source was Fanny Burney, who described Johnson as "the acknowledged Head of Literature in this kingdom" and kept a diary containing details missing from other biographies. Above all, Boswell's portrayal of Johnson is the work best known to general readers. Although critics like Donald Greene argue about its status as a true biography, the work became successful as Boswell and his friends promoted it at the expense of the many other works on Johnson's life. In criticism, Johnson had a lasting influence, although not everyone viewed him favourably. Some, like Macaulay, regarded Johnson as an idiot savant who produced some respectable works, and others, like the Romantic poets, were completely opposed to Johnson's views on poetry and literature, especially in regards to Milton.

However, some of their contemporaries disagreed: Stendhal's *Racine et Shakespeare* is based in part on Johnson's views of Shakespeare, and Johnson influenced Jane Austen's writing style and philosophy. Later, Johnson's works came into favour, and Matthew Arnold, in his *Six Chief Lives from Johnson's "Lives of the Poets"*, considered the *Lives* of Milton,

Dryden, Pope, Addison, Swift, and Gray as "points which stand as so many natural centres, and by returning to which we can always find our way again." More than a century after his death, literary critics such as G. Birkbeck Hill and T. S. Eliot came to regard Johnson as a serious critic. They began to study Johnson's works with an increasing focus on the critical analysis found in his edition of Shakespeare and *Lives of the Poets*. Yvor Winters claimed that "A great critic is the rarest of all literary geniuses; perhaps the only critic in English who deserves that epithet is Samuel Johnson". F. R. Leavis agreed and, on Johnson's criticism, said, "When we read him we know, beyond question, that we have here a powerful and distinguished mind operating at first hand upon literature.

This, we can say with emphatic conviction, really *is* criticism". Edmund Wilson claimed that "The *Lives of the Poets* and the prefaces and commentary on Shakespeare are among the most brilliant and the most acute documents in the whole range of English criticism". It is no wonder that his philosophical insistence that the language within literature must be examined became a prevailing mode of literary theory during the mid-20th century. In 1838 a statue of Johnson was erected in the Market Square in Lichfield, opposite the house where he was born. There are also statues of him in London and Uttoxeter. There are many societies formed around and dedicated to the study and enjoyment of Samuel Johnson's life and works. On the bicentennial of Johnson's death in 1984, Oxford University held a week-long conference featuring 50 papers, and the Arts Council of Great Britain held an exhibit of "Johnsonian portraits and other memorabilia". The London *Times* and *Punch* produced parodies of Johnson's style for the occasion. In 1999, the BBC Four television channel started the Samuel Johnson Prize, an award for non-fiction.

Chapter 2

Johnson on the History of the Language

"Every language," as we know, "has a time of rudeness antecedent to perfection, as well as of false refinement and declension." Now rise and fall together suggest a peak, and in this paper I'd like to discuss this linguistic trajectory by placing Johnson's comments on the history of the language in the context of other such statements from the fifteenth through the eighteenth centuries. My concern is the way these historical considerations work their way into discussions of linguistic propriety.

Johnson insists he has "studiously endeavoured to collect examples and authorities from the writers before the restoration, whose works I regard as *the wells of English undefiled*, as the pure sources of genuine diction." Purity of diction is by now a metaphor so thoroughly naturalized that it seems, if not dead, at least moribund. But it was not always so, and in calling Renaissance writers "undefiled" (a borrowing from Spenser) and "pure sources," he recalls a common habit of Renaissance humanists of castigating the undesirable as "impure." I'd like to suggest that these early humanists provide the best analogue to help us understand what Johnson had to say about the history of the English language.

Treating a language, whether classical or vernacular, as a substance capable of admitting adulteration was an idea developed for the first time in the fifteenth century, and was soon remarkably widespread. In antiquity and the Middle Ages there were ideas of *good* and *bad* Greek and Latin, but these almost never corresponded to *pure* and *corrupt*: such a dichotomy simply had not been conceived. Other divisions, of course, were common: language might be clear or muddled, decorous or inappropriate, belonging to the *genus grande* or *genus humile*. But it was not routinely conceived as a medium of "true" expression in which "false" elements served as pollutants. Only with the humanist "recovery" of "real" Latin in the fifteenth century (all these terms are, of course, hiding behind protective quotation marks) was the intervening millennium's language condemned as corrupt: scholastic philosophers and Barthollist lawyers were charged with infecting the Latin of the ancients with atrocious solecisms. In the place of these barbarians were erected monuments to the Augustan prose writers, especially Cicero, whose style became the hottest commodity in the literary marketplace.

The urge was to cure the Latin tongue by excising its tumors, to restore it to the full bloom of health it experienced in the first century B.C. In the most extreme form of this project, radical Ciceronians would restrict the legitimate vocabulary to only those words that Cicero himself had used: Longolius in fact prided himself on using only the inflected forms found in Cicero's works. Such extremism prompted reactions even from the humanists' allies; Erasmus's *Ciceronianus*, for instance, is a satire on the absurd excesses of Longolius and his kind. But a less thoroughgoing variety of Ciceronianism was widespread throughout the Renaissance.

The whole enterprise depends upon the belief in a period in which a language most nearly approaches its true genius — its peak — and the humanists believed they found this in the years between the Jugurthine War and the death of Augustus. The sixteenth century therefore produced lexicons that drew illustrative quotations almost exclusively from antiquity — not with the descriptive intentions that lie behind modern lexicographical corpora, but in the hope of regulating contemporary usage with that of the age of Cicero and Virgil. Terence's observation — "nullumst iam dictum quod non dictum sit prius" — became not a lament about the burden of the past, but a vow, a mustering of resolve, on proper style.

Even those who rejected Ciceronianism itself continued to respect the ideal of linguistic purity, plotting a palace coup to dethrone Cicero from his position as stylistic arbiter, only to replace him with a junta consisting of Seneca, Lucan, Persius, and other writers of the Silver Age. The principle of grounding modern style on that of a privileged earlier age remained intact. Whether they looked to the writers of the Augustan or the Silver Age, Renaissance thinkers grounded their conception of style on a privileged moment in the history of the language.

The Ciceronian habit survived the radical stylistic and lexical experiments of the seventeenth century, and continued, albeit in altered form, into the eighteenth. We can detect the Renaissance concern with linguistic purity, for instance, in Johnson's declaration that he has "laboured to refine our language to grammatical purity, and to clear it from colloquial barbarisms, licentious idioms, and irregular combinations." Here we see the essentially Ciceronian arguments made not about Latin but about English. The movement was in fact already underway in the Restoration. Thomas Sprat hated the florid rhetorical habits of the Renaissance, and proposed a linguistic academy, calling for "a constant Resolution, to reject all the amplifications, digressions, and swellings of style: to return back to the primitive purity." Note that the hated amplifications and swellings are the legacy of the sixteenth-century Ciceronians: but note, too, that the expurgatory metaphor is also theirs. Sprat's choice of models is different, but his insistence on "return[ing] back to the primitive purity" demonstrates exactly the same dynamic. In revealing his anxiety about linguistic "infection," he uses the same old metaphors, just as the sixteenth-century anti-Ciceronians resorted to the conceptual categories of their rivals.

A similar call for an academy appears in the most famous eighteenth-century jeremiad on linguistic impurity, Swift's *Proposal* of 1712. Swift finds "our Language ... extremely imperfect; ... its daily Improvements are by no Means in Proportion to its daily Corruptions." Now, most eighteenth-century thinkers regarded the English Renaissance as a progress away from the rudeness and imperfections of the barbarous Middle Ages. But for many, the linguistic ascent from Chaucer and Lydgate to Shakespeare and Ben Jonson had its mirror image in a subsequent decline. Dryden, for example, writes, "That an Alteration is lately made in [our language] since the Writers of the last Age ... is manifest. ... But, that this is an *Improvement* of the Language, or an alteration for the better, will not so easily be granted. For many are of a contrary opinion, that the English tongue was then in the height of its perfection; that, from *Jonsons* time to ours, it has been in a continual declination." Swift has the same fear: "From that great Rebellion to this present Time, I am apt to doubt whether the Corruptions in our Language have not, at least, equalled the Refinements of it."

Eighteenth-century writers, that is to say, saw contrary movements since the age of Elizabeth: progressive refinement toward Waller and Dryden on the one hand, yes, but a potentially unstoppable decline into babble on the other. Swift's contribution to *Tatler* 230 is well known: "I mean the continual Corruption of our *English* Tongue; which, without some timely Remedy, will suffer more by the false Refinements of Twenty Years past, than it hath been improved in the foregoing Hundred." Swift is in fact more cautious than this suggests: "the *English* Tongue," he says, "is not arrived to such a Degree of Perfection, as ... to make us apprehend any Thoughts of its Decay." But whether or not the decline had begun or was inevitable, anxiety about the threat was real, and caused the eighteenth century to inherit the humanistic idea of subjecting their own language to the discipline of a privileged earlier form, from a time before the decay began. Chesterfield therefore resolves, in the face of "All words, good and bad, ... jumbled indiscriminately together," that "The time for discrimination seems to be now come. Toleration, adoption and naturalization have run their lengths. Good order and authority are now necessary." Thus his advice to his son, in which he invokes the Terentian tag: "There is nothing truer than that old saying *Nihil dictum quod non prius dictum.*"

To judge by the front matter of the *Dictionary* alone, Johnson was attuned to this discourse of linguistic corruption.

"Every language," remember, "has a time of rudeness antecedent to perfection, as well as of false refinement and declension." Languages follow the universal arc of ascent and decline: "Language proceeds," he says, "like every thing else, thro' improvement to degeneracy." Like Swift, he withholds comment on whether the English language had already in fact begun its decline. But the metaphors of the humanist tradition fill both the Preface and the History, where Johnson describes his task as "to guard the avenues of [his] languag[e], to retain fugitives, and repulse intruders." The intruders are those without a pedigree: only those words grounded in good, old usage are considered legitimate.

The question, then, for Johnson and his contemporaries, was *which* past to choose. Rome's golden age was easy to identify, and Italy and France had already discovered their own: as early as the sixteenth century, for instance, Bembo found Petrarch and Boccaccio models for imitation. Both of these names figure prominently, along with all greats of modern Italian literature, in the table of cited authors in the Accademia della Crusca's *Vocabolario* in 1612. In France, Richelet supported his *Dictionnaire françois* with "l'usage ... des bons auteurs de la langue françoise," most from the age of Louis Quatorze. English, on the other hand, was more troublesome. Even those who agreed that language had begun to decline differed on the time of the language's peak, and the many searches for a standard by which to regulate the language resulted in competing claims for various periods from the earliest times through the age of Anne.

Johnson hints at one common choice for a model of properly pure English when he identifies the modern-day barbarians in his *Dictionary*. "The whole fabrick and scheme of the *English* language," he writes, "is *Gothick* or *Teutonick*"; but "Our language ... has ... been gradually departing from its original *Teutonick* character, and deviating towards a *Gallick* structure and phraseology." The French, then, are the invaders, the poisoners of the pure Saxon streams. English is in a unique position among the European languages in having two parents, one Germanic, one Romance. By comparison with such relatively homogeneous languages as German and French, English therefore has an obvious standard of purity. The fit was indisputably imperfect, but the need for an authorizing corpus of pure diction was enough to put Old English, at least tentatively, in the position of Augustan Latin. Interest in Saxon antiquities, to be sure, was never really popular, but scholarly interest in the roots of the English language was considerable; and from at least the late sixteenth century this study was associated with British national identity. Against such a background, additions to the language from French sources could be seen as impurities. So Johnson calls *souvenance* "A French word which with many more is now happily disused." *Gout* ("taste") is "An affected cant word"; the second sense of *to transpire* is "a sense lately innovated from *France,* without necessity"; and *ruse* is "A French word neither eloquent nor necessary."

Whatever the attraction of the old Gothic `vigour`, though, it was a troublesome standard, for Teutonic words were routinely taken to task for their barbarism. *Beowulf* was not published until 1815, and no other work was available to play the role of an authorizing Saxon classic. Many in the early part of the eighteenth century therefore sought the language's acme in the decades immediately before them. The evidence here is lexicographical. Although Johnson was the first actually to produce an English dictionary with illustrative quotations, he was not the first to consider it, and his selection of many quotations from the sixteenth and early seventeenth centuries would not have been everyone's decision. Addison, for instance, planned a dictionary in which Tillotson, "the chief standard of our language," was to have provided the quotations. After asking "whether a word is English or not" and resolving to rely on "nothing but authority," Pope too looked to the late seventeenth century for his models: "Is [the word] in Sir William Temple, or Locke, or Tillotson? If it be, you may conclude that it is right." The list of authorities for his planned dictionary includes more names from after the Restoration than before it. But many of the things that made Old English a good choice made the late seventeenth century a bad one. Johnson's reference to "false refinement" sounds like the castigation of foppish and epicene French beaux popular since the Restoration, and catches the tone of many accusations against the seventeenth century. The affectation of a frenchified culture was simply not manly enough to satisfy the need for an English golden age.

So neither was a wholly adequate surrogate for Augustan Latin. Another option, though, was more suitable: the undefiled wells of "the writers before the restoration." In collecting his own quotations, Johnson turned to the Renaissance, when he felt the language reached its zenith: specifically, the 1580s through the 1650s, from Sidney to the Restoration, between rudeness and declension. His "studious" search for "examples and authorities from the writers before the restoration" is an expression of the eighteenth-century desire to authorize the language by reference to a corpus of canonical British texts. Johnson looked to the age of Elizabeth and the authors who, as Hawkins was the first to argue, provided the models for his own style.

He wasn't alone. Edward Phillips recommends "for the avoiding of ... gross words ... onely this in general, To be ever conversant in the best Authours, as Sir *Philip Sidney*, Sir *Thomas More*, Sir *Walter Rawleigh*, my Lord *Verulam*, *Ben Johnson*." For Swift, "the Period wherein the *English* Tongue received most Improvement" could be said "to commence with the Beginning of Queen *Elizabeth*'s Reign, and to conclude with the great Rebellion in Forty-two." Even Hurd, whose temperament is often far from Johnson's, agrees with him on this point, finding "the condition of our language in the age of Elizabeth" to be "pure, strong, and perspicuous, without affectation."

Tracing the ascent of this standard and justifying the primacy of the Renaissance is the business of Johnson's Preface and History. The "time of rudeness antecedent to perfection" took more than a millennium, from the fifth century to the end of the sixteenth. Indeed, in its earliest days, English had little to recommend it. "We know nothing of the scanty jargon of our barbarous ancestors," writes Johnson. But after the introduction Christianity, the Angles, Saxons, and Jutes became by degrees acquainted with the *Roman* language, and so gained, from time to time, some knowledge and elegance, till in three centuries [after 450] they had formed a language capable of expressing all the sentiments of a civilised people.

Thus after the language "began to be adapted to civil and religious purposes," it became "artless and simple, unconnected and concise." The Norman Invasion brought about the next phase: the terms of philosophy and science entered the language along with an infusion of Norman French. Few in the eighteenth century apart from Thomas Warton had anything to say about the poetry of the eleventh through fourteenth centuries, but there was far more interest in the final stage of refinement, which began in the late fourteenth century: "From the time of Gower and Chaucer," writes Johnson, "the English writers have studied elegance, and advanced their language, by successive improvements."

By the end of the sixteenth century, the process had reached its peak, and from the writers of that time a pure and copious language may be collected:

From the authours which rose in the time of *Elizabeth*, a speech might be formed adequate to all the purposes of use and elegance. If the language of theology were extracted from *Hooker* and the translation of the Bible; the terms of natural knowledge from *Bacon*; the phrases of policy, war, and navigation from *Raleigh*; the dialect of poetry and fiction from *Spenser* and *Sidney*; and the diction of common life from *Shakespeare*, few ideas would be lost to mankind, for want of *English* words, in which they might be expressed.

Here are the same claims for Renaissance English that were made by the humanists for Augustan Latin, and also, less successfully, for Saxon and Restoration English: it plays the part of a pure native tradition. It retains the vigour of the Gothic ages but anticipates the refinement of Temple, and offers just the kind of classical purity the eighteenth century sought.

A brief excursus. When the Renaissance began to become England's golden age, its language was for the first time allowed to have a character of its own: to be more than a step on the way to something else. It achieved "a stile which never becomes obsolete, a certain mode of phraseology so consonant and congenial to the analogy and principles of its ... language as to remain settled and unaltered." It was therefore for the first time worthy of an attention not merely antiquarian. So, as Boswell writes, Johnson "disapproved of Lord Hailes, for having modernised the language of the ever- memorable John Hales of Eton.

'An authour's language, Sir, (said he,) is a characteristical part of his composition, and is also characteristical of the age in which he writes.'" This is how he justifies, for instance, the preservation of forms like *hugger-mugger* in his Shakespeare edition: "That the words now replaced are better, I do not undertake to prove; it is sufficient that they are Shakespeare's: if phraseology is to be changed as words grow uncouth by disuse, or gross by vulgarity, the history of every language will be lost; we shall no longer have the words of any authour; and ... we shall in time have very little of his meaning." "The history of our language," he says elsewhere, "and the true force of our words, can only be preserved, by keeping the text of authours free from adulteration."

This concern with a historically specific state of the language was new to the eighteenth century, but not confined to Johnson. Hughes, for instance, recognizes that the language of the English Renaissance had a distinct character, one that was worth preserving, in producing the first old-spelling edition of a modern English text. He resolves not only to preserve the Text entire, but to follow likewise, for the most part, the old Spelling. This may be thought by some too strict and precise; yet there was a Necessity for it, not only to shew the true State of our Language, as *Spenser* wrote it, but to keep the exact Sense.

Johnson carefully preserves the original orthography in his "History of the Language," though not in his illustrative quotations. The *Six Old Plays* published in 1779 are likewise in old spelling. Jonathan Richardson goes so far as to argue that the 1674 edition of *Paradise Lost* "ought to be the Model of Some Future Edition, and follow'd Letter for Letter and

Point for Point." So much for the digression; now to conclude. In the larger study of which this is a part, I explore what the age of Elizabeth meant to the age of Johnson, and try to examine it from a number of angles. One thing all these perspectives have in common is the way in which the period we now call the Renaissance was beginning to coalesce into a coherent age — not only with its own identity, but, more important, with its own cultural uses.

Johnson's age, that is to say, *used* the previous age to understand, authorize, regulate, even create itself, just as the humanists situated themselves in history by referring to their beloved antiquity and despised Middle Ages. The same thing was happening, I have argued here, with the language. As Elizabeth's age began to assume a coherent identity, writers looked backwards to understand and regulate their language: they treated a privileged point in history as a norm and regarded any deviation from it as barbaric corruption. The sixteenth century's insecurity about its Latinity was eased only by appeals to Cicero and his contemporaries; the eighteenth century's insecurities about its language likewise turned to Shakespeare and his.

Eighteenth-century linguistic histories entangle these historical judgments with logical and aesthetic judgments so tightly, in fact, that it is difficult to separate them. Languages, it seems, *need* such privileged moments, for golden ages can cut many of the Gordian knots that appeals to logic or beauty cannot untie. Johnson's own attention to "false refinement and declension," with its implication of a falling-off from a linguistic golden age, reveals one of the most important ways Johnson himself integrates historiography into considerations of the English language, hoping to "mak[e] our ancient volumes the ground-work of stile, admitting among the additions of later times, only such as may supply real deficiencies."

Chapter 3

Use, Elegance, and National Identity in Johnson's Dictionary

It's always wise to take metaphors seriously; it's doubly so with so careful a writer as Johnson; and I suggest it's trebly so in the *Dictionary*. Johnson's calling the sixteenth- and early seventeenth-century writers "undefiled" (a borrowing from Spenser) and "pure sources" suggests a concomitant corruption in others. Purity *versus* corruption was an important theme in the eighteenth century; George Campbell's 1776 *Philosophy of Rhetoric*, for instance, makes much of an unadulterated English tongue. But however much the metaphor was used in Hanoverian London, it originated neither there nor then.

Purity, in fact, is a favourite and Protean *topos* of Renaissance humanists. For the writers of the fifteenth and sixteenth centuries, impurity is always charged to barbarians. But Quattrocento barbarians, it turns out, wore many hats. Some ostensible barbarians were the comparatively innocuous Scholastic philosophers of the Middle Ages, infecting the learning and the Latin of the ancients with their own debased texts. Others, like the fifteenth-century Turks occupying Constantinople, were little better than the fifth-century Vandals and Visigoths. Still others, at least in the Protestant countries, were to be found among the villains of the Inquisition and Counter-Reformation, who sullied the early pristine Church. This is a diverse group, but they all taint and infect an otherwise pure tradition. Countless examples could be adduced, but two will serve. Linacre's motto, *ad fontes*, suggests the tenor: the desire is to arrive at the pure source, to drink from waters yet unpolluted. At the other end of the Renaissance, Milton, decked out in his full Puritan gear, develops the motif in characterizing the "threefold corruption" of the medieval bishops:

1. The best times were spreadingly infected. 2. The best men of those times fouly tainted. 3. The best writings of those men dangerously adulterated.

Though I'm not interested in identifying specific sources, I suggest that the eighteenth century inherited this Renaissance concern with purity. To judge by the front matter of the *Dictionary* alone, Johnson was attuned to their discourse of linguistic and cultural corruption; the metaphorical richness of the humanist tradition fills both the Preface and the History.

A guardian of the language, then, is charged with defending English from linguistic vandals. Johnson leaves little doubt as to the identity of these modern-day barbarians. "The whole fabrick and scheme of the *English* language," he writes, "is *Gothick* or *Teutonick*" (sig. D1r); but "Our language ... has ... been gradually departing from its original *Teutonick* character, and deviating towards a *Gallick* structure and phraseology." The French, then, are the invaders, the well-poisoners. The inversion of the hierarchy of Romance over Germanic languages, already in place in antiquity (including Tacitus) and reinforced by the sack of cultured Rome by Teutonic louts, would not likely be missed by contemporary readers.

We should be precise about the crime of which the French are accused. Though not a great etymologist, Johnson of course knew that many thousands of English words are of French origin. "Phraseology" is not a mere synonym for "words":

Single words may enter by thousands, and the fabrick of the tongue continue the same, but new phraseology changes much at once; it alters not the single stones of the building, but the order of the columns. (sig. C2v)

The danger Johnson sees is that, in the century or so before the *Dictionary*'s publication in 1755, English was being shaken at its foundations by modern authors, "by their knowledge of foreign languages, or ignorance of their own, by vanity or wantonness, by compliance with fashion, or lust of innovation" (sig. b1v).

Johnson is not, however, engaging in knee-jerk Gaul bashing. His respect for French writers, beginning with Scaliger, Thuanus, and Montaigne in the Renaissance and running through his own age, is sincere. The problem isn't that the French language is bad or dirty, but that it doesn't belong in the English language. Languages, it seems, are mutually corrupting.

The Renaissance provides not only the source of the metaphor, but a model of proper linguistic purity. Some wells, that is, remain undefiled: they are "the writers before the restoration." The *Dictionary* shows, perhaps better than any of his other works, both the depth and the breadth of Johnson's reading in these authors. Among the fifteen most-quoted authors in the *Dictionary* are seven canonical authors of the English Renaissance, who were achieving their canonical status at just this time: Shakespeare, Milton, Bacon, Spenser, Hooker, Browne, and Sidney. The thousands of quotations from the Bible come from the 1611 Authorized Version, the only translation Johnson mentions with anything other than scorn. And some of the most characteristically "Johnsonian" words — *adscititious, dignotion, vermiculation* — are owing to Johnson's professed aim in *The Rambler*: "I have familiarized the terms of philosophy by applying them to popular ideas, but have rarely admitted any word not authorized by former writers."

So it is in the "former writers" that linguistic purity is to be found, and tracing the ascent of this standard is the business of the Preface and History. "Every language," says Johnson, "has a time of rudeness antecedent to perfection," a time which took the better part of a millennium, from the middle of the eighth century to the end of the sixteenth. By then, though, the process had reached its peak, and from the writers of that time a pure and copious language may be collected:

> From the authours which rose in the time of *Elizabeth*, a speech might be formed adequate to all the purposes of use and elegance. If the language of theology were extracted from

Hooker and the translation of the Bible; the terms of natural knowledge from *Bacon*; the phrases of policy, war, and navigation from *Raleigh*; the dialect of poetry and fiction from *Spenser* and *Sidney*; and the diction of common life from *Shakespeare*, few ideas would be lost to mankind, for want of *English* words, in which they might be expressed. (sig. C1r)

The late sixteenth century, of course, probably saw a greater influx of Romance words than the middle eighth (or the middle eighteenth, for that matter), but we can set aside the question of whether Johnson's historical sense was accurate. (We must also set aside the exquisite irony of the sesquipedalian Johnson — accused in his own day of writing Latin words with English terminations — calling for a Germanic English.) The fact remains that he was concerned with erecting the age of Elizabeth as the standard of purity. And just as he inverts the centuries-old hierarchy of Romance over Germanic languages, he associates not only "use" with the basic Saxon vocabulary, but appropriates even traditionally latinate "elegance" for the English authors, leaving little to be desired from outsiders.

Johnson strives, that is, for a minimally adequate vocabulary — "admitting ... only such as may supply real deficiencies" — such as we see in the last *Rambler*: "I believe that whoever knows the English tongue in its present extent, will be able to express his thoughts without further help from other nations" (*Rambler* 208; V, 319).

I have explored some of the analogues to humanism, but with this notion of minimal sufficiency, "without further help from other nations," other possibilities may be nearer to hand.

I don't suggest that the following passage from 1684 is anything like a source for the Preface, but Johnson's writings share at least some superficial characteristics with the Marquess of Halifax's third-person comments on himself:

But for the earth of England, though perhaps inferior to that of many places abroad, to him there is divinity in it, and he would rather die than see a spire of English grass trampled down by a foreign trespasser.

This sort of nationalism, I suggest, has lexicographical

cousins. John Cannon, one of the more learned and moderate commentators on the difficult matter of Johnson's politics, is unequivocal: "In the *Dictionary*, ... a national purpose was clear from the outset." Sledd and Kolb, among the most important modern commentators on the *Dictionary*, also hear patriotic echoes not only in Johnson but in the other two great early modern lexicographical projects, the Italian *Vocabolario* and the French *Dictionnaire*. But not everyone agrees. Daisuke Nagashima uses the History of the English Language to argue that Johnson was less nationalistic than many earlier writers on language:

> In accordance with Wallis as against the linguistic nationalists from Camden to Bailey, Johnson clearly distinguishes "the Saxon (Old English)" from "the present *English*." ... Johnson's basic purpose in the history ... lies in displaying the historical changes, rather than the continuous identity, of his mother tongue.

I don't know that the recurring emphasis on the Teutonic roots of English bears out Nagashima's claim, but even if Johnson does not consistently trace English back to the age of the Egg Kings, *Elizabeth*'s England is a source of not only a linguistic normative standard, but a political one as well. The victory over the Spanish Armada, for instance, was still a defining moment in the English national story nearly two centuries later.

Cannon pithily sums up some of the traps into which we might fall when we drag nationalism into the eighteenth century: "The concept of nationalism has been almost as troublesome to historians as the practice of it has been to rulers". The conventional view was clearly formulated half a century ago: "Nationalism, as we understand it, is not older than the second half of the eighteenth century. Its first great manifestation was the French Revolution." But I suggest that if national identity proceeds through the exclusion of the foreign and the insistence on the adequacy of the national culture, it has unmistakable similarities to the discourse of purity and contamination. The early humanists, it is true, formulated a trans-European rather than a nationalistic identity, no doubt because the fragmentation of the Italian principalities (and later the thriving tramontane humanism) made identification with a single nation-state problematic. But even by the late sixteenth century, the same valorization of purity and castigation of barbarism found a place in nationalistic discourse: one needn't look further than John of Gaunt's "fortress built by nature for herself, against infection."

John Barrell may overstate the case when he argues "Johnson's appeal to the 'orthography of our fathers' is closely related to that deference to the wisdom of our political forefathers," but I think he is right when he says "good usage is to be defined nationalistically" — or at least that good usage and nationalism proceed by similar means in the eighteenth century, and that both look backwards. In both explicitly political nationalism and the celebration of "our ancient volumes," the same habit of mind is at work: both seek a foundation on which English linguistic or political authority can rest, and they work by characterizing the foreign as impure. The only difference lies in the synchronic *versus* the diachronic application of this paradigm: nationalism applies the metaphors of purity and corruption spatially; the extolling of Renaissance authors applies them chronologically. Both seek to justify and to constitute a privileged point, temporal or geographical, as normative by treating any deviation from it as barbaric corruption. Eighteenth-century writers *used* the previous age and its paradigms to understand, and even create, themselves: they used a Renaissance metaphor to valorize Renaissance authors to borrow the political glory of the Renaissance. I haven't time to argue that Johnson is in any way representative of his time, though I hope to do that elsewhere. Here I'd like only to suggest that the linguistic, national, and historical identity of an era can be constituted through the sort of cultural historiography Johnson employs in his *Dictionary*, and that this is one of the ways in which the age of Johnson worked to define itself through the age of Elizabeth.

Chapter 4

Johnson and Boswell

IT was a supreme fortune that gave Johnson the friendship of Reynolds and Boswell. His great personality is still an active and familiar force. We know him as well as if he had lived among us. But the first of Reynolds's portraits was painted when Johnson had completed *The Rambler* and was already "the great moralist," and Boswell did not meet him till after he had obtained his pension. The Johnson that we know is the Johnson "who loves to fold his legs and have his talk out." The years in which he fought poverty and gained his place in the world of letters are obscure to us, in comparison with those in which he enjoyed his hard-won leisure. He never cared, in later life, to speak about his early struggles; he never spoke much about himself at any time. Even when he wrote the lives of authors whom he had known and might have told his own experiences without disturbing the unity of his picture, he offered little more than the reflection of his feelings. Sir John Hawkins did not make full use of his great opportunity. He alone, of all Johnson's biographers, had known him almost from the start of their work in London, but he drew on his recollections fitfully and lazily. He has given enough to show how much more he might have given. Boswell, with all his pertinacious curiosity, found that he had to rely mainly on his own researches. There were in these early years subjects "too delicate to question Johnson upon." Much remained, and still remains, for others to discover.

New letters, anecdotes or facts will not disturb our idea of Johnson. They will, at most, fill gaps and settle doubts. The man himself is known. Yet the very greatness of his personality has tended to interfere with the recognition of his greatness as a man of letters. No other author whose profession was literature seems to owe so little of his fame to his books. Many writers, Dryden and Scott among others, give the impression that they were greater than anything that they have written. It has been the unique fate of Johnson to be dissociated from his works. He would have welcomed the knowledge that he was to be remembered as a man, for he had no delusions about authorship. But he is to be found in his works as he wished to be known, and as he was. If the greatest of biographies catches him at moments which he would not have recorded, it is also true that his writings give us his more intimate thoughts, and take us into regions which were denied to his conversation.

LICHFIELD, OXFORD AND BIRMINGHAM

He was born at Lichfield on 18 September, 1709, in the year in which his father, one of the chief booksellers of the midlands, was sheriff of the city. As a schoolboy, he seems to have been already distinguished by his ease in learning, his tenacity of memory, his lack of application, and delays adjusted to his power of rapid work. But the best part of his instruction he acquired for himself in his father's shop. There, he prowled about at leisure, and read as his fancy directed. He was never a laborious reader. The progress which the understanding makes through a book, he said, has more pain than pleasure in it. "Sir; do you read books through?" he once asked. There may have been few books that he read through himself. His defective eyesight had probably some bearing on what came to be an intellectual habit. But he had in a supreme degree the gift of discovering the matter and quality of a book, almost on opening its pages. The extent of his knowledge was the wonder of all his friends: Adam Smith declared that Johnson knew more books than any man alive. He had begun this knowledge by sampling his father's store. And in these days, before he had left school, he was already a good enough Latinist to be diverted from a search for apples by the discovery of a folio of Petrarch.

He was intended to follow his father's business. Hawkins

and Mrs. Piozzi both say that he could bind a book. But, after two years at home, he contrived to proceed to Oxford. He entered Pembroke college as a commoner on 31 October, 1728, and remained there continuously, with, at most, one week's break in the long vacation, till December, 1729. Thereafter, his residence was irregular, and he left the university without taking a degree. The outstanding fact of his college career was the translation of Pope's *Messiah* into Latin verse, as a Christmas exercise. This was the first of his works that was printed, being included in *A Miscellany of Poems by Several Hands* (1731), collected by J. Husbands, fellow of Pembroke college. Latin was already almost as familiar a language to him as his own. Late in life, during his tour in France, he was "resolute in speaking Latin," though he had a command of French idiom that enabled him to supply the first paragraph to Baretti's translation of *Rasselas.* "Though he is a great critic in French," said Baretti, "and knows almost as much Italian as I do, he cannot speak either language, but he talks Latin with all Cicero's fury." His knowledge of the renascence poets was unusually wide. He regretted that they were not generally known, and that Pope's attempt to rescue them from neglect by his *Selecta Poemata Italorum* had been fruitless. The first book which he himself designed was an edition of Politian, with a history of Latin poetry in the fourteenth and fifteenth centuries. Proposals for printing it by subscription were issued in August, 1734; but nothing came of the scheme, and the Latin poems of Politian still await an editor.

HIS TRANSLATION OF A VOYAGE TO ABYSSINIA

Of his five and a half years in the midlands after his residence in Oxford, the records are fragmentary. His earliest extant letter (30 October, 1731) has reference to an unsuccessful application for the post of usher in the grammar school of Stourbridge. He acted in this capacity for some time, in 1732, at Market Bosworth, in Leicestershire. Later in the same year, he paid a visit to his lifelong friend Edmund Hector, then settled as a surgeon in Birmingham; and it would appear that Birmingham was his home for the next three years. What is certain is that his hopes had now turned to writing. He contributed to *The Birmingham Journal* a number of essays, all of which are lost; he planned his edition of Politian; he offered to write for *The Gentleman's Magazine;* and he completed his first book, *A Voyage to Abyssinia, by Father Jerome Lobo. With a Continuation of the History of Abyssinia, and Fifteen Dissertations, by Mr. Le Grand. From the French.* The volume was printed in Birmingham and published in London, anonymously, in January, 1735.

FORESHADOWING OF JOHNSON'S STYLE

In this translation, there is much more of Le Grand than of Lobo. In parts, Johnson condensed freely; where he allowed himself least liberty was in the sixteen (not fifteen) dissertations, which occupy more than half the volume and deal with such subjects as the Nile, Prester John, the queen of Sheba and the religious customs of the Abyssinians. He was always an eager reader of books of travel; and it was fitting that the passion for whatever afforded views of human nature, which led him to describe his own experiences of another country and to urge others to describe theirs, should be shown in his first work. But the main interest of the volume now lies in the short preface. In the translation, he is content to convey the meaning of the original, and, while he follows in haste another's thought and language, we fail to find the qualities of his own style. But they are unmistakable in such a passage as this:

The Reader will here find no Regions cursed with irremediable Barrenness, or bless'd with Spontaneous Fecundity, no perpetual Gloom or unceasing Sunshine; nor are the Nations here described either devoid of all Sense of Humanity, or consummate in all private and social Virtues, here are no Hottentots without Religion, Polity, or Articulate Language, no Chinese perfectly Polite, and compleatly skill'd in all Sciences: He will discover, what will always be discover'd by a diligent and impartial Enquirer, that wherever Human Nature is to be found, there is a mixture of Vice and Virtue, a contest of Passion and Reason, and that the Creator doth not appear Partial in his Distributions, but has balanced in most Countries their particular Inconveniences by particular Favours.

He who writes much, Johnson said, will not easily escape a manner. But here is Johnson's manner in his first book. And here, too, is a forecast of the philosophy of *The Rambler* and *The Vanity of Human Wishes.* There are no distinct periods in Johnson's literary development, no sudden access of power, no change in his outlook, no novelties in his methods. He continued as he had begun. He grew in confidence and facility; he perfected his command of expression; but there was not any change in the spirit of his expression or in what he wished to express.

HIS MIGRATION TO LONDON

His experience of letters at Birmingham had not promised success, and, on his marriage in July, 1735, with Mrs. Elizabeth Porter, the widow of one of his Birmingham friends, he set up a school at Edial, near Lichfield. His first reference to the new enterprise is found in a letter of 25 June, 1735, recently published for the first time.

"I am going," he writes, "to furnish a House in the Country and keep a private Boarding-house for Young Gentlemen whom I shall endeavour to instruct in a method somewhat more rational than those commonly practised."

His "scheme for the classes of a grammar school," as given by Hawkins and Boswell, illustrates what he was to say about teaching in his *Life of Milton*. The school failed, and, on 2 March, 1737, he set out for London with one of his pupils, David Garrick. Henceforward, London was to be his home. Having no profession, he became by necessity an author.

IRENE AND ITS SUBSEQUENT PRODUCTION ON THE STAGE

He had no promise of work, but he looked to find employment on *The Gentleman's Magazine*, and he had hopes in the drama. He had written at Edial three acts of his tragedy *Irene*. He worked at it during his first months in London, and finished it on his visit to Lichfield to settle his affairs, in the summer of 1737.

But there remained for him "the labour of introducing it on the stage, an undertaking which to an ingenuous mind was in a very high degree vexatious and disgusting"—as he wrote of another's experience while his own tragedy was still unacted.

The goodwill of Garrick, whom he placed under a heavy debt by the great prologue which heralded his managership of Drury lane in 1774, at last brought it on the stage in February, 1749, and protracted its run to nine nights, so that there might be three third-night benefits. With all his knowledge of human nature, Johnson was unable to exhibit dramatically the shades which distinguish one character from another.

Irene is only a moral poem in a succession of dialogues on the theme that "Peace from innocence must flow" and "none are happy but the wise and virtuous." And the thought struggles with the metre. He could not divest his blank verse of the qualities of the couplet. The same faults are to be found in his translation, made many years later, of a short passage of Metastasio.

We expect the rime at the end of the line; and, when we come on it in the couplets with which each act closes, instead of feeling that they are tags, as we do in our great tragedies, we find the verse bound forward with unwonted ease. Johnson had too massive and too logical an intellect to adapt himself readily to the drama. He came to perceive this, but not till long after he had described the qualifications of a dramatist in his *Life of Savage,* and had proceeded with a second play, *Charles of Sweden,* of which the only record is an ambiguous allusion in a letter (10 June, 1742). The labour he spent on *Irene* led him to think well of it for a time; but, late in life, when he returned to it afresh, he agreed with the common verdict. He "thought it had been better." He could speak from his own experience when, in the passage on tediousness in his *Life of Prior,* he said that "unhappily this pernicious failure is that which an author is least able to discover."

HIS WORK ON THE GENTLEMAN'S MAGAZINE HIS REAL START AS A MAN OF LETTERS

It was *The Gentleman's Magazine* that gave Johnson his real start as a man of letters. Founded by Edward Cave, under the name Sylvanus Urban, in January, 1731, it had been growing steadily from small beginnings. Its original purpose was to reprint, from month to month, a selection of the more interesting matter that had appeared in the journals; and the name "magazine" was, in this its first application to a periodical, intended as a modest title for a collection which made small claim to originality. The idea was not altogether new. *The Grub-street Journal* contains a section of "domestic news" extracted from other papers, and sometimes so treated as to suggest to the modern reader the more urbane comments in the pages of *Punch.* But, as the editors of *The Grub-street Journal* complained in the preface to *Memoirs of the Society of Grub-street* (1737), their rival of *The Gentleman's Magazine* took anything he fancied—news, letters, essays or verses—and printed as much or as little of them as he pleased.

The success of the *Magazine* was never in doubt. The first number went into a fifth edition; and with success came ambition. In the number for January, 1739, a correspondent, who evidently was Johnson, observes that the extracts from the weekly journalists have "shrunk at length into a very few columns and made way for original letters and dissertations." The *Magazine* now included parliamentary reports, poetical essays, serial stories, mathematical papers, maps, songs with music, and a register of publications.

Most of the devices of modern journalism were anticipated in these early numbers. Cave had the luck and the skill to hit on what the public wanted. If we may trust the preface to the collected numbers for 1738, there were immediately "almost twenty imitations." Yet *The Gentleman's Magazine* had many features in common with *The Gentleman's Journal; or the Monthly Miscellany,* which Peter Motteux had started in January, 1692, and carried on with flagging zeal to 1694. The earlier periodical had begun on a much higher literary level and remains a work of very great interest; but its fortunes were not watched over by a man of business. It had been modelled partly on *Le Mercure Galant*. *The Gentleman's Magazine* was, in its origin, independent of both its French and its English forerunners.

REPORTS OF DEBATES IN PARLIAMENT

In the letter which Johnson sent to Cave from Birmingham in 1734, besides offering to contribute, he suggested several improvements. For "the low jests, awkward buffoonery, or the dull scurrilities of either party," which were to procure for it or its imitators a place in *The Dunciad*, might be substituted, he thought, "short literary dissertations in Latin or English, critical remarks on authors ancient or modern, or loose pieces worth preserving." Nothing came of the letter; but the suggestion that the *Magazine* should take itself more seriously accorded with Cave's business instincts, and the changes gradually introduced were in accordance with Johnson's wishes.

His first contribution, the Latin alcaics beginning *Urbane, nullis fesse laboribus*, did not appear till March, 1738. From that time, he was regularly employed; and he at once asserted some sort of literary control. There cannot be any doubt that the subsequent steady rise in the character of the *Magazine* was largely due to him. He also helped to guide its fortunes through a grave crisis. Reports of the proceedings and debates in parliament had been given in the *Magazine* since 1732; but, on 13 April, 1738, the House of Commons declared such reports to be "a notorious breach of the Privilege of this House."

The *Magazine* could not easily omit a section on which much of its popularity depended, and, in June, 1738, there appeared "debates in the Senate of Magna Lilliputia." If, as Hawkins says, the device was Cave's, it had Johnson's approval; and his hand is unmistakable in the passage in which the device is explained. He began by editing the reports, which continued to be written by William Guthrie, the first of his many Scottish friends. He was their sole author only for the thirty-six numbers and supplements from July, 1741 to March,

1744, and author rather than reporter. According to Hawkins, he had never entered either House; according to Murphy, he had once found his way into the House of Commons. He expanded in Cave's printing-office, long after the actual debates, the scanty notes supplied to him, and invested them with his own argumentative skill and eloquence. Some of the speeches are said to represent what was said by more than one speaker; others he described as the mere coinage of his imagination. His reports are, in fact, original work, and a very great work.

To us who know the secret of their authorship, it is surprising that they should not have been recognised as the work of a man of letters. They are on a high level of literary excellence, and there is an obvious uniformity in the style. Even when they succeed in suggesting the idiosyncrasies of the different speakers, they show one cast of mind and texture of language. They are Johnson's own debates on the political questions of the day, based—and based only—on the debates in parliament. He said, within a few days of his death, that he wrote them "with more velocity" than any other work—often three columns of the *Magazine* within the hour, and, once, ten pages between noon and early evening.

The wonder is, not so much that debates thus written could have been so good, as that debates so good could have been accepted as giving the words of the speakers. Johnson had not expected this; and, when he recognised it, he determined not to be any longer "accessory to the propagation of falsehood." This is the explanation given for his sudden abandonment of them in 1744. But the secret was long kept, and they continued to be regarded as genuine. There is more of Johnson than of Pitt in the famous speech about "the atrocious crime of being a young man." And two speeches entirely written by him appeared, to his amusement, in the collected works of Chesterfield.

OTHER CONTRIBUTIONS TO THE MAGAZINE

The extent of his other contributions cannot easily be determined. We have often only the evidence of style to guide us, and his editorial privileges make it difficult to apply. It is very doubtful, for instance, if the short notice, in November, 1739, of the poems of Joseph Warton and Collins printed in the previous number is, as Wooll states in his *Memoirs of Warton,* the work of Johnson. Our best authority is Boswell, but his list is only tentative. We know that he wrote the biographies of Sarpi, Boerhaave, Blake, Drake, Barretier, Lewis Morin, Burmann and Sydenham; and there are other articles about which there can be no reasonable doubt. The amount of his writing varies greatly from month to month.

In the number for December, 1740, which contains his *Essay on Epitaphs,* most of the original contributions are his; in other numbers, we cannot safely ascribe to him more than the debates. The question of authorship has never been examined thoroughly; but, even with the help of Cave's office books, there would be obstacles to a conclusive finding. In addition to his work for Cave, he had brought out, with other publishers, *Marmor Norfolciense* (April, 1739), an ironical discussion, with a political bearing, on the supposed discovery of a prophecy in "monkish rhyme," and *A Compleat Vindication of the Licensers of the Stage* (May, 1739), an ironical attack on the rejection of Brooke's *Gustavus Vasa.* Continued irony is rarely successful. Johnson did not try it again.

THE LIFE OF SAVAGE

The early series of biographies was followed by the elaborate life of a poet whom Johnson had known intimately, and whose character required protection from the insults and calumnies which it invited. Richard Savage died in the prison of Bristol at the beginning of August, 1743; and, in the number of *The Gentleman's Magazine* for the same month, Johnson announced, in an unsigned letter, that a biography of him was in preparation. He wrote it with his usual speed—once he wrote as much as forty-eight printed pages at a sitting—and had it published in February, 1744. It is a work of remarkable and varied interest, and throws light on a period of Johnson's career of which we know too little. They had suffered poverty together and forgotten it in their companionship; they had spent whole nights in the streets when their combined resources could not find them a shelter; and the description of Savage's fortunes reflects what Johnson had himself endured, and might have still to endure.

He was attracted to Savage by the story of his life, on which research had not yet cast any doubt, by his shrewd knowledge of human nature, by his social skill and experience and by his talent as a writer. Savage was eleven years older than Johnson, and in his varied life had much to tell. But the chief attraction was Savage's own character. His great capacities could not save him from his undoing. He was self-indulgent, petulant, aggressive and ungrateful; there was excuse for the indifference or resentment of those who had once been benefactors. All this Johnson brings out clearly in a narrative which, when it leans from impartiality, leans to the side of friendship. He related everything as he knew it, with no suggestion of censure, but with generous sympathy. *The Life of Savage* is one of those rare biographies which, by their perfect sincerity, tell us as much of the character of the author as of the man described. He included it, later, with only slight alterations, in *The Lives of the Poets.* It had been an adequate expression of his feelings when it was written, and he wisely decided to let well enough alone.

But it is a different *Life* from the other *Lives,* and differs from them in more than scale and method. It is the study of a personality rather than of a poet, though at no time would Johnson have tried to make such a distinction. The criticism of Savage's works is the least part of it, and has not yet all the writer's easy mastery. The style, too, which, at its best, is as good as it ever was to be, sometimes lacks its later certainty and precision. And the frequent repetition of the same ideas, though always in different language, shows a desire to give in full the content of a full mind rather than to represent it by selection. The new setting of *The Life of Savage* invites a comparison which proves that Johnson's abilities were strengthening and maturing to his seventieth year. Yet he never revealed himself more fully than in this early tribute to the memory of a difficult friend.

GREATER SCHEMES

Johnson's contributions to *The Gentleman's Magazine* had become less frequent in 1743, and they ceased in the following year. He was meditating larger schemes. And he had latterly been doing much other work.

Since the end of 1742, he had been engaged with William Oldys in cataloguing the printed books in the library of the earl of Oxford, then newly purchased by Thomas Osborne, the bookseller. The *Proposals* for printing the catalogue by subscription were written by Johnson and issued in December, 1742, and the *Account of the Harleian Library*, which they contained, was afterwards made to serve as preface to the first of the four volumes of the catalogue—*Catalogus Bibliothecae Harleianae*, 1743–4. While the catalogue was in progress, the bookseller, who had remarkable luck in having secured the services of one of the greatest of English literary antiquaries and one of the most scholarly of English critics, was persuaded to publish a collection of the more scarce and valuable tracts or pamphlets in his possession, under the title *The Harleian Miscellany*.

The bulk of the selective and editorial work fell to Oldys; but it was Johnson who, again, wrote the *Proposals*, and contributed the introduction (1744), which, when reprinted separately, he entitled *An Essay on the Origin and Importance of Small Tracts and Fugitive Pieces*. In this, his first attempt at literary history, he gives a short sketch of English pamphlets from the reformation to the reign of Charles II, and follows in the tracks of such works as *The Phenix* (1707) and *The Phoenix Britannicus* (1731), *The Critical History of Pamphlets* (1716) of Myles Davies, and the *Dissertation on Pamphlets* (1731) of his collaborator Oldys. There is no evidence of Johnson's hand in the Harleian *Collection of Voyages and Travels* (1745).

On the completion of this congenial experience in bibliography Johnson proposed to edit Shakespeare. The work was not to be undertaken for many years yet; but it was the first of the larger schemes planned by him. *Miscellaneous Observations on the Tragedy of Macbeth* (April, 1745) was intended to prepare the way. There was still room for a new edition, as Hanmer had given most thought to regularised metre and sumptuous printing, and Warburton seemed to have abandoned what he had announced as early as 1740. But, after the death of Pope and the completion of Hanmer's edition in 1744, Warburton set to work in earnest, and the prospect of early publication compelled Johnson to lay aside his scheme, which could not have had an equal chance of success, inasmuch as, like most of his work up to this time, it was anonymous. When Warburton's edition appeared, in 1747, Johnson had the meagre satisfaction of finding his *Miscellaneous Observations* singled out for praise in the vituperative preface. It was now that he turned to the *Dictionary.*

He had "long thought of it," he said; "it had grown up in his mind insensibly." The *Plan of a Dictionary of the English Language* was issued in 1747, and, at the desire of Dodsley, was addressed to the earl of Chesterfield. This year—which is, also, the year of the Drury lane prologue—marks the turn in Johnson's fortunes, though the fitful struggle with poverty was not yet over. But what was Johnson doing in 1745 and 1746? Here again the records are deficient. Of more than a thousand letters of his that are known, there is not one to throw light on either of these years. Johnson did not confine himself to the labours of the *Dictionary.* During the eight years of its preparation he wrote his greatest poem, and gave new life to the periodical essay.

JOHNSON'S EARLIER VERSE

His school verses, which were preserved by the pride of a teacher and the admiration of a friend, and printed by Boswell, are of little interest except in relation to his later work. They show the study of *The Rape of the Lock* and the translation of Homer, and they occasionally indulge in the liberties of Dryden's triple rime and alexandrine—liberties from which Johnson afterwards refrained, though he came to say that the art of concluding the sense in couplets "has perhaps been with rather too much constancy pursued." The piece entitled "The Young Authour" is a first study for the great passage in *The Vanity of Human Wishes* on the scholar's life, and, in the the music of the metre, and in the turn and balance of the expression, already discovers the quality of his mature verse. He acquired a reputation for ease in writing and for readiness to help a friend in need. His verses *Written at the request of a gentleman to whom a lady had given a sprig of myrtle* were remembered as having been made in five minutes, and those *To Miss Hickman, playing on the Spinnet,* or others like them, led the girl's father to opine that their author could write about anything. What he called "the endearing elegance of female friendship" had been, long before he met Mrs. Thrale, an effective spur to his facility.

Some of the pieces written while he was still in search of occupation in the midlands afterwards found their way into *The Gentleman's Magazine* and Mrs. Williams's *Miscellanies in Prose and Verse* (1766). None of them is more characteristic than *Friendship, An Ode.* On the other hand, the collected editions include several pieces clearly not his. He could not have written *To Lyce, an elderly Lady.* It is no less certain that, though he did write some verses *To Stella,* the chance that a piece is addressed to Stella is not, as his editors seem to have believed, an argument of his authorship. His early poems have still to be discriminated; but their chief interest will always be that they were written by the author of *London* and *The Vanity of Human Wishes.*

LONDON AND THE VANITY OF HUMAN WISHES

London: a poem, in imitation of the Third Satire of Juvenal was published in May, 1738, on the same day as Pope's *One Thousand Seven Hundred and Thirty-Eight, a Dialogue something like Horace,* and thus, accidentally, invited a comparison which appears to have gone in Johnson's favour. Here was a new author who concealed his name, rivalling Pope in the very kind of verse which, after an indisputed career, he had found best suited to his genius. The poem went into a second edition within a week; and Pope himself, who was always generous in his recognition of excellence, and had said of Johnson's youthful translation of his *Messiah* that posterity would have to decide which form of the poem was the original, declared that the unknown author of *London* could not be long concealed. The method of "imitation" adopted in this poem was described by Johnson in his *Life of Pope* as "a kind of middle composition between translation and original design, which pleases when the thoughts are unexpectedly applicable and the parallels lucky." Brought into *vogue* by Boileau, it had been practised in English by Rochester, Oldham and Dryden (in his revision of Soames's translation of Boileau's *Art Poétique*), and many others; and it had recently been perfected by Pope, who had so written that a knowledge of the original might enhance the appreciation, but should not be indispensable to it. Juvenal's *Third Satire* lent itself to imitation and had already been copied by Boileau and Oldham.

The chief criticism to be urged against Johnson's poem is that it does not show Pope's art in escaping from its model. He was still timid enough to wish to show himself scholar as well as poet. When he wrote that "falling houses thunder on your head," or that the midnight murderer "leaves unseen a dagger in your breast," he thought more of Juvenal than of modern fact. The need of a parallel forces him to say, "I cannot bear a French metropolis"; but this was not the London described in Voltaire's *Lettres Anglaises*. He himself admitted (in a manuscript note) that the description of Orgilio was "no picture of modern manners, though it might be true at Rome." His own opinion on the advantages of country life we shall find, not here, but in the passage on scenes of flowery felicity and the melody of the nightingale in *The Life of Savage*. His political views are more truly represented: the references to excise and pensions, as well as to patrons, anticipate the definitions in the *Dictionary*. But it is when Juvenal leads him to speak of poverty that he expresses his own feelings in his own person.

None of these objections can be urged against *The Vanity of Human Wishes*, written in imitation of Juvenal's *Tenth Satire* and published, with Johnson's name, in January, 1749. There is nothing in this poem to suggest to those unacquainted with the model that it is an imitation; it is, indeed, not so much an imitation as a companion study by one who, amid different circumstances, took a very similar view of life. Instead of the Roman illustrations, we have modern instances of hopes that lay in power, and learning, and war, and long life and beauty. The pictures of Wolsey and Charles of Sweden, and the description of the lot of the scholar, are distinct studies of human ambition, each complete in itself and easily taken from its setting, but all viewed in the same light, and united by the one lesson of inevitable disappointment. The poem is completely satisfying as a statement of its theme. It is not less valuable as a personal document. There is nothing in it but what Johnson consistently thought and felt. He was wont to say that there is more to be endured than enjoyed in the general condition of human life; and he had found that human happiness, if it ever comes, must come by our own effort.

The concluding lines which he supplied many years later to Goldsmith's *Traveller* state his invariable experience. In *The Life of Savage* he had said that happiness is to be placed only in virtue, which is always to be obtained; and he had said much the same in *Irene*. But there were times when he doubted even this. "Where then shall hope and fear their objects find?" In his simple piety, he gave himself to the earnest exercise of religion. His *Prayers*, which were made public after his death, will win the admiration alike of idle curiosity and of doubting reason. And so, with his habitual sincerity, he gave to *The Vanity of Human Wishes* a religious conclusion which reflected his own practice. He was no pessimist. The sense of vanity may keep us from thinking that things are better than they are, but it need not make us think that they are worse. He would maintain in talk that the world was not half so wicked as it was represented to be, that there was very little gross wickedness in it, and very little extraordinary virtue. This we are told explicitly by Mrs. Piozzi, and we may learn it for ourselves from his writings.

Shortly before he wrote *The Vanity of Human Wishes*, he had aided Dodsley in planning *The Preceptor* (April, 1748), a substantial work containing "a general course of education," and had contributed to it the preface and *The Vision of Theodore, the Hermit of Teneriffe*. He told Percy that he thought this fable the best thing he ever wrote. It states the part which he assigned to religion in the conduct of life, and should be read as a supplement to *The Vanity of Human Wishes.* It may, also, be regarded as a prelude to *The Rambler.*

This began on Tuesday, 20 March, 1750, and ended, with its 208th number, on Saturday, 14 March, 1752, three days before the death of Johnson's wife. He that condemns himself to compose on a stated day, will often bring to his task, an attention dissipated, a memory overwhelmed, an imagination embarrassed, a mind distracted with anxieties, and a body languishing with disease. So he wrote in the last number, reviewing his experiences. But the paper appeared regularly every Tuesday and Saturday, though the printer might complain of the late hour of receiving the copy. The very title was chosen in haste. Johnson meant it to announce that he would pass in each essay from subject to subject. But it was not suited to his majestic deliberations. There is nothing of the rambler in any single essay. Each pursues its way in a steady, unswerving march.

THE RAMBLER AND THE REVIVAL OF THE PERIODICAL ESSAY

The conditions amid which Johnson revived the periodical essay differed widely from those amid which it originally flourished. In the interval of forty years, there had been a development of journalistic enterprise which was not paralleled in any other country. More than 150 periodicals, of one kind or another, had been meeting the needs of the reading public, and contributing to its steady growth in size and power. Some of these were on the model of *The Spectator,* while others, written with a different purpose, or planned to include a greater variety of matter, showed its influence.

The periodical essay no longer offered any of the attractions of novelty. In its strict form, it was a type of journalism that was being crushed out of favour by politics and news. By 1750, *The Gentleman's Magazine* enjoyed a secure popularity, and had its rivals; and, in the previous year, *The Monthly Review* had been established. The time was not auspicious for beginning a paper devoted exclusively to meditations on matters of no immediate interest, without the assistance of any item of news, or of a single advertisement. But, in *The Rambler*, the periodical essay reasserted itself, and entered on the second of its two great decades, that of *The Rambler, The Adventurer, The World, The Connoisseur, The Idler* and *The Citizen of the World.*

The effect of *The Rambler* was the more remarkable, in that Johnson was deficient in the qualifications of a periodical writer. The maxim that "the drama's laws the drama's patrons give" is equally true of the essay. It was not in Johnson's nature to bow to the public, however much he believed in its ultimate verdict. He spoke in his first number as if success depended on the choice of subject. But, in the treatment of his choice, he lacked the art of going to meet his readers; and they never came in great numbers. The circulation of *The Rambler* was only about 500 copies. But it raised the literary level of the periodical essay and set a standard of excellence to such papers as *The World,* whose sale was numbered in thousands.

OPENLY DIDACTIC PURPOSE OF THE RAMBLER; SUCCESS OF THE COLLECTED EDITION

It found a larger public on being reprinted in volume form, and came to be the only periodical of the century to vie with *The Spectator* in popularity. Johnson revised it for the collected edition with unusual care. It had been his most ambitious work; and he knew that it was best suited to a leisurely perusal. Yet there is little in *The Rambler* that is now well known. Much of its literary criticism was superseded by the preface to his *Shakespeare* and by his *Lives of the Poets.* The allegories and stories have not the reputation of their models in *The Spectator.* Nor are Johnson's characters familiar as Addison's are. The explanation lies mainly in his inability to visualise. He did not number the streaks of the tulip because, in effect, he did not see them; but he remarked general properties and large appearances because he had the gift, which he assiduously developed, of viewing things in their moral aspects and human relationships. The real interest of the famous passage in *Rasselas* on the aims of the poet—a passage which, it must be remembered, leads to the humorous conclusion that "no human being can ever be a poet"—lies in its personal basis.

The best poets of his century, and the poets of all time whom he most admired, numbered the streaks when they wished. But he did not number them, because they did not enter into his experience. We do not give a face or figure to any of his characters in *The Rambler,* because he did not see either clearly himself.

Polyphilus, the quick wit without purpose; Suspirius, the fault-finder; Quisquilius, the virtuoso; Venustulus, the effeminate beau—are, each of them, bundles of habits, or a predominant habit.

Even Prospero, who might have been drawn from Garrick, represents only the social failings of the rich man who has risen in life. Johnson reverted to the methods of the character-studies of the seventeenth century. Addison had set out by continuing them, but he was at war with them at heart, and he adapted them to his purpose. The superiority of Addison in this respect will never be denied. But Johnson shows a deeper knowledge of human nature "in all its gradations," and, while he lacks the familiar elegance which alone can play with foibles and frivolities, he offers a richer harvest of deep observation.

And Johnson had not the desire, even had he possessed the ability, to disguise his purpose. Addison, too, had been frankly didactic; he had said that he meant to bring philosophy to dwell on tea-tables and in coffee-houses. But he kept his readers from suspecting that they were being taught or reformed.

Johnson's lessons are obvious. His aim was "only the propagation of truth"; it was always his "principal design to inculcate wisdom or piety." The great moralist lavishes the best instruction he can offer, the instruction of a man of the world who knows what the world cannot give; but he does not offer it in a way to attract unwilling attention. He recognised this himself and admitted that "the severity of dictatorial instruction has been too seldom relieved." His deep humour is present throughout, and is occasionally given scope, as in the essay on the advantages of living in a garret; but it is always controlled by the serious purpose.

A DICTIONARY OF THE ENGLISH LANGUAGE; NEW FEATURES OF ITS DESIGN; DISTINCTIVE MERITS OF THE WORK: THE DEFINITIONS

In concluding *The Rambler,* he stated that he had laboured "to refine our language to grammatical purity, and to clear it from colloquial barbarisms, licentious idioms, and irregular combinations." At this time he was in the midst of a similar and greater task in his *Dictionary of the English Language.* Most of the earlier English dictionaries, to the beginning of the eighteenth century, had been dictionaries of "hard words." Then, Nathan Bailey, in his *Universal Etymological English Dictionary* (1721), had aimed at a record of all English words, irrespective of their *vogue* or repute. Johnson purposely omitted "many terms appropriated to particular occupations," and thought not so much of the reader as of the writer and the purity of the language. His *Plan* clearly states his objects, and it is cleverly supplemented in Chesterfield's two papers in *The World.* He set out to perform, singlehanded, for the English language what the French Academy, a century before, had undertaken for French.

It was to be "a dictionary by which the pronunciation of our language may be fixed, and its attainment facilitated; by which its purity may be preserved, its use ascertained, and its duration lengthened." So Johnson hoped; and Chesterfield was ready to acknowledge him as a dictator who would free the language from its anarchy. But, when he came to write the preface, he had found that "no dictionary of a living tongue can ever be perfect, since, while it is hastening to publication, some words are budding, and some falling away." None the less, the mistaken hope gave the *Dictionary* its peculiar value. By aiming at fixing the language, he succeeded in giving the standard of reputable use. Though there are many words in Bailey's dictionary which Johnson omitted, a hasty comparison will show that he added a large number. He held that the golden age of our language began with the reign of Elizabeth, and that the writers in the century before the restoration were "the pure sources of genuine diction."

As his earliest authorities, he chose Sidney and Spenser. When he avowedly included obsolete words, they were to be found in wellknown authors, or appeared to deserve revival. "Cant words," as he called them, were occasionally admitted, because of their *vogue;* others were described as "low." But the most interesting departure from the rigid exclusiveness of an academic dictionary is his treatment of dialect. There is a much larger infusion of provincialisms than might have been expected. The great majority of these are Scottish, no doubt because five of his six amanuenses, as Boswell has proudly recorded, were "natives of North Britain"; but he was also affectionately disposed to words with which he had been familiar in his native county. With all his care for current reputable use, he had too great respect for the native stock to ignore its humbler members, and his selection and description of these have a clear historical value. His main fear for the language was that it would be corrupted by French. It seemed to him to have been, since the restoration, "deviating towards a Gallick structure and phraseology," and to be threatening to "reduce us to babble a dialect of France." So he set himself to denounce "the folly of naturalising useless foreigners to the injury of the natives." It was no vain boast that the book was devoted to the honour of his country. "We have long preserved our constitution, let us make some struggles for our language."

It appears from Spence's *Anecdotes* that Pope had discussed the plan of a dictionary, and had drawn up a list of authors, beginning with Hooker and Spenser, from whom words should be collected. The list is referred to in Johnson's *Plan;* and in terms which suggest a closer relationship than is now known to have existed. But there is nothing to show that Pope had favoured the inclusion of quotations. This was Johnson's most notable innovation in English lexicography. He had hoped that every quotation would serve a further purpose than that of illustrating the use of a word; but he found, as he proceeded, that he had to abandon the idea of combining a dictionary with an anthology. The quotations were frequently from memory and are seldom accompanied with exact references; but, considering the slightness of the assistance which he received, they supply a remarkable proof of the range of his knowledge, and they have a different kind of interest from those in other dictionaries, which, based on more scientific principles, record the use of a word with no attention to the quality of the writer. But the chief worth of the *Dictionary* lies where it should. Johnson had a supreme talent for definition. When it is remembered that the definitions are his own, that he was the first to attempt a thorough distinction of the different meanings (such words as *come* and *go* being each subdivided into more than fifty sections), and that the highest praises he has received have been paid by his successors, the extent of his services to the survey of the language will readily be estimated.

The few explanations in which he gave play to his prejudice or indulged his humour were only a remission of the continued exercise of his keen and muscular intellect. Occasionally, he obscured a simple meaning; and no better statement is to be found than in his preface, of the difficulties of defining the obvious. He had, like every one in his century, little etymological knowledge to help him. But his common sense often kept him right in giving the original meaning of a word and distinguishing its later uses, where his successors, previously to the much later advance in philological science, by aiming at refinement introduced confusion and error.

LESSER WORK

The publication of the *Dictionary* in eight years was a remarkable achievement of industry, and the more remarkable in that he had been doing much other work. Apart from his duties to his own *Rambler*, he held himself ready to assist his friends. He contributed a paper about once a fortnight, from March, 1753, to Hawkesworth's *Adventurer*. He helped Lauder, unsuspectingly, with a preface and postscript to his Miltonic hoax, and dictated his confession (1750–1); and he wrote the dedication for Mrs. Lennox's *Female Quixote* (1752) and

Shakespear Illustrated (1753). He contributed the life of Cheynel to *The Student* (1751), and the life of Cave to *The Gentleman's Magazine* (1754). He composed Zachariah Williams's *Account of an Attempt to ascertain the Longitude at Sea,* (1755). And he furnished the *Dictionary* with a "History of the English Language" and a "Grammar of the English Tongue," including a section on prosody, as well as with its noble preface.

And all this had been accomplished "amidst inconvenience and distraction, in sickness and in sorrow." He had so great a capacity for work, and when he had once started moved with so much ease, that he did not recognise his rapidity to be uncommon. The extreme concentration compelled periods of relaxation which he allowed to weigh on his conscience. He, too, was subject to the common delusion that his best was his normal. As he was, in all matters, a man of the most sensitive morality, it became a habit with him to be distressed at his idleness; and it has become a habit with us to speak of his constitutional indolence. He certainly had to make an effort to begin. But to the activity of the eight years from his thirty-eighth to his forty-sixth, it is not easy to find a parallel.

DEDICATIONS

The *Dictionary* has the accidental interest of having occasioned the letter to the earl of Chesterfield, which is sometimes said to have given the death-blow to literary patronage. Though always an object of curiosity, the letter was first made public by Boswell in 1790. In refusing to dedicate the *Dictionary,* Johnson adhered to his regular practice, from which only motives of business had suggested a departure. The *Plan* was a letter "addressed" to Chesterfield. Only once had he dedicated a work of his own—*The Voyage to Abyssinia,* and that was dedicated in the person of the Birmingham bookseller. But, though he made a rule for himself, he did not condemn the custom. He accepted dedications, and he continued to supply other writers with theirs. He told Boswell that he "believed he had dedicated to all the Royal family round." He excelled in dedications.

JOURNALISTIC PROJECTS AND LABOURS

His next scheme was a journal that should record the progress of European studies, and he planned it while the zest that came from completing the *Dictionary* concealed how far he had drawn on his energies. Such periodicals as *The Present State of the Republic of Letters* (1728–36) and *The History of the Works of the Learned* (1737–43) had now long ceased after having shown, at most, the possibility of success; and, since 1749, their place had been taken by *The Monthly Review*, of which, in its early years, Johnson had no reason to think highly. He now intended an English periodical that would rival those of Le Clerc and Bayle. But this scheme for "the Annals of Literature, foreign as well as domestic," was to yield to an older project. In June, 1756, he issued new *Proposals* for an edition of Shakespeare, and he hoped to have the work completed by the end of the following year. The long strain, however, had begun to tell. He had difficulty in facing any continuous work, and he suffered gravely from the mental depression to which he was always liable. He has described his unhappy condition in his Latin verses entitled [char] *post Lexicon Anglicanum auctum et emendatum*, which give a more intimate account of his feelings than he ever allowed himself in the publicity of English; and stronger evidence is to be found in his prayers, and in the reports of his friends.

It was now that he confirmed himself in the habit of seeking relief in company, and, by encouraging the calls of anyone who wished for his help, established his personal authority in literature. Only the need of money made him write, and none of his work at this time required long effort. He brought out an abridgment of his *Dictionary* (January, 1756), but he probably had assistance in this mechanical labour. Having abandoned the idea of a critical periodical of his own, he contributed to the early numbers of Kit Smart's *Universal Visiter* (1756), and then undertook the control of *The Literary Magazine* (May, 1756–7). Here, he made his famous defence of tea; and, here, he exposed the shallow optimism of Soame Jenyns's *Free Enquiry into the Nature and Origin of Evil*, in an essay which, written with the convincing ease that had come from the experience of much painful thought, is an unsurpassed example of his method and power in argument. Another piece of journalistic work, at this time, was the introductory column of Dodsley's evening paper, *The London Chronicle* (1 January, 1757), which was to be distinguished from all other journals, probably on his advice, by its "account of the labours and productions of the learned."

He also helped his friends with their books. He wrote a life of Sir Thomas Browne, with a criticism of Browne's style, for his own edition of *Christian Morals* (1756).

With it may be grouped the later life of Ascham in the edition of Ascham's works nominally prepared by James Bennet (1761). The variety of his writings for some years after the completion of his *Dictionary* helps to explain how he found his memory unequal to producing a perfect catalogue of his works.

THE IDLER

His assistance was, once again, sought to give weight and dignity to a new periodical, and the starting of *The Universal Chronicle, or Weekly Gazette* was the occasion of his second series of essays, *The Idler.* They began 15 April, 1758, and appeared every Saturday till 5 April, 1760. The fact that *The Idler* was not an independent publication, but merely a section of a journal, will account for most of the differences between it and the *Rambler.* The papers are much shorter and do not show the same sense of sole responsibility. In one respect, however, they have a clear superiority. Their lighter touch is better suited to portraiture. Dick Minim the critic, Johnson's only character that may still be said to live, is a perfect example of his art at its best; nor can there be any difference of opinion about the shorter sketches of Jack Whirler and Tom Restless, or of Mr. Sobre, in which the author represented himself. That the characters should no longer bear Latin names indicates a wider change. The critical papers also show the growth of ease and confidence. There is an obvious interest in those on "Hard Words," "Easy Writing" and "The Sufficiency of the English Language."

RASSELAS AND ITS LESSON

While *The Idler* was in progress, Johnson's mother died, and her death was the occasion both of his paper on the loss of a friend and of his solemn novel on the choice of life, *Rasselas, Prince of Abyssinia* (April, 1759). No work of his has been more frequently translated or is better known by name; but none has met with more contradictory judgments, or is a stricter test of the reader's capacity to appreciate the peculiar qualities of Johnson's thought and manner. There is little or no story, no crisis, no conclusion; there is little more than a succession of discussion and disquisitions on the limitations of life. *Rasselas* may be called the prose *Vanity of Human Wishes;* and it is the fullest, gravest and most intimate statement of his common theme.

It has been said that Addison would have written a novel, could he have cast the Coverly papers in a different form. Johnson proposed to write a novel, and produced an expanded essay. There are five "oriental tales" in *The Rambler,* and three were yet to appear in *The Idler*. They suited his purpose in their vagueness of background and their free scopt for didactic fancies. *Rasselas* is another of these tales, elaborated to enforce his lesson by a greater range of observation. The first requirement of the story was a happy valley. Older writers would have placed it in Arcadia; Johnson takes us to the same undiscovered country, but calls it Abyssinia. He had not forgotten his early translation.

The name "Rasselas" was suggested by it, and other instances of recollection are equally certain. There were "impassable forests and inaccessible cliffs" in the real Abyssinia, and why not a happy valley behind them? But one of the attractions of Lobo's narrative had been that the reader found in it no regions blessed with spontaneous fecundity or unceasing sunshine. Johnson knew, quite as well as the critics who stumble at local and ethnographical discrepancies, that there is no happy valley; but he asked its existence to be granted as a setting for a tale which would show that "human life is every where a state in which much is to be endured, and little to be enjoyed." The gloom is heavy, but, to those who can appreciate Johnson, it is never depressing. He had cleared his mind of cant, and he wrote to give his readers the strength that comes from the honesty of looking straight at things as they are.

He pursues his way relentlessly through the different conditions that seem to offer happiness openhanded, and works to a climax in the story of the astronomer; "Few can attain this man's knowledge, and few practise his virtues, but all may suffer his calamity. Of the uncertainties of our present state, the most dreadful and alarming is the uncertain continuance of reason." This is one of the many passages which emphasise his perfect sincerity. The book ends in resignation to the futility of searching for happiness, and in resolution to pursue life as it is found. Stated in these words, the lesson may appear a commonplace. But so are the real things of human experience. And never was the lesson stated with more sympathetic knowledge, and enlivened with a greater wealth of aphoristic wisdom.

Meanwhile, the edition of Shakespeare was at a stand. Some of the plays—evidently, those in the first volume—had been printed by March, 1758; but, during the next four years, there was no sign of progress. In addition to *The Idler* and *Rasselas* Johnson had been writing dedications, prefaces, introductions and reviews, engaging in unsuccessful controversy on the structure of the new bridge at Blackfriars, and helping to lay the Cock lane ghost. The discontent of his subscribers, roughly expressed in Churchill's *Ghost* (1762), at last roused him to complete his work; and the financial ease that had come with his pension of £300 (1762) gave him what time he needed. The edition was published, in eight volumes, in October, 1765.

ON SHAKESPEARE: VALUE OF ITS TEXT AND NOTES

There was nothing new in Johnson's methods as an editor. He aimed only at doing better what had been done already, and produced an edition of the old fashion at a time when the science of Shakespearean editing was about to make a distinct advance. But he had qualifications sometimes wanting in editors with more painful habits or more ostentatious equipment—a good knowledge of Elizabethan English, and imperturbable common sense. Like almost every text of Shakespeare that had yet appeared, or was to appear till our own day, it was based on the text of the most recent edition. What he sent to the printer was Warburton's text revised. But he worked on the "settled principle that the reading of the ancient books is probably true," and learned to distrust conjecture. His collation was never methodical; his weak eyesight was a serious hindrance to an exacting task. But he restored many of the readings of the first folio, and, carrying on the system of combination that had been started by Pope, was the first to detect and admit many of the readings of the quartos.

He produced a text which, with all its shortcomings, was nearer the originals than any that had yet appeared. Some of his emendations, which are always modest and occasionally minute, find an unsuspected place in our modern editions. Though his text has long been superseded, the advance of scholarship will never impair the value of his notes. It was a proud boast that not a single passage in the whole work had appeared to him corrupt which he had not endeavoured to restore, or obscure which he had not endeavoured to illustrate; and it did not go beyond the truth. No edition, within its limits, is a safer guide to Shakespeare's meaning. The student who searches the commentators for help in difficulties, soon learns to go straight to Johnson's note as the firm land of common sense in a sea of ingenious fancies. The same robust honesty gives the preface a place by itself among critical pronouncements on Shakespeare. He did not hesitate to state what he believed to be Shakespeare's faults.

Yet Shakespeare remained to him the greatest of English authors, and the only author worthy to be ranked with Homer. He, also, vindicated the liberties of the English stage. After conforming to the "unities" in his own *Irene,* and then suggesting his doubts of them in *The Rambler,* he now proved that they are "not essential to a just drama." The guiding rule in his criticism was that "there is always an appeal open from criticism to nature." A generation later, the French "romantics" found their case stated in his preface, and they did not better what they borrowed.

POLITICAL PAMPHLETS

Hereafter, Johnson did not, on his own initiative, undertake any other large work. "Composition is, for the most part," he said, "an effort of slow diligence and steady perseverance, to which the mind is dragged by neccessity or resolution." His pension had removed the necessity, and, for the next twelve years, his best work lay in talk. In 1763, he met Boswell; in 1764, he founded with Reynolds "The Club"—not known till long after as "The Literary Club"; in 1765, he gained the friendship of the Thrales. Companionship and elegant comforts provided the relief that was still needed to his recurring depressions. He wrote little, but he engaged in personal kindnesses, and talked his best, and exerted an influence which spread far beyond the circle of his conversation. He was still, as at all times, ready to contribute to the publications of his friends, and even dictated the arguments in some of Boswell's law cases; but he did not undertake any writing that required resolution or has added to his fame.

His four political tracts—*The False Alarm* (1770), *Falkland's Islands* (1771), *The Patriot* (1774) and *Taxation no Tyranny* (1775)—are known, so far as they are known, because he was their author. Since his early work on the debates in *The Gentleman's Magazine,* he had always taken a keen interest in politics. Most of his essays in *The Literary Magazine* had been on political topics. Towards the end of 1765, he had undertaken to supply "single-speech" Hamilton with his views on questions that were being discussed in parliament and had written for him, in November, 1766, *Considerations on the Corn Laws.* But now, he wrote as a pamphleteer. The most judicious of the four tracts is *Falkland's Islands,* which makes a just defence of the policy towards Spain and is notable for its picture of the horrors of war and for its reference to Junius.

The best thing in *The False Alarm,* his thoughts on the present discontents, is the satirical picture of the progress of a petition. In *Taxation no Tyranny,* his "answer to the Resolutions and Address of the American Congress," he asks "how is it that we hear the loudest yelps for liberty among the drivers of negroes?"

A JOURNEY TO THE WESTERN ISLANDS OF SCOTLAND

The prejudice in *A Journey to the Western Islands of Scotland* is of a different kind, and never displeasing. It is only the natural prejudice of John Bull as a tourist. He makes many acute observations which even the most perfervid Scot must have recognised to be just; but his impartiality is occasionally impeded by a want of knowledge which he himself was the first to admit. He had been conducted round Scotland by Boswell from August to November, 1773, and the book—which was published in January, 1775—is not so much a record of the ninety-four days of "vigorous exertion" as a series of thoughts on a different civilisation. It had a different purpose from that of Pennant's *Tour in Scotland* (1771), which Johnson praised highly. He had taken the opportunity of enquiring into the authenticity of the poems of Ossian, and convinced himself that "they never existed in any other form than that which we have seen."

This is the best known section of his book; but the reader may find more interest in the remarks on the superstitions of the Highlands, on American emigration and on the Scottish universities. In July and August, 1774, he made a tour in north Wales with his friends the Thrales, and kept a diary which might have served as the groundwork of a companion volume to his Scottish *Journey;* but he did not make any use of it, and it remained in MS. till 1816. The beauty of the Welsh scenery had greatly impressed him, and this diary must not be neglected in any estimate of his feeling for wild landscape. The fragmentary records of his tour in France with the Thrales in 1775 were left to be printed by Boswell. Johnson was content to pass the rest of his days in leisure, working only as the mood prompted, when, on Easter Eve, 1777, a deputation of booksellers asked him to undertake, at the age of sixty-seven, what was to prove his masterpiece.

THE LIVES OF THE POETS: THEIR ORIGINAL PLAN AND DISTINCTIVE FEATURES

The Lives of the Poets arose out of a business venture. The London booksellers were anxious to drive out of the market an Edinburgh reprint of the English poets and to protect their own copyright; and, besides producing an edition superior in accuracy and elegance, they determined to add biographical prefaces by some writer of authority. The scheme took some time to mature, and Percival Stockdale had hopes of the editorship. But Johnson was given the first offer and at once accepted. Writing to Boswell, on 3 May, 1777, he says he is engaged "to write little Lives and little Prefaces, to a little edition of the English Poets." The work proved so congenial that he wrote at greater length than he had intended; and, when the edition was completed, the prefaces were issued without the texts under the title *The Lives of the Poets* (1781). Their independent publication, and the title by which they are now known, were alike afterthoughts; in origin, *The Lives of the Poets* is only editorial matter. It is even more important to remember that this great body of critical opinion—perhaps the greatest in the English language—was written on invitation and in conformity with conditions controlled by others.

When he found the complete series labelled "Johnson's Poets," he was moved to write on a scrap of paper which has happily been preserved: "It is great impudence to put Johnson's Poets on the back of books which Johnson neither recommended nor revised." Of the fifty-two poets, five, at most, were included on his suggestion. In the life of Watts, he says that the readers of the collection are to impute to him whatever pleasure or weariness they may find in the perusal of Blackmore, Watts, Pomfret and Yalden; but it would also appear from the letter to Boswell cited above that he "persuaded the booksellers to insert something of Thomson." There is no evidence that he advised any omission. For only one of the fifty-two lives was he indebted to another hand–the life of Young by Sir Herbert Croft. He included his early life of Savage, with insignificant changes, and worked up his article on Roscommon in *The Gentleman's Magazine* for May, 1748. The other lives he now wrote specially for the booksellers, availing himself here and there of what he had written already, such as the "Dissertation on Pope's Epitaphs" in *The Universal Visiter* (1756), and the character of Collins in Fawkes and Woty's *Poetical Calendar* (1763).

The original plan had evidently been to include "all the English poets of reputation from Chaucer to the present day." It is no matter for regret that this scheme was curtailed. The poets of the seventeenth and eighteenth centuries, besides affording him ample scope for expounding his views on poetry, possessed for him the personal interest which was always a stimulus to his criticism. But, even could he be shown to have recommended Cowley as the starting point, it would be an error to infer that this was the limit to his knowledge and appreciation. Such an inference would neglect his preface to Shakespeare, his work on the Elizabethans for the *Dictionary* and his statement in *The Idler* that "we consider the whole succession from Spenser to Pope as superior to any names which the Continent can boast." Of the earlier writers, he had not the knowledge possessed by Thomas Warton and other of his friends. But he wrote on Ascham, and corresponded on the manuscripts of Sir Thomas More, and devoted to him a considerable section of the introductory matter of his *Dictionary;* and he was always alert to any investigation, whether in modern English, or Old English, or northern antiquities. His comprehensive knowledge of English literature may be described as beginning with the reign of Henry VIII. In an interview with George III, he was enjoined to add Spenser to *The Lives of the Poets;* and he would readily have complied, could he have obtained new material.

In the earlier interview which Boswell has recorded, many years before *The Lives of the Poets* was thought of, George III proposed that Johnson should undertake the literary biography of his country. It was a happy courtesy, for, though there had been good lives of individual poets since Sprat's *Life of Cowley*, the collections that had yet appeared had shown that much remained to be accomplished, and Johnson was specially fitted to write the lives of authors. Even had he not said so, we should have suspected that the biographical part of literature was what he loved most. The best of these collections had been *The Lives of the Poets of Great Britain and Ireland* (1753), nominally by "Mr. Cibber" (Theophilus), but really by Robert Shiels, *The Royal and Noble Authors* (1758), of Horace Walpole, which is a "catalogue," and the literary articles in the very unequal *Biographia Britannica*. It was left to Johnson to impart a sustained excellence to this kind of writing, and, by engaging in what had not yet occupied an author of his authority, to raise it to a new level as an English literary form.

EQUIPOISE OF BIOGRAPHY AND CRITICISM

The most obvious features of *The Lives of the Poets* is the equipoise of biography and criticism. Johnson states the facts simply, but connects them with his impression of the writer, and, when he passes to the examination of poems, he is still thinking of their relation to the writer's personality. He finds the man behind the work. The truth is that he was much more interested in the man than in that part of him which is the author. Of "mere poets," he thought little; and, though he championed the dignity of authorship, he claimed for it no exclusive privileges, nor held that the poet was a man apart to be measured by standards inapplicable to other men.

If the enduring freshness of *The Lives of the Poets* is due to any one quality more than to another, it is to Johnson's inexhaustible interest in the varieties of human nature. As detailed biographies, they have been superseded, though they remain our only authority for many facts and anecdotes, and include much that had been inaccessible. He made researches; but they were limited to his immediate needs. It is often easy to trace the sources of his information. He criticised Congreve's plays without having read them for many years, and he refused for a time to hear Lord Marchmont's recollections of Pope. Though, in general, he welcomed new details, his aim was to know enough to describe the man and to bring out his individuality in the estimate of his work.

INFLUENCE OF PERSONAL FEELING

The common result of this method in criticism is that the critic is at his best when he is in sympathy with the writer. Johnson meant to be scrupulously judicial; but he showed personal feelings. He disliked the acrimonious politics of Milton, the querulous sensitiveness of Swift and the timid foppery of Gray. This personal antipathy underlies his criticisms, though it is qualified, at times, even generously. Had Gray written often as in the *Elegy,* he says "it had been vain to blame and useless to praise him"; and *Paradise Lost* "is not the greatest of heroic poems only because it is not the first." Of Dryden and Pope he wrote in friendship, and there exists no finer criticism of them. But no critic has been severer on Dryden's negligences, or spoken more ruthlessly of the *Essay on Man.*

The passage on *Lycidas* is generally regarded as an error of judgment which marks Johnson's limitations as a critic. With his usual courage, he stated a deliberate opinion. He gave his reasons—the artificiality of the pastoral convention, the confusion of the allegory with actual fact and sacred truth, and the absence of the feeling of real sorrow. But there is the further explanation that he was opposed to some recent tendencies in English poetry. That he had more than *Lycidas* in his mind is shown by the emphasis of his statement. The same ideas reappear in his criticism of Collins and Gray. He objected to the habit of inverting the common order of words, and, on one occasion, cited Thomas Warton's "evening gray"; he might also have cited "mantle blue." It was Warton who occasioned his extempore verses beginning—

Whereso'er I turn my view,
All is strange, yet nothing new;

and Warton imitated, as well as edited, the early poems of Milton. Warton was one of many in whom he found faults which he traced to Milton as their original. In criticising *Lycidas,* he had in mind his own contemporaries. When the new tendencies had prevailed, he was said to have judged by a rigorous code of criticism. This code would have been difficult to reconcile with the preface to his edition of Shakespeare; with the praise given by him to Homer's heroes, that they are not described but develop themselves; with his statement that "real criticism" shows "the beauty of thought as formed on the workings of the human heart"; and with his condemnation of "the cant of those who judge by principles rather than perception."

His views on the matter of poetry are shown in his criticism of Gray's *Bard:* "To select a singular event, and swell it to a giant's bulk by fabulous appendages of spectres and predictions, has little difficulty, for he that forsakes the probable may always find the marvellous." The common growth of mother earth sufficed for him as for Wordsworth. The distinction which he draws between the *Elegy* and *The Bard* was that which ultimately divided Wordsworth and Coleridge. There was enough for him in life as he knew it. And there was a personal reason why, more than the other writers of his century, he should tend to limit nature to human experience. The tumult in his mind was allowed no direct expression in his writings; but it made him look upon the world as the battle ground of thought, and passion, and will.

JOHNSON'S LAST YEARS AND DEATH

With the revision of *The Lives of the Poets,* Johnson's career as an author closed. In the three years of failing health which were left to him, he lived his accustomed life, honoured for the authority of his opinion, generous in his help to younger writers, and active in domestic benevolence. He revised Crabbe's *Village,* and dictated much to Boswell. Death removed some who had played a great part in his later life—Thrale, whose house at Streatham had been a second home, and two of the pensioners in his own house at Bolt-court, Levett and Mrs. Williams. The tribute to Levett, noble in its restrained emotion, is the tenderest of his poems. The sadness of loss was embittered by Mrs. Thrale's marriage to Piozzi and the irreparable break in the long and happy friendship. He had so far recovered from a paralytic seizure as to be able, at the close of 1783, to found the Essex-Head club. By its ease of access, the old man sought to supply the need of new company. He dined at The Club, for the last time, in June, 1784. Next month, he set out for his native city, and returned by Birmingham and Oxford, the cities of his youth. His health had not found any relief, and, when he reached London in November, was rapidly declining. He died 13 December, and, on the 20th, was buried in Westminster abbey. Shortly before his death, he had destroyed his papers.

HIS LITERARY GROWTH, AND ADVANCE IN EASE OF STYLE

His long career had been uniform in its aim and methods, and the distinctions between his earlier and later writings are those which come from experience and confidence. The author of the preface to *A Voyage to Abyssinia* is unmistakably the author of *The Rambler* and *The Lives of the Poets,* with the same tastes and habits of thought, but younger, with a shorter reach and less precision in his skill. There had been no discipleship, and no time of searching where his strength lay; and no new influences had modified his purpose. The changes to be found in his work of forty-five years are those of a natural and undisturbed development, so steady that its stages cannot be minutely marked by us, and were probably imperceptible to himself. As he grew older, he related all art more and more to life. Though careful to give his thoughts their best expression, and severe on improprieties in others, he became impatient of mere proficiency in technique; and, though a scholar, he recognised the insufficiency of scholarship and the barrenness of academic pursuits. He had the "purposes of life" ever and increasingly before him, and his criticisms of the English poets are the richest of his works in worldly wisdom.

THE WEIGHT OF HIS WORDS CARRIED BY THE STRENGTH OF HIS THOUGHT

At the same time, his style became easier. The Latin element is at its greatest in *The Rambler*. He was then engaged on his *Dictionary*. But he always tended to use long words most when he wrote in haste; and his revision was towards simplicity. He used them in conversation, where alone he allowed himself the liberty of a daring coinage.

They were in no sense embroidery, but part of the very texture of his thought. "Difference of thoughts," he said, "will produce difference of language.

He that thinks with more extent than another will want words of larger meaning; he that thinks with subtlety will seek for terms of more nice discrimination." As we read him and accustom our minds to move with his, we cease to notice the diction. The strength of his thought carries the weight of his words. His meaning is never mistaken, though it may not be fully grasped at a glance; for he puts much in small compass, and the precision of his language requires careful reading for its just appreciation.

"Familiar but not coarse, and elegant but not ostentatious"; "vanity produced a grotto where necessity enforced a passage"—could the thought be put more pointedly, or adequately, or shortly? When Latin diction cannot be changed without loss, or without affecting the tenor of the thought, it has made good its right. His humour and irony found an aid in the dignified phraseology. But he also used simple words. Wit is "that which he that never found it wonders how he missed"; "what he does best he soon ceases to do"; "a rage for saying something when there is nothing to be said"—these, also, are typical of his style. The letter to Chesterfield reaches its climax in the homeliest of English: "till I am known, and do not want it."

ILL SUCCESS OF HIS PARODISTS

His parodists have been peculiarly unsuccessful. We lose their meaning in a jumble of pedantries; and we do not lose Johnson's. They inflate their phraseology; but Johnson is not tumid. And they forget that his balance is a balance of thought. His own explanation still holds good: "the imitators of my style have not hit it. Miss Aikin has done it the best; for she has imitated the sentiment as well as the diction." This was said in 1777. But better than Miss Aikin's essay "On Romances" in the style of *The Rambler,* and the best of all the parodies, is *A Criticism on the Elegy written in a Country Church-yard* (1783), composed by John Young, the versatile professor of Greek at Glasgow, and designed as a continuation of *The Life of Gray.* The long list of his serious imitators begins with Hawkesworth and extends to Jeffrey, who started by training himself in the school of the periodical essayists. Others, who did not take him as a model, profited by the example of a style in which nothing is negligent and nothing superfluous. He was the dominating influence in English prose throughout the second half of the eighteenth century. The lesson of discipline required to be taught, and it was learned from him by many whose best work shows no traces of his manner.

EFFECT OF JOHNSON'S DEATH; MRS. PIOZZI'S ANECDOTES AND SIR JOHN HAWKINS'S LIFE

His death, says Murphy, "kept the public mind in agitation beyond all former example. No literary character ever excited so much attention." Collections of stories about him had begun to appear in his lifetime, and now his friends competed in serious biography. When Mrs. Piozzi wrote her account, she had heard of nine others already written or in preparation. Her *Anecdotes of the late Samuel Johnson* (1786) has a place by itself. It preserves much that would have been lost; but its importance lies chiefly in its picture of Johnson's character, and in its illustration of the qualities by which he was attracted. She writes with amiable pride in the ties that bound him to the hospitality of Streatham, and with an honest effort to rise above their quarrel.

If her detractors can find evidence of artfulness, no one can deny the clearness of her vision; and, if, at times, her little vanities prevented her from seeing the true bearing of Johnson's remarks, she must, at least, be admitted to have been happy in the selection of what she has recorded. There is no work of the same size as her *Anecdotes* that gives a better portrait of Johnson. In strong contrast is the *Life* (1787) by Sir John Hawkins. It is the solid book of an "unclubbable" magistrate and antiquary, who has much knowledge and little intuition. He had known Johnson for over forty years and, on many points, is our chief authority. Much of the value of his book lies in the lengthy digressions on contemporary literature. His lack of sympathy made him unsuited for biography; but we are under a debt to him for the facts which he threw together.

BOSWELL'S EARLIER EXPERIENCES AND WRITINGS

The merits of Mrs. Piozzi and Hawkins were united and augmented by Boswell. He had been collecting material since his first interview in 1763. He had told Johnson his purpose by 1772, and he had spoken definitely of his *Life* in a letter of 1775. After Johnson's death, he set to work in earnest and spared himself no trouble. "You cannot imagine," he wrote in 1789, "what labour, what perplexity, what vexation I have endured in arranging a prodigious multiplicity of materials, in supplying omissions, in searching for papers buried in different masses, and all this besides the exertion of composing and polishing: many a time have I thought of giving it up."

But he was confident in the result. It was to be not merely the best biography of Johnson, but the best biography ever written. "I am absolutely certain," he said, "that my mode of biography, which gives not only a *History* of Johnson's *visible* progress through the world, and of his publications, but a *view* of his mind in his letters and conversations, is the most perfect that can be conceived, and will be more of a Life than any work that has ever yet appeared."

When the book at last came out, in May, 1791, the same confidence was expressed in the opening paragraphs. There, he admits that the idea of interspersing letters had been taken from Mason's life of Gray. He had made a careful study of the art of biography; and the *Anecdotes* of Mrs. Piozzi, which had shown the necessity of a careful handling of intimate material, and the facts of Hawkins, which had proved the inadequacy of simple narrative, had reassured him that he was engaged on the real life of his friend.

Johnson owes much to Boswell; but it was Johnson who

gave us Boswell. His life is the story of failure turned to success by an irresistible devotion. He had always been attracted by whatever won the public attention, partly from scientific curiosity, as when he visited Mrs. Rudd, and partly with a view to his own advancement. In the first of his letters, he says that Hume "is a very proper person for a young man to cultivate an acquaintance with." He comes to know Wilkes, but doubts "if it would be proper to keep a correspondence with a gentleman in his present capacity." The chief pleasure that he foresaw in his continental tour was his meeting with Voltaire and Rousseau. Then, he proceeded to Corsica and became the friend and enthusiastic champion of Paoli.

Having received a communication on Corsican affairs from the earl of Chatham, he asks: "Could your lordship find time to honour me now and then with a letter?" Again, he is found thinking of a life of lord Kames and satisfying himself that "he has eminence enough to merit this." There was cause for the sturdy laird of Auchinleck to complain, according to Sir Walter Scott's anecdote, that his irresponsible son was always pinning himself to the tail of somebody or other. But, of all his heroes, Johnson alone brought out the best qualities in his volatile character, and steadied him to the worthy use of his rare gifts. When Johnson is absent, his writings possess no remarkable merit, though they have always the interest of being the pellucid expression of his singular personality. The *Life* is the devoted and flawless recognition of an influence which he knew that his nature had required.

AN ACCOUNT HIS LATER LIFE

Born at Edinburgh in 1740, the son of a Scottish advocate who took his title as a judge from his ancient estate of Auchinleck in Ayrshire, Boswell reluctantly adopted the family profession of law, and, after studying at Edinburgh, Glasgow and Utrecht, was called to the Scottish bar in 1766. His heart was never in a legal career, and, to the last, he had a fond belief in sudden and splendid success in literature or politics. His earliest work appeared in *The Scots Magazine,* but has not been identified. He wrote much verse and published *An Elegy on the death of an amiable young lady* (1761), *An Ode to Tragedy,* dedicated to himself (1761), and *The Cub at Newmarket,* a humorous description of his experiences as the guest of the Jockey club (1762).

Several of his earliest pieces are printed in *A Collection of Original Poems, by the Rev. Mr. Blacklock and other Scotch Gentlemen* (1760–2), the second volume of which he edited. He frequented the literary society of Edinburgh, founded the jovial "Soaping Club" and engaged in regular correspondence with his friends.

The *Letters between the Hon. Andrew Erskine and James Boswell Esq.,* in which, also, there is much verse, he published in 1763. "They have made ourselves laugh," says the advertisement; "we hope they will have the same effect upon other people." They were hardly worth publishing, though we should be sorry now not to have them. In the description of a long series of daydreams, given with the characteristic vanity which is always saved by its frankness, he says:

I am thinking of the perfect knowledge which I shall acquire of men and manners, of the intimacies which I shall have the honour to form with the learned and ingenious in every science, and of the many amusing literary anecdotes which I shall pick up.

This was published, from Flexney's shop in Holborn, in the very month that he met Johnson in Davies's parlour. Shortly before this, he had brought out, with Erskine and George Dempster, his two associates in much of his early work, the rare *Critical Strictures* on Mallet's *Elvira.* He returned to Edinburgh from his continental travels in 1766, and, being admitted to the bar in the midst of the excitement about the Douglas cause, found in it material for *Dorando* (June, 1767), which recounts the points at issue under a Spanish disguise, and appeared immediately before the thirteen Scottish judges, by a majority of one, arrived at a decision contrary to his wishes.

The little story went into three editions within a fortnight, but it now disappoints the hopes excited by its rarity. As the case was sent up to the House of Lords, where the decision was ultimately reversed, Boswell continued to write about it and brought out the more serious *Essence of the Douglas Cause* (November, 1767). He took an energetic part in the riotous controversy concerning the Edinburgh stage and supplied the prologue for the opening of the first licensed theatre in Scotland.

At the same time, he was engaged on his Corsican experiences. *An Account of Corsica* had been read by Lord Hailes in manuscript in June, 1767, and was issued in March, 1768.

It is Boswell's first considerable book, and, indeed, his only book, apart from those concerned with Johnson, that had a chance of being remembered on its merits. It won what he calls "amazing celebrity"; he could boast that he was "really the great man now."

His head was full of Corsica and was not to be emptied of it, even on Johnson's advice. He made a collection of twenty letters by himself and others, and published them under the title *British Essays in favour of the Brave Corsicans* (January, 1769); and, in the following September, he appeared at the Shakespeare festival at Stratford in the dress of an armed Corsican chief and recited a poem that "preserved the true Corsican character."

A description of the proceedings, an account of himself, and the poem were immediately contributed by him to *The London Magazine*. Two months later, he married, and then tried to settle to his legal practice.

From this time, the influence of Johnson, already evident in *An Account of Corsica*, grew steadily stronger. He was not satisfied with Edinburgh after the splendour of London. "The unpleasing tone, the rude familiarity, the barren conversation," he complains, "really hurt my feelings." But he had to content himself with lengthy visits to London in vacation, which was the more indispensable when Johnson had procured his election to The Club, and he had become a proprietor of *The London Magazine*. He contributed to it, monthly, a series of seventy periodical essays called *The Hypochondriack* (1777–83), for which he found much material in himself. There is also much in them that was inspired by the dominating friendship. They take *The Rambler* as their model, and are the most Johnsonian of his writings. After the death of his father and his own succession to Auchinleck, in 1782, he turned to politics, and carried out his ambition of becoming a member of the English bar, but to no purpose.

He stood for parliament, and published two letters "to the people of Scotland"; one, *On the Present State of the Nation* (1783), and the other, *On the Alarming Attempt to infringe the Articles of the Union* (1785). All he obtained was the recordership of Carlisle, which he soon resigned.

In his last years, which were saddened by the loss of his wife and troubled with financial difficulties, he is still found hoping that practice may come at any time and expecting "a capital prize."

He confesses that he no longer lives with a view to have surprising incidents, though he is still desirous that his life "should *tell*." But he begins to waken from the long delusion and, in a melancholy moment, admits: "I certainly am constitutionally unfit for any employment." He was then on the point of achievement. His life was to tell better than he knew, and in another way than he had hoped. His friendship for Johnson was helping him in these years to do what he was unable to do for himself. Without Johnson, he relapses to the level of his early verse in *No Abolition of Slavery; or the Universal Empire of Love* (April, 1791).

And, when the effort of producing the great work is over, there remains only the record of steady decline, varied by new schemes of matrimony, and cheered by large sales and the preparation of new editions. He died in London, 19 May, 1795. From 1758 to within a few weeks of his death, he had corresponded regularly with William Johnson Temple, a fellow student in the Greek class at Edinburgh who became vicar of St. Gluvias in Cornwall; and these letters, which had been sold by a hawker at Boulogne and were rescued to be published in 1857, give us his real autobiography. They tell us much more than the many descriptions of himself, from his *Ode to Tragedy* to the "Memoirs" in the *European Magazine* of 1791. If they show why his descendants decided on a holocaust of his papers, they also explain the attraction which he exerted on those who took the trouble to try to understand him.

HIS LIFE OF JOHNSON, WITH THE JOURNAL OF A TOUR TO THE HEBRIDES, HIS ENDURING TITLE TO FAME

But, if Boswell without Johnson would have been forgotten, it was his own talent that gave the *Life* its surpassing excellence. Whenever he writes of Johnson, he succeeds in giving the impression that he saw things as they were, and not through the spectacles of his own personality.

He never tried to conceal the part that he played; and yet, despite his vanities, and they were many, he knew how to make his readers think that they are looking at the facts for themselves.

The very freedom from self-consciousness which was no help to his career was a great part of the secret of his skill in description. It also provided him with material denied to less sympathetic natures.

"No man," he said, "has been more successful in making acquaintance easily than I have been. I even bring people quickly on to a degree of cordiality." Johnson, too, tells us that "Mr. Boswell's frankness and gaiety made every body communicative."

He never tired of arranging new situations, in order to see what they would bring forth; and his interpretations of what he found are strong testimony to his insight into character and to his judgment.

Minute as his observations are, he never offers a meaningless detail.

It is easy to understand why Johnson made him postpone the *Journal of a Tour to the Hebrides,* which was intended as a supplement to his own *Journey.*

He had given "notions rather than facts"; but Boswell had contrived to make the facts give Johnson. The reproduction of his sayings and experiences was too minute to be published during his lifetime, and was more decently delayed till the year after his death. The *Life* does not surpass the *Journal* in the sense of actuality; but it is a greater achievement. He had met Johnson only on some two hundred and seventy days, scattered over twenty-one years, and his material had to be gathered from many sources.

He selects and arranges; he places his facts in the light and perspective that will create the situation; and Johnson lives in his pages.

And he had the gift of the perfect style for his kind of biography—a style of no marked individuality, but easy, clear and flexible, which does its duty without attracting attention, and requires to be examined to have its excellence recognised.

Chapter 5

Johnson, Spenser, and Literary Progress

Neat "meta-narratives" of literary history are a favourite target of recent critics, justly suspicious of teleological accounts of literary development. One of the most significant of these meta-narratives is the Renaissance, the progression from Medieval barbarism toward modern enlightenment, but this notion of an emergence from rudeness to refinement has come under fire from recent critics.

The nineteenth century has so far provided much of the ammunition for this revisionary assault, and it is only natural that Schiller, Burckhardt, Pater, Hegel, and Marx should be central in the project.

But Augustan critics were formulating their own ideas about the Renaissance, and we can gain a great deal of insight by looking at their approach to, say, Shakespeare or Milton. We can perhaps gain even more by looking at the problem cases. The third member of the English Renaissance poetic triumvirate, Edmund Spenser, was manifestly one of these problems, and he fit uneasily in the eighteenth century's progressive version of the Renaissance.

Spenser was much on the mind of Samuel Johnson, one of the most active and important of those developing our notion of the Renaissance — not in any extended treatment, but in scattered comments from the 1730s through the '80s. Spenser's position in Johnson's thought has received little attention, but tugging on these Spenserian loose ends reveals a thread woven across the entire fabric of Johnson's criticism.

Focusing on Johnson and his age may help us better understand the meta-narrative called the Renaissance, and focusing on the rise of the Renaissance may in turn help us better understand Johnson and his age.

The word "Renaissance" was not englished until around 1840, but the lack of the term did not prevent Johnson's contemporaries from recognizing the phenomenon. Johnson himself refers, for instance, to "the Revival of Learning in Europe," and dates "the golden age of our language" from "the accession of Elizabeth."

The metaphors used for this period show the importance of progression: "refinement," for instance, a metaphor from metallurgy, suggests that modern purity came from burning away the imperfections of the past; "cultivation" suggests our arable land once lay fallow. Impressing readers with the darkness of the Dark Ages was *de rigueur* for early eighteenth-century writers such as Addison, for whom the Middle Ages were a time of "Darkness and Superstition." Critics whose interest in Medieval authors extended beyond mere antiquarianism valued only their anticipation of what was to come. Winstanley, for instance, finds Gower "the first refiner of our *English* Tongue," and praises Chaucer's "earnest desire to enrich and beautifie our *English* Tongue, which in those days was very rude and barren." Writers who were not part of this march from rudeness to refinement were ill regarded. Skelton, for example, is "now accounted only a Rhymer," and "Whoso reads him, will find he hath a miserable, loose, rambling Style; ... yet were good Poets so scarce in his Age, that he had the good fortune to be chosen Poet Laureat."

Like Skelton, Spenser sat uncomfortably in a tradition that valued forward-looking authors, and he was therefore a problem for the eighteenth century. Spenser, somewhere between Medieval rudeness and modern civilization, perversely refused to let go of what appeared to be vulgar errors, and could not be reconciled with progressive Augustan critical bromides. This peculiar failure of Spenser's judgment led to scathing attacks, of which Addison's dismissal is typical: "But now the mystic tale, that pleas'd of yore,/ Can charm an understanding age no more." The lapses in Spenser's taste can be arranged under three heads: design, allegory, and language. Most upsetting is his disregard for the Aristotelian unity of action.

The romance design, with its Ariostan *entrelacement* and multiple heroes, was no more appreciated by early eighteenth-century critics than by those of the Renaissance. Allegory, another holdover from the Dark Ages, was also scorned: as Addison complains, "The long-spun allegories fulsome grow,/ While the dull moral lies too plain below." And Spenser's metrical "imperfections" and his archaic diction were considered more perverse than charming before mid-century.

This paradox frustrated eighteenth-century critics, who found that his poetical power, for all its faults, could be neither denied nor resisted. Spenser, educated in the classics in an enlightened age, rejected many aesthetic principles the eighteenth century held not only dear but self-evident. Johnson's censure of Spenser's "studied barbarity" is one expression of this frustration; Hughes's account is another: "It may seem strange indeed, since *Spenser* appears to have been well acquainted with the best Writers of Antiquity, that he has not imitated them."

Even Spenser's defenders had to admit he was incompatible with the Renaissance-as-progression paradigm, and this contributed to the changes in critical sensibility over the course of the century. Hughes was among the first to formulate an aesthetics different from the classical inheritance, an early stage in the development of a new Romantic sensibility. He begins with an architectural metaphor picked up from Rymer, who confesses "I have thought our Poetry of the last Age was as rude as our Architecture." What was censure in Rymer is praise in Hughes:

> Indeed the whole Frame of it wou'd appear monstrous, if it were to be examin'd by the Rules of Epick Poetry. ... But ... the Author never design'd it by these Rules. ... To compare it therefore with the Models of Antiquity, wou'd be like drawing a Parallel between the *Roman* and the *Gothick* Architecture. ... Tho the former is more majestick in the whole, the latter may

be very surprizing and agreeable in its Parts. This Gothic aesthetic grew, with the help of others like Warton and Hurd, over the course of the century. Spenser provided, along with Percy's ballads, a rallying-cry for a generation of Romantic critics engaged in rewriting the eighteenth century's version of literary history.

Samuel Johnson not only witnessed this change; he was a major participant in it. But he was also an important representative of the earlier sensibility, who in many ways agrees with the progressive paradigm for the Renaissance. He contrasts the na‹vet, of earlier ages with Elizabethan enlightenment: in the Preface to the *Dictionary*, for instance, he writes, "Every language has a time of rudeness antecedent to perfection." Likewise the Preface to Shakespeare: "Nations, like individuals, have their infancy. ... The study of those who then aspired to plebeian learning was laid out upon adventures, giants, dragons, and enchantments." The best Renaissance writers slew these dragons, and "*Sidney*'s work" is therefore "the boundary, beyond which I make few excursions. From the authors which rose in the time of *Elizabeth*, a speech might be formed adequate to all the purposes of use and elegance."

Spenser is a major figure in this age of awakening, and Johnson's interest — even fascination — with Spenser was lifelong. In *Idler* 91, for instance, Johnson "consider[s] the whole succession [of poets] from Spenser to Pope, as superiour to any names which the continent can boast." Spenser appears nearly three thousand times in the *Dictionary*, and gives Johnson his designation for "the writers before the restoration, whose works I regard as *the wells of English undefiled*."

But for all his fondness of Spenser, Johnson saw the same problems as his contemporaries, and they produced in him the same tensions. He refused, however, to let *a priori* notions of periodization direct his reading. His comment on the object of critical inquiry is well known: "It is ... the task of criticism to establish principles; to improve opinion into knowledge." This task includes rendering the past intelligible by building historical narratives. But though the rules and schemata have their place, the empiricist critic must also distinguish those means of pleasing which depend upon known causes and rational deduction, from the nameless and inexplicable elegancies ... which may well be termed the enchantresses of the soul. Criticism reduces those regions of literature under the dominion of science, which have hitherto known only the anarchy of ignorance, the caprices of fancy, and the tyranny of prescription.

Johnson wants, where possible, to explain away the "enchantresses of the soul" by annexing their territory into the realm of literary history, but he recognizes — perhaps uncomfortably — that some authors cannot, and should not, be subdued. Guarding against "the tyranny of prescription," therefore, is as important as reducing literature to rules. Of the three categories considered above — design, allegory, and language — Johnson says nothing about Spenser's design, but we can speculate on his opinion. Though he was instrumental in removing the unities of time and place from English criticism, he preserved one Neoclassical unity — "nothing is essential to the fable, but unity of action" — and here Spenser is manifestly deficient. But up rises Johnson's empiricism: "Since the end of poetry is pleasure, that cannot be unpoetical with which all are pleased," and this critical honesty accounts for his fondness for Medieval romances.

This honesty accounts for many of his departures from the taste of his age. Though allegory was widely condemned, Spenser the allegorist was dear to Johnson. Boswell notes that he "praised John Bunyan highly," and that Johnson said "There is reason to think that he had read Spenser." His own allegorical writings owe much to Spenser; the personified Truth and Falsehood of *Rambler* 96, for instance, and "the 'Gulph of Intemperance,' a dreadful whirlpool, interspersed with rocks" in *Rambler* 102 echo specific passages in *The Faerie Queene*. His *Vision of Theodore* is especially reminiscent of Spenser's allegory, while the title of his never-completed *"Palace of Sloth, — a vision"* has an unmistakable Spenserian ring.

Language is a more considerable problem than design or

allegory. No party-line ancient or modern, Johnson considers language neither degenerative nor progressive, but he does see in it a kind of development or trajectory: "Every language has a time of rudeness antecedent to perfection, as well as of false refinement and declension."

This is not historical relativism but its opposite; it suggests a trans-historical linguistic ideal, an ideal to which ages succeed or fail in attaining. The Renaissance marks the beginning of this linguistic perfection.

Johnson's concern for this ideal made him uneasy at seeing "the imitation of Spenser ... likely to gain upon the age," and Spenser's unmusical stanza and versification were especially loathsome: the imitators seem to conclude, that when they have disfigured their lines with a few obsolete syllables, they have accomplished their design. ... Perhaps ... the stile of Spenser might by long labour be justly copied; but life is surely given us for higher purposes than to gather what our ancestors have wisely thrown away.

Johnson here is able to "conside[r] the metrical art simply as a science," a positivist science in which the clear failures of the past should be abandoned, and in which modern poets can advance by degrees beyond their precursors. Johnson also faults Spenser's diction, which he, like Ben Jonson, found to be "no language." *The Shepheardes Calender* draws Johnson's scorn for its "obsolete terms and rustick words, which they very learnedly call Dorick"; this "studied barbarity" calls forth Johnson's most devastating sarcasm: "Surely at the same time that a shepherd learns theology," he writes acidly, "he may gain some acquaintance with his native language." Johnson's dismissal of Spenser's archaism shows the critical tension Johnson felt at discovering major failings in a major poet, a poet who could not be rescued from "the nameless and inexplicable elegancies which appeal wholly to the fancy." It shows, in short, the limits of systematic criticism.

That Spenser could draw both the highest approbation and the most stinging sarcasm leads us to seek Johnson's particular notion of the Renaissance, one that admits Spenserian allegory but not Spenser's language. A candidate for the kind of progress he saw in the Renaissance appears throughout his works; one especially clear statement comes in his praise of Homer:

His positions are general, and his representations natural, with very little dependence on local or temporary customs, on those changeable scenes of artificial life, which, by mingling original with accidental notions, and crowding the mind with images which time effaces, produce ambiguity in diction, and obscurity in books. To this open display of unadulterated nature it must be ascribed, that Homer has fewer passages of doubtful meaning than any other poet either in the learned or in modern languages.

Here is one of Johnson's favourite pairs of polar opposites, generality *versus* "accident," and I suggest Johnson saw the Renaissance as Europe's passage from one pole to the other. Faux Medieval diction is a recollection of the "remote allusions and obscure opinions" of a justly forgotten age. These are Johnson's targets in his attacks on Spenser's obfuscatory archaism, which leads only to "obscurity in books," and which time justly "effaces."

Generality and "unadulterated nature," on the other hand, are dissociated from "changeable scenes of artificial life" with their "accidental notions" — the very business of allegory, which works by moving from the specific to the general. Allegory educates us in generality, teaching us not to depend on the "local and temporary customs" of the Middle Ages. The "revival of learning" amounts to the revival of general nature, the nature that appears in Shakespeare at his most "universal."

The Renaissance is therefore Europe's maturity, its accession to general nature, its abandonment of the peculiarities of archaism. But even the most mature literature has room for the generality of allegory, the bridge between the details consigned to antiquarians and the universal nature valuable to every reader, just as the Renaissance is the bridge between darkness and light. Spenser more than any other poet is the wedge that splits allegory from archaism, and forces Johnson's empirical criticism to come to terms with Renaissance poetic progress.

A DICTIONARY OF THE ENGLISH LANGUAGE

English writer and lexicographer, the son of Michael Johnson, bookseller and magistrate of Lichfield, who married in 1706 Sarah Ford. Michael's abilities and attainments seem to have been considerable. He was so well acquainted with the contents of the volumes which he exposed for sale that the country rectors of Staffordihire and Worcestershire thought him an oracle on points of learning. Between him and the clergy, indeed, there was a strong religious and political sympathy. He was a zealous churchman, and, though he had qualified himself for municipal office by taking the oaths to the sovereigns in possession, was to the last a Jacobite in heart. The social position of Samuel's paternal grandfather, William Johnson, remains obscure; his mother was the daughter of Cornelius Ford, "a little Warwickshire Gent."

At a house (now the Johnson Museum) in the Market Square, Lichfield, Samuel Johnson was born on the 18th of September 1709 and baptized on the same day at St. Mary's, Lichfield. In the child the physical, intellectual and moral peculiarities which afterwards distinguished the man were plainly discernible: great muscular strength accompanied by much awkwardness and many infirmities; great quickness of parts, with a morbid propensity to sloth and procrastination; a kind and generous heart, with a gloomy and irritable temper. He had inherited from his ancestors a scrofulous taint, and his parents were weak enough to believe that the royal touch would cure him. In his third year he was taken up to London, inspected by the court surgeon, prayed over by the court chaplains and stroked and presented with a piece of gold by Queen Anne.

Her hand was applied in vain. The boy's features, which were originally noble and not irregular, were distorted by his malady. His cheeks were deeply scarred. He lost for a time the sight of one eye; and he saw but very imperfectly with the other. But the force of his mind overcame every impediment. Indolent as he was, he acquired knowledge with such ease and rapidity that at every school (such as those at Lichfield and Stourbridge) to which he was sent he was soon the best scholar.

From sixteen to eighteen he resided at home, and was left to his own devices. He learned much at this time, though his studies were without guidance and without plan. He ransacked his father's shelves, dipped into a multitude of books, read what was interesting, and passed over what was dull.

An ordinary lad would have acquired little or no useful knowledge in such a way; but much that was dull to ordinary lads was interesting to Samuel. He read little Greek; for his proficiency in that language was not such that he could take much pleasure in the masters of Attic poetry and eloquence. But he had left school a good Latinist, and he soon acquired an extensive knowledge of Latin literature. He was peculiarly attracted by the works of the great restorers of learning. Once, while searching for some apples, he found a huge folio volume of Petrarch's works. The name excited his curiosity, and he eagerly devoured hundreds of pages. Indeed, the diction and versification of his own Latin compositions show that he had paid at least as much attention to modern copies from the antique as to the original models.

While he was thus irregularly educating himself, his family was on the most part impoverished. Michael Johnson was much better qualified to pore over books, and to talk about them, than to trade in them. His business declined; his debts increased; it was with difficulty that the daily expenses of his household were defrayed. It was out of his power to support his son at either university; but a wealthy neighbor offered assistance; and, in reliance on promises which proved to be of very little value, Samuel was entered at Pembroke College, Oxford. When the young scholar presented himself to the rulers of that society, they were amazed not more by his ungainly figure and eccentric manners than by the quantity of extensive and curious information which he had picked up during many months of desultory but not unprofitable study. On the first day of his residence he surprised his teachers by quoting Macrobius; and one of the most learned among them declared that he had never known a freshman of equal attainments.

At Oxford Johnson resided barely over two years, possibly less. He was poor, even to raggedness; and his appearance excited a mirth and a pity which were equally intolerable to his haughty spirit. He was driven from the quadrangle of Christ Church by the sneering looks which the members of that aristocratical society cast at the holes in his shoes. Some charitable person placed a new pair at his door; but he spurned them away in a fury. Distress made him, not servile, but reckless and ungovernable. The needy scholar was generally to be seen under the gate of Pembroke, a gate now adorned with his effigy, haranguing a circle of lads, over whom, in spite of his tattered gown and dirty linen, his wit and audacity gave him an undisputed ascendancy. In every mutiny against the discipline of the college he was the ringleader. Much was pardoned, however, to a youth so highly distinguished by abilities and acquirements. He had early made himself known by turning Alexander Pope's "Messiah" into Latin verse. The style and rhythm, indeed, were not exactly Virgilian; but the translation found many admirers, and was read with pleasure by Pope himself.

The time drew near at which Johnson would, in the ordinary course of things, have become a Bachelor of Arts; but he was at the end of his resources. Those promises of support on which he had relied had not been kept. His family could do nothing for him. His debts to Oxford tradesmen were small indeed, yet larger than he could pay. In the autumn of 1731 he was under the necessity of quitting the university without a degree. In the following winter his father died. The old man left but a pittance; and of that pittance almost the whole was appropriated to the support of his widow. The property to which Samuel succeeded amounted to no more than twenty pounds.

His life, during the thirty years which followed, was a struggle with poverty. The misery of that struggle needed no aggravation, but was aggravated by the sufferings of an unsound body and an unsound mind. Before the young man left the university, his hereditary malady had broken forth in a singularly cruel form. He had become an incurable hypochondriac. He said long after that he had been mad all his life, or at least not perfectly sane; and, in truth, eccentricities less strange than his have often been thought ground sufficient for absolving felons and for setting aside wills. His grimaces, his gestures, his mutterings, sometimes diverted and sometimes terrified people who did not know him. At a dinner table he would, in a fit of absence, stoop down and twitch off a lady's shoe.

He would amaze a drawing-room by suddenly ejaculating a clause of the Lord's Prayer. He would conceive an unintelligible aversion to a particular alley, and perform a great circuit rather than see the hateful place. He would set his heart on touching every post in the streets through which he walked. If by any chance he missed a post, he would go back a hundred yards and repair the omission. Under the influence of his disease, his senses became morbidly torpid, and his imagination morbidly active. At one time he would stand poring on the town clock without being able to tell the hour. At another he would distinctly hear his mother, who was many miles off, calling him by his name. But this was not the worst. A deep melancholy took possession of him, and gave a dark tinge to all his views of human nature and of human destiny. Such wretchedness as he endured has driven many men to shoot themselves or drown themselves. But he was under no temptation to commit suicide. He was sick of life; but he was afraid of death; and he shuddered at every sight or sound which reminded him of the inevitable hour. In religion he found but little comfort during his long and frequent fits of dejection, for his religion partook of his own character.

With such infirmities of body and of mind, he was left, at 22, to fight his way through the world. He remained during about five years in the midland counties. At Lichfield, his birthplace and early home, he had inherited some friends and acquired others. He was kindly noticed by Henry Hervey, an officer of noble family, who happened to be quartered there. Gilbert Walmesley, registrar of the ecclesiastical court of the diocese, did himself honor by patronizing the young adventurer, whose repulsive person, unpolished manners and squalid garb moved many of the petty aristocracy of the neighborhood to laughter or disgust. At Lichfield, however, Johnson could find no way of earning a livelihood. He became usher of a grammar school in Leicestershire; he resided as a humble companion in the house of a country gentleman; but a life of dependence was insupportable to his haughty spirit. He repaired to Birmingham, and there earned a few guineas by literary drudgery. In that town he printed a translation, little noticed at the time, and long forgotten, of a Latin book about Abyssinia. He then put forth proposals for publishing by subscription the poems of Politian, with notes containing a history of modern Latin verse; but subscriptions did not come in, and the volume never appeared.

While leading this vagrant and miserable life, Johnson fell in love. The object of his passion was Mrs. Elizabeth Porter, widow of Harry Porter, whose daughter Lucy was born only six years after Johnson himself. To ordinary spectators the lady appeared to be a short, fat, coarse woman, heavy makeup, dressed in gaudy colors, and fond of exhibiting provincial airs and graces which were not exactly those of the Queensberrys and Lepels. To Johnson, however, whose passions were strong, whose eyesight was too weak to distinguish rouge from natural bloom, and who had seldom or never been in the same room with a woman of real fashion, his Tetty, as he called her, was the most beautiful, graceful and accomplished of her sex. That his admiration was unfeigned cannot be doubted; she had, however, a jointure of £600 and perhaps a little more; she came of a good family, and her son Jervis commanded H.M.S. "Hercules." The marriage, in spite of occasional wranglings, proved happier than might have been expected. The lover continued to be under the illusions of the wedding day (July 9, 1735) until the lady died in her sixty-fourth year. On her monument at Bromley he placed an inscription extolling the charms of her person and of her manners; and when, long after her decease, he had occasion to mention her, he exclaimed with a tenderness half ludicrous, half pathetic, "Pretty creature!"

His marriage made it necessary for him to exert himself

more strenuously than he had hitherto done. He took a house at Edial near Lichfield and advertised for pupils. But eighteen months passed away, and only three pupils came to his academy. The "faces" that Johnson habitually made (probably nervous contortions due to his disorder) may well have alarmed parents. Good scholar though he was, these twitchings had lost him usherships in 1735 and 1736. David Garrick, who was one of the pupils, used, many years later, to throw the best company of London into convulsions of laughter by mimicking the master and his lady.

At length Johnson, in the twenty-eighth year of his age, determined to seek his fortune in London as a literary adventurer. He set out with a few guineas, three acts of his tragedy of *Irene* in manuscript, and two or three letters of introduction from his friend Walmesley. Never since literature became a calling in England had it been a less gainful calling than at the time when Johnson took up his residence in London. In the preceding generation a writer of eminent merit was sure to be munificently rewarded by the Government.

The least that he could expect was a pension or a sinecure place; and, if he showed any aptitude for politics, he might hope to be a member of parliament, a lord of the treasury, an ambassador, a secretary of state. But literature had ceased to flourish under the patronage of the great, and had not yet begun to flourish under the patronage of the public. One man of letters, indeed, Pope, had acquired by his pen what was then considered as a handsome fortune, and lived on a footing of equality with nobles and ministers of state. But this was a solitary exception.

Even an author whose reputation was established, and whose works were popular — such an author as James Thomson, whose *Seasons* was in every library, such an author as Henry Fielding, whose *Pasquin* had had a greater run than any drama since *The Beggar's Opera* — was sometimes glad to obtain, by pawning his best coat, the means of dining on tripe at a cookshop underground, where he could wipe his hands, after his greasy meal, on the back of a Newfoundland dog. It is easy, therefore, to imagine what humiliations and privations must have awaited the novice who had still to earn a name. One of the publishers to whom Johnson applied for employment measured with a scornful eye that athletic though uncouth frame, and exclaimed, "You had better get a porter's knot and carry trunks." Nor was the advice bad, for a porter was likely to be as plentifully fed, and as comfortably lodged, as a poet.

Some time appears to have lapsed before Johnson was able to form any literary connection from which he could expect more than bread for the day which was passing over him. He never forgot the generosity with which Hervey, who was now residing in London, relieved his wants during this time of trial. "Harry Hervey", said Johnson many years later, "was a vicious man; but he was very kind to me. If you call a dog Hervey, I shall love him." At Hervey's table Johnson sometimes enjoyed feasts which were made more agreeable by contrast. But in general he dined, and thought that he dined well, on sixpenny-worth of meat and a pennyworth of bread at an alehouse near Drury Lane.

About a year after Johnson had begun to reside in London he was fortunate enough to obtain regular employment from Edward Cave on the *Gentleman's Magazine*. That periodical, just entering on the ninth year of its long existence, was the only one in the kingdom which then had what would now be called a large circulation. Johnson was engaged to write the speeches in the "Reports of the Debates of the Senate of Lilliput", under which thin disguise the proceedings of parliament were published. He was generally furnished with notes, meagre indeed and inaccurate, of what had been said; but sometimes he had to find arguments and eloquence both for the ministry and for the opposition.

He was himself a Tory, not from rational conviction — for his serious opinion was that one form of government was just as good or as bad as another — but from mere passion, such as inflamed the Capulets against the Montagues. In his infancy he had heard so much talk about the villainies of the Whigs, and the dangers of the Church, that he had become a furious partisan when he could scarcely speak. Before he was three he had insisted on being taken to hear Sacheverel preach at Lichfield Cathedral, and had listened to the sermon with as much respect and probably with as much intelligence, as any Staffordshire squire in the congregation. The work which had been begur in the nursery had been completed by the university. Oxford, when Johnson resided there, was the most Jacobitical place in England; and Pembroke was one of the most Jacobitical colleges in Oxford.

The prejudices which he brought up to London were scarcely less absurd than those of his own Tom Tempest. Charles II and James II were two of the best kings that ever reigned. William Laud was a prodigy of parts and learning over whose tomb Art and Genius still continued to weep. Hampden deserved no more honorable name than that of the "zealot of rebellion." He long had an aversion to the Scots, an aversion of which he could not remember the commencement, but which, he owned, had probably originated in his abhorrence of the conduct of the nation during the Great Rebellion. It is easy to guess in what manner debates on great party questions were likely to be reported by a man whose judgment was so much disordered by party spirit. A show of fairness was indeed necessary to the prosperity of the *Magazine*. But Johnson long afterwards owned that, though he had saved appearances, he had taken care that the Whig dogs should not have the best of it; and, in fact, every passage which has lived, every passage which bears the marks of his higher faculties, is put into the mouth of some member of the opposition.

A few weeks after Johnson had entered on these obscure labors, he published a work which at once placed him high among the writers of his age. It is probable that what he had suffered during his first year in London had often reminded him of some parts of the satire in which Juvenal had described the misery and degradation of a needy man of letters, lodged among the pigeon's nests in the tottering garrets which overhung the streets of Rome. Pope's admirable imitations of Horace's *Satires* and *Epistles* had recently appeared, were in every hand, and were by many readers thought superior to the originals. What Pope had done for Horace, Johnson aspired to do for Juvenal.

Johnson's *London* appeared without his name in May 1738. He received only ten guineas for this stately and vigorous poem; but the sale was rapid and the success complete. A second edition was required within a week. Those small critics who are always desirous to lower established reputations ran about proclaiming that the anonymous satirist was superior to Pope in Pope's own peculiar department of literature. It ought to be remembered, to the honour of Pope, that he joined heartily in the applause with which the appearance of a rival genius was welcomed. He made inquiries about the author of *London*. Such a man, he said, could not long,be concealed. The name was soon discovered; and Pope, with great kindness, exerted himself to obtain an academical degree and the mastership of a grammar school for the poor young poet. The attempt failed, and Johnson remained a bookseller's hack.

It does not appear that these two men, the most eminent writer of the generation which was going out, and the most eminent writer of the generation which was coming in, ever saw each other. They lived in very different circles, one surrounded by dukes and earls, the other by starving pamphleteers and index-makers. Among Johnson's associates at this time may be mentioned Boyse, who, when his shirts were pledged, scrawled Latin verses sitting up in bed with his arms through two holes in his blanket, who composed very respectable sacred poetry when he was sobre, and who was at last run over by a hackney coach when he was drunk; Hoole, surnamed the metaphysical tailor, who, instead of attending to his measures, used to trace geometrical diagrams on the board where he sat cross-legged; and the penitent impostor, George Psalmanazar, who, after poring all day in a humble lodging on the folios of Jewish rabbis and Christian fathers, indulged himself at night with literary and theological conversation at an alehouse in the City.

But the most remarkable of the persons with whom at this time Johnson consorted was Richard Savage, an earl's son, a shoemaker's apprentice, who had seen life in all its forms, who had feasted among blue ribands in St. James's Square, and had lain with fifty pounds weight of irons on his legs in the condemned ward of Newgate. This man had, after many vicissitudes of fortune, sunk at last into abject and hopeless poverty. His pen had failed him. His patrons had been taken away by death, or estranged by the riotous profusion with which he squandered their bounty, and the ungrateful insolence with which he rejected their advice. He now lived by begging.

He dined on venison and champagne whenever he had been so fortunate as to borrow a guinea. If his questing had been unsuccessful, he appeased the rage of hunger with some scraps of broken meat, and lay down to rest under the piazza of Covent Garden in warm weather, and, in cold weather, as near as he could get to the furnace of a glass house. Yet in his misery he was still an agreeable companion. He had an inexhaustible store of anecdotes about that gay and brilliant world from which he was now an outcast. He had observed the great men of both parties in hours of careless relaxation, had seen the leaders of opposition without the mask of patriotism, and had heard the prime minister roar with laughter and tell stories not over-decent. During some months Savage lived in the closest familiarity with Johnson; and then the friends parted, not without tears. Johnson remained in London to drudge for Cave. Savage went to the west of England, lived there as he had lived everywhere, and in 1743 died, penniless and heartbroken, in Bristol Jail.

Soon after his death, while the public curiosity was strongly excited about his extraordinary character and his not less extraordinary adventures, a life of him appeared widely different from the catchpenny lives of eminent men which were then a staple article of manufacture in Grub Street. The style was indeed deficient in ease and variety; and the writer was evidently too partial to the Latin element of our language. But the little work, with all its faults, was a masterpiece. No finer specimen of literary biography existed in any language, living or dead; and a discerning critic might have confidently predicted that the author was destined to be the founder of a new school of English eloquence. The *Life of Savage* was anonymous; but it was well known in literary circles that Johnson was the writer.

During the three years which followed, he produced no important work; but he was not, and indeed could not be, idle. The fame of his abilities and learning continued to grow. William Warburton pronounced him a man of parts and genius; and the praise of Warburton was then no light thing. Such was Johnson's reputation that, in 1747, several eminent booksellers combined to employ him in the arduous work of preparing a *Dictionary of the English Language*, in two folio volumes. The sum which they agreed to pay him was only fifteen hundred guineas; and out of this sum he had to pay several poor men of letters who assisted him in the humbler parts of his task.

The prospectus of the *Dictionary* he addressed to the earl of Chesterfield. Chesterfield had long been celebrated for the politeness of his manners, the brilliancy of his wit, and the delicacy of his taste. He was acknowledged to be the finest speaker in the House of Lords. He had recently governed Ireland, at a momentous conjuncture, with eminent firmness, wisdom and humanity; and he had since become secretary of state. He received Johnson's homage with the most winning affability, and requited it with a few guineas, bestowed doubtless in a very graceful manner, but was by no means desirous to see all his carpets blackened with the London mud, and his soups and wines thrown to right and left over the gowns of fine ladies and the waistcoats of fine gentlemen, by an absent, awkward scholar, who gave strange starts and uttered strange growls, who dressed like a scarecrow and ate like a cormorant. During some time Johnson continued to call on his patron, but, after being repeatedly told by the porter that his lordship was not at home, took the hint, and ceased to present himself at the inhospitable door.

Johnson had flattered himself that he should have completed his *Dictionary* by the end of 1750; but it was not until 1755 that he at length gave his huge volumes to the world. During the seven years which he passed in the drudgery of penning definitions and marking quotations for transcription, he sought for relaxation in literary labour of a more agreeable kind. In January 1749 he published *The Vanity of Human Wishes*, an excellent imitation of the tenth satire of Juvenal, for which he received fifteen guineas.

A few days after the publication of this poem, his tragedy of *Irene*, begun many years before, was brought on the stage by his old pupil, David Garrick, now manager of Drury Lane Theatre. The relation between him and his old preceptor was of a very singular kind. They repelled each other strongly, and yet attracted each other strongly. Nature had made them of very different clay; and circumstances had fully brought out the natural peculiarities of both. Sudden prosperity had turned Garrick's head. Continued adversity had soured Johnson's temper. Johnson saw with more envy than became so great a man the villa, the plate, the china, the Brussels carpet, which the little mimic had got by repeating, with grimaces and gesticulations, what wiser men had written; and the exquisitely sensitive vanity of Garrick was galled by the thought that, while all the rest of the world was applauding him, he could obtain from one morose cynic, whose opinion it was impossible to despise, scarcely any compliment not acidulated with scorn.

Yet the two Lichfield men had so many early recollections in common, and sympathized with each other on so many points on which they sympathized with nobody else in the vast population of the capital, that, though the master was often provoked by the monkey-like impertinence of the pupil, and the pupil by the bearish rudeness of the master, they remained friends until they were parted by death. Garrick now brought *Irene* out, with alterations sufficient to displease the author, yet not sufficient to make the piece pleasing to the audience. After nine representations the play was withdrawn. The poet however cleared by his benefit nights, and by the sale of the copyright of his tragedy, about three hundred pounds, then a great sum in his estimation.

About a year after the representation of *Irene*, he began to publish a series of short essays on morals, manners and literature. This species of composition had been brought into fashion by the success of the *Tatler*, and by the still more brilliant success of the *Spectator*.

A crowd of small writers had vainly attempted to rival Joseph Addison. The *Lay Monastery*, the *Censor*, the *Freethinker*, the *Plain Dealer*, the *Champion*, and other works of the same kind had had their short day. At length Johnson undertook the adventure in which so many aspirants had failed. In the thirty-sixth year after the appearance of the last number of the *Spectator* appeared the first number of the *Rambler*. From March 1750 to March 1752 this paper continued to come out every Tuesday and Saturday.

From the first the *Rambler* was enthusiastically admired by a few eminent men. Samuel Richardson, when only five numbers had appeared, pronounced it equal if not superior to the *Spectator*. Young and Hartley expressed their approbation not less warmly. In consequence probably of the good offices of Bubb Dodington, who was then the confidential adviser of Prince Frederick, two of his royal highness's gentlemen carried a gracious message to the printing office, and ordered seven copies for Leicester House. But Johnson had had enough of the patronage of the great to last him all his life, and was not disposed to haunt any other door as he had haunted the door of Chesterfield.

By the public the *Rambler* was at first very coldly received. Though the price of a number was only twopence, the sale did not amount to five hundred. The profits were therefore very small. But as soon as the flying leaves were collected and reprinted they became popular. The author lived to see thirteen thousand copies spread over England alone. Separate editions were published for the Scotch and Irish markets. A large party pronounced the style perfect, so absolutely perfect that in some essays it would be impossible for the writer himself to alter a single word for the better. Another party, not less numerous, vehemently accused him of having corrupted the purity of the English tongue. The best critics admitted that his diction was too monotonous, too obviously artificial, and now and then turgid even to absurdity. But they did justice to the acuteness of his observations on morals and manners, to the constant precision and frequent brilliancy of his language, to the weighty and magnificent eloquence of many serious passages, and to the solemn yet pleasing humour of some of the lighter papers.

The last *Rambler* was written in a sad and gloomy hour. Mrs. Johnson had been given over by the physicians. Three days later she died. She left her husband almost broken-hearted. Many people had been surprised to see a man of his genius and learning stooping to every drudgery, and denying himself almost every comfort, for the purpose of supplying a silly, affected old woman with superfluities, which she accepted with but little gratitude. But all his affection had been concentrated on her. He had neither brother nor sister, neither son nor daughter. Her opinion of his writings was more important to him than the voice of the pit of Drury Lane Theatre, or the judgment of the *Monthly Review*. The chief support which had sustained him through the most arduous labour of his life was the hope that she would enjoy the fame and the profit which he anticipated from his *Dictionary*. She was gone; and in that vast labyrinth of streets, peopled by eight hundred thousand human beings, he was alone. Yet it was necessary for him to set himself, as he expressed it, doggedly to work. After three more laborious years, the *Dictionary* was at length complete.

It had been generally supposed that this great work would be dedicated to the eloquent and accomplished nobleman to whom the prospectus had been addressed. Lord Chesterfield well knew the value of such a compliment; and therefore, when the day of publication drew near, he exerted himself to soothe, by a show of zealous and at the same time of delicate and judicious kindness, the pride which he had so cruelly wounded. Since the *Rambler* had ceased to appear, the town had been entertained by a journal called the *World*, to which many men of high rank and fashion contributed. In two successive numbers of the *World*, the *Dictionary* was puffed with wonderful skill.

The writings of Johnson were warmly praised. It was proposed that he should be invested with the authority of a dictator, nay, of a pope, over our language, and that his decisions about the meaning and the spelling of words should be received as final. His two folios, it was said, would of course be bought by everybody who could afford to buy them. It was soon known that these papers were written by Chesterfield. But the just resentment of Johnson was not to be so appeased. In a letter written with singular energy and dignity of thought and language, he repelled the tardy advances of his patron. The *Dictionary* came forth without a dedication. In the Preface the author truly declared that he owed nothing to the great, and described the difficulties with which he had been left to struggle so forcibly and pathetically that the ablest and most malevolent of all the enemies of his fame, Horne Tooke, never could read that passage without tears.

Johnson's *Dictionary* was hailed with an enthusiasm such as no similar work has ever excited. It was indeed the first dictionary which could be read with pleasure. The definitions show so much acuteness of thought and command of language, and the passages quoted from poets, divines and philosophers are so skilfully selected, that a leisure hour may always be very agreeably spent in turning over the pages. The faults of the book resolve themselves, for the most part, into one great fault. Johnson was a wretched etymologist. He knew little or nothing of any Teutonic language except English, which indeed, as he wrote it, was scarcely a Teutonic language; and thus he was absolutely at the mercy of Junius and Skinner.

The *Dictionary*, though it raised Johnson's fame, added nothing to his pecuniary means. The fifteen hundred guineas which the booksellers had agreed to pay him had been advanced and spent before the last sheets issued from the press. It is painful to relate that twice in the course of the year which followed the publication of this great work he was arrested and carried to sponging-houses, and that he was twice indebted for his liberty to his excellent friend Richardson. It was still necessary for the man who had been formerly saluted by the highest authority as dictator of the English language to supply his wants by constant toil.

He abridged his *Dictionary*. He proposed to bring out an

edition of Shakespeare by subscription, and many subscribers sent in their names and laid down their money; but he soon found the task so little to his taste that he turned to more attractive employments. He contributed many papers to a new monthly journal, which was called the *Literary Magazine*. Few of these papers have much interest; but among them was one of the best things that he ever wrote, a masterpiece both of reasoning and of satirical pleasantry, the review of Jenyns' *Inquiry into the Nature and Origin of Evil*.

In the spring of 1758 Johnson put forth the first of a series of essays, entitled the *Idler*. During two years these essays continued to appear weekly. They were eagerly read, widely circulated, and indeed impudently pirated, while they were still in the original form, and had a large sale when collected into volumes. The *Idler* may be described as a second part of the *Rambler*, somewhat livelier and somewhat weaker than the first part.

While Johnson was busied with his *Idlers*, his mother, who had accomplished her ninetieth year, died at Lichfield. It was long since he had seen her, but he had not failed to contribute largely out of his small means to her comfort. In order to defray the charges of her funeral, and to pay some debts which she had left, he wrote a little book in a single week, and sent off the sheets to the press without reading them over. A hundred pounds were paid him for the copyright, and the purchasers had great cause to be pleased with their bargain, for the book was *Rasselas*, and it had a great success.

The plan of *Rasselas* might, however, have seemed to invite severe criticism. Johnson has frequently blamed Shakespeare for neglecting the proprieties of time and place, and for ascribing to one age or nation the manners and opinions of another. Yet Shakespeare has not sinned in this way more grievously than Johnson. Rasselas and Imlac, Nekayah and Pekuah, are evidently meant to be Abyssinians of the 18th century; for the Europe which Imlac describes is the Europe of the 18th century, and the inmates of the Happy Valley talk familiarly of that law of gravitation which Isaac Newton discovered and which was not fully received even at

Cambridge until the 18th century. Johnson, not content with turning filthy savages, ignorant of their letters, and gorged with raw steaks cut from living cows, into philosophers as eloquent and enlightened as himself or his friend Edmund Burke, and into ladies as highly accomplished as Mrs. Lennox or Mrs. Sheridan, transferred the whole domestic system of England to Egypt.

Into a land of harems, a land of polygamy, a land where women are married without ever being seen, he introduced the flirtations and jealousies of our ballrooms. In a land where there is boundless liberty of divorce, wedlock is described as the indissoluble compact. "A youth and maiden meeting by chance, or brought together by artifice, exchange glances, reciprocate civilities, go home, and dream of each other. Such", says Rasselas, "is the common process of marriage." A writer who was guilty of such improprieties had little right to blame the poet who made Hector quote Aristotle, and represented Julio Romano as flourishing in the days of the Oracle of Delphi.

By such exertions as have been described Johnson supported himself until the year 1762. In that year a great change in his circumstances took place. He had from a child been an enemy of the reigning dynasty. His Jacobite prejudices had been exhibited with little disguise both in his works and in his conversation. Even in his massy and elaborate *Dictionary* he had, with a strange want of taste and judgment, inserted bitter and contumelious reflexions on the Whig party. The excise, which was a favourite resource of Whig financiers, he had designated as a hateful tax. He had railed against the commissioners of excise in language so coarse that they had seriously thought of prosecuting him. He had with difficulty been prevented from holding up the lord privy seal by name as an example of the meaning of the word "renegade."

A pension he had defined as pay given to a state hireling to betray his country; a pensioner as a slave of state hired by a stipend to obey a master. It seemed unlikely that the author of these definitions would himself be pensioned. But that was a time of wonders. George III had ascended the throne, and had, in the course of a few months, disgusted many of the old friends, and conciliated many of the old enemies of his house. The city was becoming mutinous; Oxford was becoming loyal. Cavendishes and Bentincks were murmuring; Somersets and Wyndhams were hastening to kiss hands. The head of the treasury was now Lord Bute, who was a Tory, and could have no objection to Johnson's Toryism. Bute wished to be thought a patron of men of letters; and Johnson was one of the most eminent and one of the most needy men of letters in Europe. A pension of £300 a year was graciously offered, and with very little hesitation accepted.

This event produced a change in Johnson's whole way of life. For the first time since his boyhood he no longer felt the daily goad urging him to the daily toil. He was at liberty, after thirty years of anxiety and drudgery, to indulge his constitutional indolence, to lie in bed until two in the afternoon, and to sit up talking until four in the morning, without fearing either the printer's devil or the sheriff's officer.

One laborious task indeed he had bound himself to perform. He had received large subscriptions for his promised edition of Shakespeare; he had lived on those subscriptions during some years; and he could not without disgrace omit to perform his part of the contract. His friends repeatedly exhorted him to make an effort, and he repeatedly resolved to do so. But, notwithstanding their exhortations and his resolutions, month followed month, year followed year, and nothing was done. He prayed fervently against his idleness; he determined, as often as he received the sacrament, that he would no longer doze away and trifle away his time; but the spell under which he lay resisted prayer and sacrament. Happily for his honour, the charm which held him captive was at length broken by no gentle or friendly hand.

He had been weak enough to pay serious attention to a story about a ghost which haunted a house in Cock Lane, and had actually gone himself, with some of his friends, at one in the morning, to St. John's Church, Clerkenwell, in the hope of receiving a communication from the perturbed spirit. But the spirit, though adjured with all solemnity, remained obstinately silent; and it soon appeared that a naughty girl of eleven had been amusing herself by making fools of so many philosophers. Charles Churchill, who, confident in his powers, drunk with popularity, and burning with party spirit, was looking for some man of established fame and Tory politics to insult, celebrated the Cock Lane ghost in three cantos, nicknamed Johnson Pomposo, asked where the book was which had been so long promised and so liberally paid for, and directly accused the great moralist of cheating. This terrible word proved effectual, and in October 1765 appeared, after a delay of nine years, the new edition of Shakespeare.

This publication saved Johnson's character for honesty, but added nothing to the fame of his abilities and learning. The Preface, though it contains some good passages, is not in his best manner. The most valuable notes are those in which he had an opportunity of showing how attentively he had during many years observed human life and human nature. The best specimen is the note on the character of Polonius. Nothing so good is to be found even in Wilhelm Meister's admirable examination of *Hamlet*. But verdict on Johnson's work is mixed. Macaulay condemns it, and others praise Johnson's grasp of human nature and insight into the dramatist's meanings. Johnson had, in his prospectus, told the world that he was peculiarly fitted for the task which he had undertaken, because he had, as a lexicographer, been under the necessity of taking a wider view of the English language than any of his predecessors.

But, unfortunately, he had altogether neglected that very part of our literature with which it is especially desirable that an editor of Shakespeare should be conversant. In the two folio volumes of the *English Dictionary* there is not a single passage quoted from any dramatist of the Elizabethan age except Shakespeare and Ben Jonson. Even from Ben the quotations are few. Johnson might easily in a few months have made himself well acquainted with every old play that was extant. But it never seems to have occurred to him that this was a necessary preparation for the work which he had undertaken. He would doubtless have admitted that it would be the height of absurdity in a man who was not familiar with the works of

Aeschylus and Euripides to publish an edition of Sophocles. Yet he ventured to publish an edition of Shakespeare, without having ever in his life, as far as can be discovered, read a single scene of Massinger, Ford, Dekker, Webster, Marlow, Beaumont or Fletcher. His detractors were noisy and scurrilous. He had, however, acquitted himself of a debt which had long lain heavy on his conscience and he sank back into the repose from which the sting of satire had roused him. He long continued to live upon the fame which he had already won. He was honored by the University of Oxford with a doctor's degree, by the Royal Academy with a professorship, and by the king with an interview, in which his majesty most graciously expressed a hope that so excellent a writer would not cease to write. In the interval between 1765 and 1775 Johnson published only two or three political tracts.

But, though his pen was now idle, his tongue was active. The influence exercised by his conversation, directly upon those with whom he lived, and indirectly on the whole literary world, was altogether without a parallel. His colloquial talents were indeed of the highest order. He had strong sense, quick discernment, wit, humour, immense knowledge of literature and of life, and an infinite store of curious anecdotes. As respected style, he spoke far better than he wrote. Every sentence which dropped from his lips was as correct in structure as the most nicely balanced period of the *Rambler*. But in his talk there were no pompous triads, and little more than a fair proportion of words in -osity and -ation. All was simplicity, ease and vigour. He uttered his short, weighty, and pointed sentences with a power of voice, and a justness and energy of emphasis, of which the effect was rather increased than diminished by the rollings of his huge form, and by the asthmatic gaspings and puffings in which the peals of his eloquence generally ended. Nor did the laziness which made him unwilling to sit down to his desk prevent him from giving instruction or entertainment orally. To discuss questions of taste, of learning, of casuistry, in language so exact and so forcible that it might have been printed without the alteration of a word, was to him no exertion, but a pleasure.

He loved, as he said, to fold his legs and have his talk out. He was ready to bestow the overflowings of his full mind on anybody who would start a subject: on a fellow-passenger in a stage coach, or on the person who sat at the same table with him in an eating-house. But his conversation was nowhere so brilliant and striking as when he was surrounded by a few friends, whose abilities and knowledge enabled them, as he once expressed it, to send him back every ball that he threw. Some of these, in 1764, formed themselves into a club, which gradually became a formidable power in the commonwealth of letters. The verdicts pronounced by this conclave on new books were speedily known over all London, and were sufficient to sell off a whole edition in a day, or to condemn the sheets to the service of the trunkmaker and the pastrycook. Oliver Goldsmith was the representative of poetry and light literature, Joshua Reynolds of the arts, Edmund Burke of political eloquence and political philosophy. There, too, were Edward Gibbon the greatest historian and Sir William Jones the greatest linguist of the age. David Garrick brought to the meetings his inexhaustible pleasantry, his incomparable mimicry, and his consummate knowledge of stage effect. Among the most constant attendants were two high-born and high-bred gentlemen, closely bound together by friendship, but of widely different characters and habits — Bennet Langton, distinguished by his skill in Greek literature, by the orthodoxy of his opinions, and by the sanctity of his life, and Topham Beauclerk, renowned for his amours, his fastidious taste and his sarcastic wit.

Among the members of this celebrated body was one to whom it has owed the greater part of its celebrity, yet who was regarded with little respect by his brethren, and had not without difficulty obtained a seat among them. This was James Boswell, a young Scots lawyer, heir to an honorable name and a fair estate. That he was a coxcomb and a bore, weak, vain, pushing, curious, garrulous, was obvious to all who were acquainted with him. To a man of Johnson's strong understanding and irritable temper, the silly egotism and adulation of Boswell must have been as teasing as the constant buzz of a fly. Johnson hated to be questioned; and Boswell was eternally catechizing him on all kinds of subjects, and sometimes propounded such questions as, "What would you do, sir, if you were locked up in a tower with a baby?" Johnson was a water-drinker and Boswell was a wine-bibber, and indeed little better than an habitual sot. It was impossible that there should be perfect harmony between two such companions. Indeed, the great man was sometimes provoked into fits of passion, in which he said things which the small man, during a few hours, seriously resented.

Every quarrel, however, was soon made up. During twenty years the disciple continued to worship the master; the master continued to scold the disciple, to sneer at him, and to love him. The two friends ordinarily resided at a great distance from each other. Boswell practiced in the Parliament House of Edinburgh, and could pay only occasional visits to London. During those visits his chief business was to watch Johnson, to discover all Johnson's habits, to turn the conversation to subjects about which Johnson was likely to say something remarkable, and to fill quarto notebooks with minutes of what Johnson had said. In this way were gathered the materials out of which was afterwards constructed the most interesting biographical work in history. Soon after the club began to exist, Johnson formed a connection less important indeed to his fame, but much mere important to his happiness, than his connection with Boswell. Henry Thrale, one of the most opulent brewers in the kingdom, a man of sound and cultivated understanding, rigid principles, and liberal spirit, was married to one of those clever, kind-hearted, engaging, vain, pert young women who are perpetually doing or saying what is not exactly right, but who, do or say what they may, are always agreeable.

In 1765 the Thrales became acquainted with Johnson, and the acquaintance ripened fast into friendship. They were astonished and delighted by the brilliancy of his conversation. They were flattered by finding that a man so widely celebrated preferred their house to any other in London. Johnson soon had an apartment at the brewery in Southwark, and a still more pleasant apartment at the villa of his friends on Streatham Common. A large part of every year he passed in those abodes, which must have seemed magnificent and luxurious indeed, when compared with the dens in which he had generally been lodged. But his chief pleasures were derived from what the astronomer of his Abyssinian tale called "the endearing elegance of female friendship." Mrs. Thrale rallied him, soothed him, coaxed him, and if she sometimes provoked him by her flippancy, made ample amends by listening to his reproofs with angelic sweetness of temper. When he was diseased in body and in mind, she was the most tender of nurses. No comfort that wealth could purchase, no contrivance that womanly ingenuity, set to work by womanly compassion, could devise, was wanting to his sick room. It would seem that a full half of Johnson's life during about sixteen years was passed under the roof of the Thrales.

He accompanied the family sometimes to Bath, and sometimes to Brighton, once to Wales and once to Paris. But he had at the same time a house in one of the narrow and gloomy courts on the north of Fleet Street. In the garrets was his library, a large and miscellaneous collection of books, falling to pieces and begrimed with dust. On a lower floor he sometimes, but very rarely, regaled a friend with a plain dinner — a veal pie, or a leg of lamb and spinach, and a rice pudding. Nor was the dwelling uninhabited during his long absences. It was the home of the most extraordinary assemblage of inmates that ever was brought together. At the head of the establishment Johnson had placed an old lady named Williams, whose chief recommendations were her blindness and her poverty. But, in spite of her murmurs and reproaches, he gave an asylum to another lady who was as poor as herself, Mrs. Desmoulins, whose family he had known many years before in Staffordshire. Room was found for the daughter of Mrs. Desmoulins, and for another destitute damsel, who was generally addressed as Miss Carmichael, but whom her generous host called Polly. An old quack doctor named Levett, who had a wide practice, but among the very poorest class, poured out Johnson's tea in the morning and completed this strange menagerie. All these poor creatures were at constant war with each other, and with Johnson's Negro servant Frank.

Sometimes, indeed, they transferred their hostilities from the servant to the master, complained that a better table was not kept for them, and railed or maundered until their benefactor was glad to make his escape to Streatham or to the Mitre Tavern. And yet he, who was generally the haughtiest and most irritable of mankind, who was but too prompt to resent anything which looked like a slight on the part of a purse-proud bookseller, or of a noble and powerful patron, bore patiently from mendicants, who, but for his bounty, must have gone to the workhouse, insults more provoking than those for which he had knocked down Osborne and bidden defiance to Chesterfield. Year after year Mrs. Williams and Mrs. Desmoulins, Polly and Levett, continued to torment him and to live upon him. The course of life which has been described was interrupted in Johnson's sixty-fourth year by an important event. He had early read an account of the Hebrides, and had been much interested by learning that there was so near him a land peopled by a race which was still as rude and simple as in the Middle Ages. A wish to become intimately acquainted with a state of society so utterly unlike all that he had ever seen frequently crossed his mind. But it is not probable that his curiosity would have overcome his habitual sluggishness, and his love of the smoke, the mud, and the cries of London, had not Boswell importuned him to attempt the adventure, and offered to be his squire.

At length, in August 1773, Johnson crossed the Highland line, and plunged courageously into what was then considered, by most Englishmen, as a dreary and perilous wilderness. After wandering about two months through the Celtic region, sometimes in rude boats which did not protect him from the rain, and sometimes on small shaggy ponies which could hardly bear his weight, he returned to his old haunts with a mind full of new images and new theories. During the following year he employed himself in recording his adventures. About the beginning of 1775 his *Journey to the Hebrides* was published, and was, during some weeks, the chief subject of conversation in all circles in which any attention was paid to literature. His prejudice against the Scots had at length become little more than matter of jest; and whatever remained of the old feeling had been effectually removed by the kind and respectful hospitality with which he had been received in every part of Scotland. It was, of course, not to be expected that an Oxonian Tory should praise the Presbyterian polity and ritual, or that an eye accustomed to the hedgerows and parks of England should not be struck by the bareness of Berwickshire and East Lothian. But even in censure Johnson's tone is not unfriendly.

The most enlightened Scotsmen, with Lord Mansfield at their head, were well pleased. But some foolish and ignorant Scotsmen were moved to anger by a little unpalatable truth which was mingled with much eulogy, and assailed him whom they chose to consider as the enemy of their country with libels much more dishonorable to their country than anything that he had ever said or written. They published paragraphs in the newspapers, articles in the magazines, sixpenny pamphlets, five-shilling books. One scribbler abused Johnson for being blear-eyed, another for being a pensioner; a third informed the world that one of the doctor's uncles had been convicted of felony in Scotland, and had found that there was in that country one tree capable of supporting the weight of an Englishman. James Macpherson, whose *Fingal* had been treated in the *Journey* as an impudent forgery, threatened to take vengeance with a cane. The only effect of this threat was that Johnson reiterated the charge of forgery in the most contemptuous terms, and walked about, during some time, with a cudgel.

Of other assailants Johnson took no notice whatever. He had early resolved never to be drawn into controversy; and he adhered to his resolution with a steadfastness which is the more extraordinary because he was, both intellectually and morally, of the stuff of which controversialists are made. In conversation he was a singularly eager, acute and pertinacious disputant. When at a loss for good reasons, he had recourse to sophistry; and when heated by altercation, he made unsparing use of sarcasm and invective. But when he took his pen in his hand, his whole character seemed to be changed. A hundred bad writers misrepresented him and reviled him; but not one of the hundred could boast of having been thought by him worthy of a refutation, or even of a retort. One Scotsman, bent on vindicating the fame of Scots learning, defied him to the combat in a detestable Latin hexameter: "Maxime, si tu vis, cupio contendere tecum." But Johnson took no notice of the challenge.

He always maintained that fame was a shuttlecock which could be kept up only by being beaten back as well as beaten forward, and which would soon fall if there were only one battledore. No saying was oftener in his mouth than that fine apophthegm of Richard Bentley, that no man was ever written down but by himself. Unhappily, a few months after the appearance of the *Journey to the Hebrides,* Johnson did what none of his envious assailants could have done, and to a certain extent succeeded in writing himself down. The disputes between England and her American colonies had reached a point at which no amicable adjustment was possible. War was evidently impending; and the ministers seem to have thought that the eloquence of Johnson might with advantage be employed to inflame the nation against the opposition at home, and against the rebels beyond the Atlantic. He had already written two or three tracts in defence of the foreign and domestic policy of the government; and those tracts, though hardly worthy of him, were much superior to the crowd of pamphlets which lay on the counters of Almon and Stockdale. But his *Taxation no Tyranny* was a pitiable failure.

Even Boswell was forced to own that in this unfortunate piece he could detect no trace of his master's powers. The general opinion was that the strong faculties which had produced the *Dictionary* and the *Rambler* were beginning to feel the effect of time and of disease, and that the old man would best consult his credit by writing no more. But this was a great mistake. Johnson had failed, not because his mind was less vigorous than when he wrote *Rasselas* in the evenings of a week, but because he had foolishly chosen, or suffered others to choose for him, a subject such as he would at no time have been competent to treat. He was in no sense a statesman. He never willingly read or thought or talked about affairs of state. He loved biography, literary history, the history of manners; but political history was positively distasteful to him. The question at issue between the colonies and the mother country was a question about which he had really nothing to say. Happily, Johnson soon had an opportunity of proving most signally that his failure was not to be ascribed to intellectual decay.

On Easter Eve 1777 some persons, deputed by a meeting which consisted of forty of the first booksellers in London, called upon him. Though he had some scruples about doing business at that season, he received his visitors with much civility. They came to inform him that a new edition of the English poets, from Cowley downwards, was in contemplation, and to ask him to furnish short biographical prefaces. He readily undertook the task for which he was pre-eminently qualified. His knowledge of the literary history of England since the Restoration was unrivalled. That knowledge he had derived partly from books, and partly from sources which had long been closed: from old Grub Street traditions; from the talk of forgotten poetasters and pamphleteers, who had long been lying in parish vaults; from the recollections of such men as Gilbert Walmesley, who had conversed with the wits of Button, Cibber, who had mutilated the plays of two generations of dramatists, Orrery, who had been admitted to the society of Swift and Savage, who had rendered services of no very honorable kind to Pope. The biographer therefore sat down to his task with a mind full of matter. He had at first intended to give only a paragraph to every minor poet, and only four or five pages to the greatest name. But the flood of anecdote and criticism overflowed the narrow channel.

The work, which was originally meant to consist only of a few sheets, swelled into ten volumes — small volumes, it is true, and not closely printed. The first four appeared in 1779, the remaining six in 1781. The *Lives of the Poets* are, on the whole, the best of Johnson's works. The narratives are as entertaining as any novel. The remarks on life and on human nature are eminently shrewd and profound. The criticisms are often excellent, and, even when grossly and provokingly unjust, well deserve to be studied. *Savage's Life* Johnson reprinted nearly as it had appeared in 1744. Whoever, after reading that life, will turn to the other lives will be struck by the difference of style. Since Johnson had been at ease in his circumstances he had wrtten little and had talked much. When therefore he, after the lapse of years, resumed his pen, the mannerism which he had contracted while he was in the constant habit of elaborate composition was less perceptible than formerly, and his diction frequently had a colloquial ease which it had formerly wanted. The improvement may be discerned by a skilful critic in the *Journey to the Hebrides,* and in the *Lives of the Poets* is so obvious that it cannot escape the notice of the most careless reader.

Among the *Lives* the best are perhaps those of Cowley, Dryden and Pope. The very worst is, beyond all doubt, that of Gray; the most controverted that of Milton. This great work at once became popular. There was, indeed, much just and much unjust censure; but even those who were loudest in blame were attracted by the book in spite of themselves. Malone computed the gains of the publishers at five or six thousand pounds. But the writer was very poorly remunerated. Intending at first to write very short prefaces, he had stipulated for only two hundred guineas. The booksellers, when they saw how far his performance had surpassed his promise, added only another hundred. Indeed Johnson, though he did not despise or affect to despise money, and though his strong sense and long experience ought to have qualified him to protect his own interests, seems to have been singularly unskilful and unlucky in his literary bargains. He was generally reputed the first English writer of his time. Yet several writers of his time sold their copyrights for sums such as he never ventured to ask. To give a single instance, William Robertson received £4500 for the *History of Charles V.*

Johnson was now in his seventy-second year. The infirmities of age were coming fast upon him. That inevitable event of which he never thought without horror was brought near to him; and his whole life was darkened by the shadow of death.

The strange dependants to whom he had given shelter, and to whom, in spite of their faults, he was strongly attached by habit, dropped off one by one; and, in the silence of his home, he regretted even the noise of their scolding matches. The kind and generous Thrale was no more; and it was soon plain that the old Streatham intimacy could not be maintained upon the same footing.

Mrs. Thrale herself confessed that without her husband's assistance she did not feel able to entertain Johnson as a constant inmate of her house. Free from the yoke of the brewer, she fell in love with a music master, high in his profession, from Brescia, named Gabriel Piozzi, in whom nobody but herself could discover anything to admire. The secret of this attachment was soon discovered by Fanny Burney, but Johnson at most only suspected it.

In September 1782 the place at Streatham was from motives of economy let to Lord Shelburne, and Mrs. Thrale took a house at Brighton, to where Johnson accompanied her; they remained for six weeks on the old familiar footing. In March 1783 Boswell was glad to discover Johnson well looked after and staying with Mrs. Thrale in Argyll Street, but in a bad state of health. Impatience of Johnson's criticisms and infirmities had been steadily growing with Mrs. Thrale since 1774. She now went to Bath with her daughters, partly to escape his supervision. Johnson was very ill in his lodgings during the summer, but he still corresponded affectionately with his mistress and received many favors from her. He retained the full use of his senses during the paralytic attack, and in July he was sufficiently recovered to renew his old club life and to meditate further journeys. In June 1784 he went with Boswell to Oxford for the last time. In September he was in Lichfield. On his return his health was rather worse; but he would submit to no dietary regime. His asthma tormented him day and night, and dropsical symptoms made their appearance. His wrath was excited in no measured terms against the re-marriage of his old friend Mrs. Thrale, the news of which he heard this summer.

The whole dispute seems entirely uncalled-for, but the marriage aroused some of Johnson's strongest prejudices. He wrote inconsiderately on the subject, but we must remember that he was at the time afflicted in body and mentally haunted by dread of impending change. Throughout all his troubles he had clung vehemently to life. The feeling described in that fine but gloomy paper which closes the series of his idlers seemed to grow stronger in him as his last hour drew near. He fancied that he should be able to draw his breath more easily in a southern climate, and would probably have set out for Rome and Naples but for his fear of the expense of the journey. That expense, indeed, he had the means of defraying; for he had laid up about £2000, the fruit of labors which had made the fortune of several publishers. But he was unwilling to break in upon this hoard, and he seems to have wished even to keep its existence a secret. Some of his friends hoped that the government might be induced to increase his pension to £600 a year, but this hope was disappointed, and he resolved to stand one English winter more.

That winter was his last. His legs grew weaker; his breath grew shorter; the fatal water gathered fast, in spite of incisions which he, courageous against pain but timid against death, urged his surgeons to make deeper and deeper. Though the tender care which had mitigated his sufferings during months of sickness at Streatham was withdrawn, and though Boswell was absent, he was not left desolate. The ablest physicians and surgeons attended him, and refused to accept fees from him. Burke parted from him with deep emotion. Windham sat much in the sick-room. Frances Burney, whom the old man had cherished with fatherly kindness, stood weeping at the door; while Langton, whose piety eminently qualified him to be an adviser and comforter at such a time, received the last pressure of his friend's hand within. When at length the moment, dreaded through so many years, came close, the dark cloud passed away from Johnson's mind. Windham's servant, who sat up with him during his last night, declared that "no man could appear more collected, more devout or less terrified at the thoughts of the approaching minute." At hour intervals, often of much pain, he was moved in bed and addressed himself vehemently to prayer.

In the morning he was still able to give his blessing, but in the afternoon he became drowsy, and at a quarter past seven in the evening on the 13th of December 1784, in his seventy-sixth year, he passed away.

He was laid, a week later, in Westminster Abbey, among the eminent men of whom he had been the historian — Cowley and Denham, Dryden and Congreve, Gay, Prior and Addison.

Chapter 6

Samuel Johnson and Metaphorical Propriety

There is a famous passage in Samuel Johnson's Life of Denham which has confused critics and produced a variety of interpretations. I.A. Richards, Allen Tate, Jean Hagstrum and William Edinger, have tried to decipher the passage. I will consider the comments of each in an attempt to arrive at some sound conclusions about the meaning of Johnson's statement. It is my view that this difficult passage, if read properly, will help to establish a better understanding of Johnson's concept of metaphorical propriety.

Johnson analyzes the following lines from Sir John Denham's "Cooper's Hill":

O could I flow like thee, and make thy stream
My great example, as it is my theme!
Though deep, yet clear: though gentle, yet not dull;
Strong without rage, without o'erflowing full. (qtd. in Lives 34)

Johnson admires the passage but qualifies his praise with the following criticism:

The lines are in themselves not perfect; for most of the words, thus artfully opposed, are to be understood simply on one side of the comparison, and metaphorically on the other; and if there be any language which does not express intellectual operations by material images, into that language they cannot be translated.

The cryptic formulation of Johnson's language has vexed his readers for a long time. The confusion partly results from

Johnson's decision to treat the tenor of the conceit as the "intellectual operations" of the poet rather than poetic style. Poetic style is evaluated by its effect on the listener. It is a result of the oral effects and aural impressions of diction, syntax and meter. This is distinguished from "intellectual operations," or purely cognitive processes, which are understood abstractly. In the Life of Cowley, Johnson uses the same phrase in an apparent binary sense: "They neither copied nature nor life; neither painted the forms of matter nor represented the operations of the intellect". This pronouncement suggests that Johnson may have considered any non-material activity or process, such as the flow of a poem, to be an "intellectual operation." Nonetheless, poetic style is far more analogous to the flow of a river insofar as its effects are realized through sense experience. Poetic style therefore can be aligned with material processes more easily than can pure thought or cognition. The problem with the conceit is that Denham's tenor seems to alternate between poetic style and mental process. Denham invokes the river as a model for the "flow" of his poetic style; yet his first descriptive clause, "Though deep, yet clear," suggests a profound mind rather than a smooth poetic style. Certainly the imaginative faculty, from which poetic style flows, may be considered as an operation of the intellect. And since Denham initially seems to describe the mind, Johnson's treatment of the tenor as "intellectual operations" is perhaps understandable. But after the initial descriptive clause, the rest of the terms all apply to style far more directly than if they were applied to the intellect.

If we consider Johnson's own analytical style, as exemplified in the Lives of the Poets, we find that he exhibits a critical habit of mind very similar to Denham's method in the Thames conceit. Johnson's tendency in his moral and critical writings to use parallel and antithetical constructions to separate praiseworthy qualities from their corresponding faults accounts for his high estimation of the passage. According to Johnson, "...[T]he particulars of resemblance are so perspicaciously collected, and every mode of excellence separated from its adjacent fault by so nice a line of limitation;

the different parts of the sentence are so accurately adjusted.... This principle of analysis is prevalent in the Lives of the Poets. In the memorable, encomiastic closing to the Life of Addison, Johnson describes his style as "familiar but not coarse, and elegant but not ostentatious". In the Life of Milton, speaking of the poet's depiction of Adam and Eve, Johnson states, "In the first state, their affection is tender without weakness, and their piety sublime without presumption". Johnson uses this style for negative criticism as well, as in Life of Cowley, where he complains of the "metaphysical poets": "Their thoughts are often new, but seldom natural; they are not obvious, but neither are they just".

In the Life of Pope, Johnson says of Warburton's poetry, "His style is copious without selection, and forcible without neatness". In each example, we see Johnson using antithesis in a manner similar to Denham's. In the last example, his descriptive words are very similar in meaning to those used by Denham. "Forcible without neatness" is essentially an inverted version of Denham's "strong without rage." "Copious without selection," is almost a perfect analogue, though constructed as a negative, to Denham's "without o'er-flowing full." In light of Johnson's negative comments, Tate suggests, "His remark that the 'particulars of resemblance are perspicaciously collected,' seems incomprehensible". But if we consider Johnson's own tendency to separate "mode[s] of excellence" from "adjacent fault[s]," it is not difficult to see why Johnson admired Denham's lines. The confusing part of Johnson's comment is the criticism.

Before we can assess Johnson's exact meaning, we must determine what he refers to when he uses the word "comparison." William Edinger supposes that the "comparison" Johnson refers to is the antithesis of terms in each clause. He correctly points out, "The words 'artfully opposed' include 'deep' versus 'clear,' 'gentle' versus 'not dull,' 'strong' versus 'without rage,' and 'full' versus 'without o'erflowing'". This point is obvious enough, but he proceeds to the questionable conclusion that the "comparison" Johnson refers to is each antithesis taken individually. According to

Edinger, "If Johnson's observation that one side of each comparison is to be understood 'simply' i.e., literally, and the other side metaphorically were true of all, then 'deep,' 'gentle,' 'strong,' and 'full' would describe the Thames, while 'clear,' 'not dull,' 'without rage,' and 'without o'erflowing' would only describe qualities of style, Denham's 'tenor.'". Here Edinger has interpreted Johnson's statement to mean that, in each antithesis the first term literally applies to the river and the second term metaphorically applies to the intellect. He goes on to say, "Johnson does not, however, make this claim, saying only that 'most' of the antitheses are to be understood in this way. An unmistakable instance is 'gentle, not dull,' where gentle can apply both to the river and to style... but dull can apply only to style... Other instances are more open to question." Edinger's assumption that Johnson refers to the antitheses when he uses the word "comparison" leads him to a shaky interpretation. He acknowledges that only one of the four "comparisons" seems to legitimately fit his reading of Johnson's comment.

And he does seem to recognize the problem when, to support his reading, he points out that Johnson qualifies his statement by saying that "most" of the words function this way. Even with Johnson's qualification, Edinger would have to demonstrate that more than one of the antithetical clauses can clearly exemplify his reading. One out of four comparisons would not justify Johnson's use of the term "most." It seems doubtful that Johnson is censuring Denham, as Edinger supposes, for a failure of the visual side of the metaphor to afford images. Edinger's problematic reading proceeds from a mistaken interpretation of the word "comparison." He is perhaps confused by the structure of Johnson's sentence. Following the implied logic of apposition, Edinger assumes Johnson's insertion of the qualifying phrase "thus artfully opposed" implies that the comparison he refers to is each individual antithesis formed by the artful opposition of terms. A more reasonable conclusion is that the "comparison" Johnson refers to is the whole conceit—the comparison of the river with the poet's style. The two sides of the comparison are not the first and second term of each antithesis, but rather the vehicle on one side and the tenor on the other: the river and the poet's style.

If we accept that Johnson means the entire conceit when he refers to the "comparison," we see that, in Johnson's view, most of the words in Denham's conceit are literally applicable to the river but only figuratively describe the intellect. As we've already considered, the tenor of the conceit is more appropriately thought of as poetic style, with the exception of the first descriptive clause which would seem to apply to the mind; nonetheless, I will take Johnson on his own terms—as Tate, Hagstrum and Richards have each done in their respective discussions of the passage—in an attempt to elucidate his meaning and infer a principle from it. Johnson's criticism suggests that the ground of the comparison is obscure because Denham's conceit employs a vehicle to elucidate a tenor which is already figurative. For Johnson, this represents an impropriety in the structure of the analogical relationship of the metaphorical components because that which is figurative, the intellect or imagination, is transferred over to an image, the river, where the descriptive terms have a different literal meaning.

Jean Hagstrum interprets Johnson's criticism in terms of Addison's concept of "mixed wit". According to Addison, "Mixt Wit... is a Composition of Punn and true Wit, and is more or less perfect as the Resemblance lies in the Ideas or in the Words". His examples are taken from passages where poets have formed metaphors based on the common use of "fire" and "flame" as figures for the passion of love. He states, "...[T]he Poet mixes the Qualities of Fire with those of Love; and in the same Sentence speaking of it both as a Passion and as real Fire, surprises the Reader with those seeming Resemblances or Contradictions that make up all the Wit in this kind of Writing". Johnson was influenced by Addison's theories about metaphor and quoted his comments on "mixed wit" in the Life of Cowley. The concept of "mixed wit" is helpful in understanding Johnson's critique of Denham because in Denham's metaphor the descriptive terms, which form the comparison, function simultaneously on both sides of the analogy. For a resemblance to be found, as Addison supposes, in the words, the metaphor must employ the same words in different senses on both sides of the metaphor. It is important to recognize the difference between a pun, which Addison terms "false wit," which is simply an accidental coincidence of language, and an instance of "mixed wit," where the double entendre is formed by a secondary, figurative sense of the word that proceeds from a perceived resemblance to its primary meaning. This form of wit is "mixed" rather than "false" in Addison's view because there is in fact a partial correspondence between the two meanings without which the figurative sense would not have arisen.

Furthermore, Addison acknowledges the possibility of a mixed-wit metaphor having propriety when he states that such a metaphor "is more or less perfect as the Resemblance lies in the Ideas or in the Words" (emphasis added). Based on this concept, Hagstrum argues, "The assertion about the river is clear; but the assertion about the poet himself is not... [N]o words in the comparison literally and clearly explain the poet's mental operations". Allen Tate similarly suggests, "The imperfection... lies in its failure to work both ways; that is, the qualities that Denham would like to achieve cannot be found literally in the river". Addison's theory, which defines a specific type of metaphor in which the analogy is partly true and partly a verbal felicity, provides a plausible basis for Johnson's criticism of Denham's lines.

The crux problem he detects is that words like "deep," "clear," "gentle," "strong," "o'erflowing," and "full" have literal meanings in a material context, but the abstract transference of those terms into an immaterial context, such as creative processes of the intellect, requires the terms to function figuratively. The terms must perform a double role, with literal meaning on one side of the conceit and figurative meaning on the other. Understood in terms of "mixed wit," the analogy is built partly upon puns that exploit the double meanings of the descriptive terms. What is said of the river is said of the poet's style; the illusion of analogical correspondence is created by the double meaning of each descriptive term. A degree of correspondence in the nature of the two things may exist, but the poet has only hinted at such a correspondence.

Tate construes Johnson's complaint the following way: "The tenor of the figure, in order to be convincing, ought to have translatability into a high degree of abstraction; it ought to be detachable from the literal image of the flowing river". This means that all of the descriptive terms should literally apply to the immaterial side of the conceit. Johnson's judgment that the lines are imperfect reveals something important about his idea of metaphorical propriety. His remarks on "Cooper's Hill," implicitly demand a strictly literal correspondence in any metaphor that compares material and immaterial processes. The problem with this stricture is that the ground of a comparison of physical and mental operations cannot achieve a perfectly literal correspondence because qualities of the intellect cannot be visualized or understood by the senses except through the use of figurative language.

Even if we treat Denham's tenor as poetic style and distinguish that from "intellectual operations," the difference is only a matter of degree. A phrase like "without o'erflowing, full" may be more directly applicable to style than to the intellect, but it is still somewhat figurative. It is not as literal in reference to style as it is in reference to the river. As Richards suggests, "...[M]etaphor is the omnipresent principle of language". It is precisely this facility with which we revert to figurative language which Johnson mistrusts in the structure of metaphors such as Denham's, where words are pressed into functioning both literally and figuratively at the same time. We inherently rely on figurative language in describing the processes of the mind. Johnson recognizes this and expects the poet to observe a greater degree of care and clarity in his use of figurative language when the objective is to exemplify an unexpected but accurate resemblance of different entities.

The problem with Johnson's idea of metaphoric literalism is that all languages "express intellectual operations by material images." This is precisely why Johnson's hypothetical language, which does not express operations of the intellect in material images, is only hypothetical. Abstract terminology results from the human intellect's ability to grasp intuitively a resemblance of immaterial qualities of the mind to the material processes of the physical world. As Richards points out, "...

Historians of language have long taught that we can find no word or description for any of the intellectual operations which, if its history is known, is not seen to have been taken, by metaphor, from a description of some physical happening". This is precisely the point which renders Johnson's criticism of Denham's lines problematic and necessitates his use of a hypothetical language devoid of figures of speech to elucidate his point. The words we use exclusively in reference to mental qualities have been so distinctly separated from their original literal meaning that we mistake their abstract meanings for primary ones. Johnson himself offers a pertinent reflection on this feature of language in the preface to his Dictionary of the English Language:

The original sense of words is often driven out of use by their metaphorical acceptations, yet must be inserted for the sake of a regular origination. Thus I know not whether *ardour* is used for *material heat,* or whether *flagrant,* in English, ever signifies the same with *burning*; yet such are the primitive ideas of these words, which are therefore set first, though without examples, that the figurative senses may be commodiously deduced.

A perfect example of this would be the word Johnson uses to praise the manner in which Denham's "resemblances" are collected: "perspicaciously." It is incidentally noteworthy that two of the first three examples of the word "perspicaciously" in the OED are from Johnson. The third example is the exact sentence which I am currently discussing from the "Life of Denham." The OED defines "perspicacious" as follows: "Of eyes, sight, etc.: keen, sharp; clear-sighted. Chiefly *fig.*"; "Of a person, wit, etc.: penetrating; perceptive, discerning."; "Clear, transparent. *Obs. rare.*". Definition 2 is an abstract application of the term which relies on other abstract terms taken from material processes, such as "penetrating," "perceptive" and "discerning" to define its meaning.

Another particularly pertinent example of this relationship between material and abstract terminology can be seen in one of the problem words from Denham's conceit discussed earlier: "dull." As I noted, Edinger suggests that the word "dull," as it is used in Denham's conceit, only applies to the intellect. Richards, on the other hand suggests that the term describes the river literally but the intellect only derivatively. The disagreement over the signification of "dull" in Denham's line suggests the reciprocity of mental and physical qualities. Common usage can easily give rise to a material application of a term where the common signification is mental. Here is the OED's first definition for "dull": "Not quick in intelligence or mental perception; slow of understanding; not sharp of wit; obtuse, stupid, inapprehensive. In early use, sometimes: Wanting wit, fatuous, foolish" (def. 1).

Here too, we see how an apparently abstract term is inherently reliant upon material images to elucidate its meaning. The OED definition employs physical terms, such as "quick", "slow" and "sharp" to explain the mental signification of "dull," supporting Richards's contention about the physical origin of abstract terms. Also supporting Richards' interpretation of the word "dull" as descriptive of the river, here is the OED's third entry for "dull": "Slow in motion or action; not brisk; inert, sluggish, inactive; heavy, drowsy" (def. 3a). And the following example is cited from Spenser, where "dull" is applied to moving water: "Thenceforth her waters wexed dull and slow" (def. 3a). Johnson himself quotes this same passage from Spenser to exemplify the sixth entry for "dull" in his Dictionary.

The figurative, verbal structure of the analogy which Johnson recognizes is apparent, but Johnson's judgment that the lines are thus imperfect indicates a narrow view of metaphorical decorum. The ingenuity of Denham's metaphor is in the use of an image that allows him to exemplify the relational aspects of the intellectual qualities he aspires to. Richards suggests, "What the lines say of the mind is something that does not come from the river. But the river is not a mere excuse, or a decoration only, a gilding of the moral pill. The vehicle is still controlling the mode in which the tenor forms" (Philosophy 122-23). By this he means that although an overly scrupulous reading of the conceit would recognize a lack of perfect analogical propriety in the terms of the metaphor, the arrangement and structure of the metaphor is such that the relations of the terms on both sides of the conceit make sense to the reader. The fidelity of the analogy is not found in the terms taken individually but in the antithetical relations of the terms to each other. The bottom of the river is mysterious as is the bottom of a profound idea. Just as the river's clearness is all the more surprising considered in relation to its depth, a profound intellect is all the more impressive for its ability to express itself lucidly.

This relation can only be visualized in the image of the river, but the tenuous relation of depth and clarity—the difficulty of achieving both—may be appropriately applied to the river and the intellect in a way that is acceptable and even felicitous by Johnson's standards. Similarly, the river is "strong, without rage." This means that the river flows powerfully but stays within the limit of its banks. Similarly, Denham's ideal style of poetic expression is forceful but tempered and focused. Although the correspondence is not literal, the relation of the terms is analogically fit to describe both the river and the poet's style. These relational analogies, the separations of virtues from concomitant faults, are the resemblances which Johnson celebrates as "perspicaciously collected."

The metaphor is not simply a verbal felicity that compares a set of literal qualities with a corresponding set of figurative qualities; it is not simply an instance of Addison's mixed wit. It is a collection of analogous antithetical relations of qualities. It would seem that although Johnson is troubled by the figurative application of Denham's terms to the intellect, he recognizes the fitness of the antithetical relations of the terms in both the vehicle and the tenor.

Edinger cites one of Johnson's own images from "The

Vanity of Human Wishes" as an example of a metaphor which observes his own guidelines for a proper metaphor. The image of fireworks to represent the transience of worldly prominence affords an opportunity to analyse Johnson on his own terms, but with perhaps a different conclusion than Edinger's:

Unnumber's suppliants crowd Preferment's gate,
Athirst for wealth, and burning to be great;
Delusive Fortune hears th' incessant call,
They mount, they shine, evaporate, and fall (Vanity 73-76).

Edinger says that this image "fulfills all the requirements we have inferred from his criticism" because "Johnson's particulars function on both the metaphoric and descriptive levels" and afford a striking image with visual propriety. This conclusion relies on Edinger's assumption that Johnson criticized Denham for a "failure of the visual". But the use of terms that "are to be understood simply on one side of the comparison, and metaphorically on the other," which Edinger observes as the propriety of Johnson's metaphor, is precisely Johnson's complaint about Denham's lines. The words, "mount," "shine," "evaporate," and "fall," are all derived from material processes. They are literally applicable to an image of fireworks, just as Denham's terms do, in spite of Edinger's claims, afford a literal image of the river. But, like the terms in Denham's conceit, Johnson's four verbs, "mount," "shine," "evaporate," and "fall," are to be understood figuratively when applied to the tenor. The structure of the metaphor is similar to that of Denham's insofar as the verbs perform a double function, which is literal on the side of the vehicle and figurative on the side of the tenor.

The figurative sense of words like "mount," "shine" and "fall" is so common to the language that one easily forgets they are figurative at all. In this sense, the words, as they function in Johnson's metaphor, bear a similarity to Addison's mixed wit. What Johnson makes evident with this conceit, he fails to acknowledge in his criticism of Denham: namely, that the analogy of an abstract process to a material one can be evinced by the use of figurative speech—and this can be the proper ground of a successful metaphor. Johnson's verbs are no more literally true of worldly ascension and decline than Denham's qualities are literally descriptive of the intellect. Johnson's tenor is no less dependent on the visual image of the fireworks to elucidate the meaning of the analogy than Denham's is on the river. To say that someone who has risen to prominence "shines" would be as meaningless as Denham's conceit in a language that does not express abstract operations by material images. "[E]vaporate" is a particularly problematic word from Johnson's image because it is a technical, scientific term which is only understood in Johnson's metaphor because of its position between two other common, figurative terms.

It may be true that Johnson's analogy is more clear and direct than Denham's. But this is simply a matter of degree. As Addison suggested, mixed-wit metaphors may exhibit a range of analogical propriety between the illusory verbal resemblance and true resemblance. As a type of metaphor, the structure of Johnson's fireworks image is similar to that of Denham's Thames conceit. In Denham's metaphor, it is not the qualities themselves, but the analogous relations of the terms in each of the four antitheses that accounts for the fidelity of the comparison. In Johnson's image, it is the arching figure formed by the chronological relation of the four verbs which is analogous in the vehicle and the tenor. Both conceits rely on the vehicle not to explain a perfect analogy of operations but to provide a concise unifying power of summation. Both images establish a mode in which the figurative terms make sense.

It is difficult to see why Edinger chose the fireworks metaphor as an example of Johnson observing his own critical precepts. If Denham's image suffers from a failure of literalness in the tenor, the same can be said of Johnson's. Perhaps a better example, one which avoids the qualities which Johnson censures in Denham, can be found in the Life of Cowley where he criticizes the methods of the metaphysical poets: "Their attempts were always analytic; they broke every image into fragments; and could no more represent, by their slender conceits and laboured particularities, the prospects of nature, or the scenes of life, than he who dissects a sunbeam with a prism can exhibit the wide effulgence of a summer noon". Here we have a metaphor with a different structure from Denham's Thames conceit. There is sufficient abstraction because none of the terms function on both sides of the comparison, thus avoiding Addison's problem of mixed wit. Each of the elements of the tenor lines up neatly with the features of the vehicle. The vehicle is perfectly suited to exemplify the actions and qualities of the tenor. The image of a scientist using a prism to divide sunlight into a narrow view of the refracted light spectrum exemplifies the style of analysis that Johnson found distasteful in the metaphysical poets.

According to Richards, "A metaphor may be illustrative or diagrammatical, providing a concrete instance of a relation which would otherwise have to be stated in abstract terms" (Principles 239). The image from the Life of Cowley avoids the problems Johnson discusses in Denham's conceit because it is a simile that does not require any of its terms to function simultaneously on both sides of the metaphor. In Denham's lines, depth and clarity of the river are compared with depth and clarity of intellect, pressing the terms to function both figuratively and literally. Likewise, in the fireworks image, the terms "mount," "shine," "evaporate" and "fall" function on both sides of the comparison. In both metaphors, it is up to the reader to see the figurative relationship of the terms to the tenor. Johnson seems to prefer the diagrammatical form of analogy. Of course, he could not avoid the use of figurative language to exemplify resemblances of material and abstract processes any more than other poets can.

WAS JOHNSON A CONSERVATIVE, OR A LIBERAL

People frequently try to understand Johnson in terms of being a conservative or a liberal — because it's often easier to understand the world if you can chunk it and classify it. It's perfectly natural. Difficulties sometimes arise, though, on the basis of how much they do or don't know about Johnson. To anyone whose knowledge is largely grounded in Boswell's *Life of Johnson*, it would seem as if Johnson would obviously be a 21st century conservative. Knowing what Johnson actually wrote, however, leads to a more complex picture. As a result, Johnson is loved by both Conservatives and Liberals.

Keep in mind, the entire question is hypothetical, and perhaps invalid. Why? Well, to transpose Johnson's opinions directly into the 21st century denies him awareness of the entire dialog that's happened in the last 200 years. And then, to extrapolate from them, into new areas of discourse, is even more tenuous. Johnson was a dynamic man, and to deny him the benefit of all that's happened since his death is unfair to his memory.

Chapter 7

Anecdotes of Samuel Johnson

To urge my distance from England as an excuse for the book's being ill-written would be ridiculous; it might indeed serve as a just reason for my having written it at all; because, though others may print the same aphorisms and stories, I cannot here be sure that they have done so. As the Duke says, however, to the Weaver, in A Midsummer Night's Dream, "Never excuse; if your play be a bad one, keep at least the excuses to yourself." I am aware that many will say I have not spoken highly enough of Dr. Johnson; but it will be difficult for those who say so to speak more highly. If I have described his manners as they were, I have been careful to show his superiority to the common forms of common life. It is surely no dispraise to an oak that it does not bear jessamine; and he who should plant honeysuckle round Trajan's column would not be thought to adorn, but to disgrace it.

When I have said that he was more a man of genius than of learning, I mean not to take from the one part of his character that which I willingly give to the other. The erudition of Mr. Johnson proved his genius; for he had not acquired it by long or profound study: nor can I think those characters the greatest which have most learning driven into their heads, any more than I can persuade myself to consider the River Jenisca as superior to the Nile, because the first receives near seventy tributary streams in the course of its unmarked progress to the sea, while the great parent of African plenty, flowing from an almost invisible source, and unenriched by any extraneous waters, except eleven nameless rivers, pours his majestic torrent into the ocean by seven celebrated mouths.

But I must conclude my preface, and begin my book, the first I ever presented before the public; from whose awful appearance in some measure to defend and conceal myself, I have thought fit to retire behind the Telamonian shield, and show as little of myself as possible, well aware of the exceeding difference there is between fencing in the school and fighting in the field.

Studious, however, to avoid offending, and careless of that offence which can be taken without a cause, I here not unwillingly submit my slight performance to the decision of that glorious country, which I have the daily delight to hear applauded in others, as eminently just, generous, and humane.

Too much intelligence is often as pernicious to biography as too little; the mind remains perplexed by contradiction of probabilities, and finds difficulty in separating report from truth. If Johnson then lamented that so little had ever been said about Butler, I might with more reason be led to complain that so much has been said about himself; for numberless informers but distract or cloud information, as glasses which multiply will for the most part be found also to obscure. Of a life, too, which for the last twenty years was passed in the very front of literature, every leader of a literary company, whether officer or subaltern, naturally becomes either author or critic, so that little less than the recollection that it was once the request of the deceased, and twice the desire of those whose will I ever delighted to comply with, should have engaged me to add my little book to the number of those already written on the subject.

I used to urge another reason for forbearance, and say, that all the readers would, on this singular occasion, be the writers of his life: like the first representation of the Masque of Comus, which, by changing their characters from spectators to performers, was acted by the lords and ladies it was written to entertain. This objection is, however, now at an end, as I have found friends, far remote indeed from literary questions, who may yet be diverted from melancholy by my description of Johnson's manners, warmed to virtue even by the distant reflection of his glowing excellence, and encouraged by the relation of his animated zeal to persist in the profession as well as practice of Christianity.

Samuel Johnson was the son of Michael Johnson, a bookseller at Lichfield, in Staffordshire; a very pious and worthy man, but wrong-headed, positive, and afflicted with melancholy, as his son, from whom alone I had the information, once told me: his business, however, leading him to be much on horseback, contributed to the preservation of his bodily health and mental sanity, which, when he stayed long at home, would sometimes be about to give way; and Mr. Johnson said, that when his workshop, a detached building, had fallen half down for want of money to repair it, his father was not less diligent to lock the door every night, though he saw that anybody might walk in at the back part, and knew that there was no security obtained by barring the front door. "*This,*" says his son, "*was madness, you may see, and would have been discoverable in other instances of the prevalence of imagination, but that poverty prevented it from playing such tricks as riches and leisure encourage*".

Michael was a man of still larger size and greater strength than his son, who was reckoned very like him, but did not delight in talking much of his family: "*One has,*" says he, "*SO little pleasure in reciting the anecdotes of beggary.*" One day, however, hearing me praise a favourite friend with partial tenderness as well as true esteem: "*Why do you like that man's acquaintance so?*" said he. "*Because,*" replied I, "*he is open and confiding, and tells me stories of his uncles and cousins; I love the light parts of a solid character.*" "*Nay, if you are for family history,*" says Mr. Johnson, good-humouredly, "*I can fit you: I had an uncle, Cornelius Ford, who, upon a journey, stopped and read an inscription written on a stone he saw standing by the wayside, set up, as it proved, in honour of a man who had leaped a certain leap thereabouts, the extent of which was specified upon the stone: 'Why now,' says my uncle, 'I could leap it in my boots;' and he did leap it in his boots. I had likewise another uncle, Andrew,*" continued he, "*my father's brother, who kept the ring in Smithfield (where they wrestled and boxed) for a whole year, and never was thrown or conquered. Here now are uncles for you, Mistress, if that's the way to your heart."* Mr. Johnson was very conversant in the art of attack and defence by boxing, which science he had learned from this uncle Andrew, I believe; and I have heard him descant upon the age when people were received, and when rejected, in the schools once held for that brutal amusement, much to the admiration of those who had no expectation of his skill in such matters, from the sight of a figure which precluded all possibility of personal prowess; though, because he saw Mr. Thrale one day leap over a cabriolet stool, to show that he was not tired after a chase of fifty miles or more, he suddenly jumped over it too, but in a way so strange and so unwieldy, that our terror lest he should break his bones took from us even the power of laughing.

Michael Johnson was past fifty years old when he married his wife, who was upwards of forty, yet I think her son told me she remained three years childless before he was born into the world, who so greatly contributed to improve it. In three years more she brought another son, Nathaniel, who lived to be twenty-seven or twenty-eight years old, and of whose manly spirit I have heard his brother speak with pride and pleasure, mentioning one circumstance, particular enough, that when the company were one day lamenting the badness of the roads, he inquired where they could be, as he travelled the country more than most people, and had never seen a bad road in his life. The two brothers did not, however, much delight in each other's company, being always rivals for the mother's fondness; and many of the severe reflections on domestic life in Rasselas took their source from its author's keen recollections of the time passed in his early years.

Their father, Michael, died of an inflammatory fever at the age of seventy-six, as Mr. Johnson told me, their mother at eighty-nine, of a gradual decay. She was slight in her person, he said, and rather below than above the common size. So excellent was her character, and so blameless her life, that when an oppressive neighbour once endeavoured to take from her a little field she possessed, he could persuade no attorney to undertake the cause against a woman so beloved in her narrow circle: and it is this incident he alludes to in the line of his " *Vanity of Human Wishes,*" calling her "*The general favourite as the general friend.*" Nor could any one pay more willing homage to such a character, though she had not been related to him, than did Dr. Johnson on every occasion that offered: his disquisition on Pope's epitaph placed over Mrs. Corbet is a proof of that preference always given by him to a noiseless life over a bustling one; but however taste begins, we almost always see that it ends in simplicity; the glutton finishes by losing his relish for anything highly sauced, and calls for his boiled chicken at the close of many years spent in the search of dainties; the connoisseurs are soon weary of Rubens, and the critics of Lucan; and the refinements of every kind heaped upon civil life always sicken their possessors before the close of it.

At the age of two years Mr. Johnson was brought up to London by his mother, to be touched by Queen Anne for the scrofulous evil, which terribly afflicted his childhood, and left such marks as greatly disfigured a countenance naturally harsh and rugged, beside doing irreparable damage to the auricular organs, which never could perform their functions since I knew him; and it was owing to that horrible disorder, too, that one eye was perfectly useless to him; that defect, however, was not observable, the eyes looked both alike. As Mr. Johnson had an astonishing memory, I asked him if he could remember Queen Anne at all? "He had," he said, "*a confused, but somehow a sort of solemn, recollection of a lady in diamonds, and a long black hood.*"

The christening of his brother he remembered with all its circumstances, and said his mother taught him to spell and pronounce the words 'little Natty,' syllable by syllable, making him say it over in the evening to her husband and his guests. The trick which most parents play with their children, that of showing off their newly-acquired accomplishments, disgusted Mr. Johnson beyond expression. He had been treated so himself, he said, till he absolutely loathed his father's caresses, because he knew they were sure to precede some unpleasing display of his early abilities; and he used, when neighbours came o' visiting, to run up a tree that he might not be found and exhibited, such, as no doubt he was, a prodigy of early understanding.

His epitaph upon the duck he killed by treading on it at five years old— *"Here lies poor duck That Samuel Johnson trod on; If it had liv'd it had been good luck, For it would have been an odd one"*— is a striking example of early expansion of mind and knowledge of language; yet he always seemed more mortified at the recollection of the bustle his parents made with his wit than pleased with the thoughts of possessing it. *"That,"* said he to me one day, *"is the great misery of late marriages; the unhappy produce of them becomes the plaything of dotage. An old man's child,"* continued he, *"leads much such a life. I think, as a little boy's dog, teased with awkward fondness, and forced, perhaps, to sit up and beg, as we call it, to divert a company, who at last go away complaining of their disagreeable entertainment."*

In consequence of these maxims, and full of indignation against such parents as delight to produce their young ones early into the talking world, I have known Mr. Johnson give a good deal of pain by refusing to hear the verses the children could recite, or the songs they could sing, particularly one friend who told him that his two sons should repeat Gray's "Elegy" to him alternately, that he might judge who had the happiest cadence. "No, pray, sir," said he, *"let the dears both speak it at once; more noise will by that means be made, and the noise will be sooner over."* He told me the story himself, but I have forgot who the father was.

Mr. Johnson's mother was daughter to a gentleman in the country, such as there were many of in those days, who possessing, perhaps, one or two hundred pounds a year in land, lived on the profits, and sought not to increase their income. She was, therefore, inclined to think higher of herself than of her husband, whose conduct in money matters being but indifferent, she had a trick of teasing him about it, and was, by her son's account, very importunate with regard to her fears of spending more than they could afford, though she never arrived at knowing how much that was, a fault common, as he said, to most women who pride themselves on their economy. They did not, however, as I could understand, live ill together on the whole. "*My father,*" says he, "*could always take his horse and ride away for orders when things went badly.*" The lady's maiden name was Ford; and the parson who sits next to the punch-bowl in Hogarth's "Modern Midnight Conversation" was her brother's son.

This Ford was a man who chose to be eminent only for vice, with talents that might have made him conspicuous in literature, and respectable in any profession he could have chosen. His cousin has mentioned him in the lives of Fenton and of Broome; and when he spoke of him to me it was always with tenderness, praising his acquaintance with life and manners, and recollecting one piece of advice that no man surely ever followed more exactly: "*Obtain,*" says Ford, "*some general principles of every science; he who can talk only on one subject, or act only in one department, is seldom wanted, and perhaps never wished for, while the man of general knowledge can often benefit, and always please.*"

He used to relate, however, another story less to the credit of his cousin's penetration, how Ford on some occasion said to him, "*You will make your way the more easily in the world, I see, as you are contented to dispute no man's claim to conversation excellence; they will, therefore, more willingly allow your pretensions as a writer.*" Can one, on such an occasion, forbear recollecting the predictions of Boileau's father, when stroking the head of the young satirist?—"Ce petit bon homme," says he, "n'a point trop d'esprit, mais il ne dira jamais mal de personne." Such are the prognostics formed by men of wit and sense, as these two certainly were, concerning the future character and conduct of those for whose welfare they were honestly and deeply concerned; and so late do those features of peculiarity come to their growth, which mark a character to all succeeding generations.

Dr. Johnson first learned to read of his mother and her old maid Catharine, in whose lap he well remembered sitting while she explained to him the story of St. George and the Dragon. I know not whether this is the proper place to add that such was his tenderness, and such his gratitude, that he took a journey to Lichfield fifty-seven years afterwards to support and comfort her in her last illness; he had inquired for his nurse, and she was dead. The recollection of such reading as had delighted him in his infancy made him always persist in fancying that it was the only reading which could please an infant; and he used to condemn me for putting Newbery's books into their hands as too trifling to engage their attention. "*Babies do not want,*" said he, "*to hear about babies; they like to be told of giants and castles, and of somewhat which can stretch and stimulate their little minds.*"

When in answer I would urge the numerous editions and quick sale of "Tommy Prudent" or "Goody Two-Shoes." "*Remember always,*" said he, "*that the parents buy the books, and that the children never read them.*" Mrs. Barbauld, however, had his best praise, and deserved it; no man was more struck than Mr. Johnson with voluntary descent from possible splendour to painful duty. At eight years old he went to school, for his health would not permit him to be sent sooner; and at the age of ten years his mind was disturbed by scruples of infidelity, which preyed upon his spirits and made him very uneasy, the more so as he revealed his uneasiness to no one, being naturally, as he said, "*of a sullen temper and reserved disposition.*"

He searched, however, diligently but fruitlessly, for evidences of the truth of revelation; and at length, recollecting a book he had once seen in his father's shop, entitled "De Veritate Religionis," etc., he began to think himself highly culpable for neglecting such a means of information, and took himself severely to task for this sin, adding many acts of voluntary, and to others unknown, penance. The first opportunity which offered, of course, he seized the book with avidity, but on examination, not finding himself scholar enough to peruse its contents, set his heart at rest; and, not thinking to inquire whether there were any English books written on the subject, followed his usual amusements, and considered his conscience as lightened of a crime. He redoubled his diligence to learn the language that contained the information he most wished for, but from the pain which guilt had given him he now began to deduce the soul's immortality, which was the point that belief first stopped at;

and from that moment, resolving to be a Christian, became one of the most zealous and pious ones our nation ever produced.

When he had told me this odd anecdote of his childhood, *"I cannot imagine,"* said he, *"what makes me talk of myself to you so, for I really never mentioned this foolish story to anybody except Dr. Taylor, not even to my dear, dear Bathurst, whom I loved better than ever I loved any human creature; but poor Bathurst is dead!"* Here a long pause and a few tears ensued. *"Why, sir,"* said I, *"how like is all this to Jean Jacques Rousseau—as like, I mean, as the sensations of frost and fire, when my child complained yesterday that the ice she was eating burned her mouth."* Mr. Johnson laughed at the incongruous ideas, but the first thing which presented itself to the mind of an ingenious and learned friend whom I had the pleasure to pass some time with here at Florence was the same resemblance, though I think the two characters had little in common, further than an early attention to things beyond the capacity of other babies, a keen sensibility of right and wrong, and a warmth of imagination little consistent with sound and perfect health. I have heard him relate another odd thing of himself too, but it is one which everybody has heard as well as me: how, when he was about nine years old, having got the play of Hamlet in his hand, and reading it quietly in his father's kitchen, he kept on steadily enough till, coming to the Ghost scene, he suddenly hurried upstairs to the street door that he might see people about him.

Such an incident, as he was not unwilling to relate it, is probably in every one's possession now; he told it as a testimony to the merits of Shakespeare. But one day, when my son was going to school, and dear Dr. Johnson followed as far as the garden gate, praying for his salvation in a voice which those who listened attentively could hear plain enough, he said to me suddenly, *"Make your boy tell you his dreams: the first corruption that entered into my heart was communicated in a dream." "What was it, sir?"* said I. *"Do not ask me,"* replied he, with much violence, and walked away in apparent agitation. I never durst make any further inquiries. He retained a strong aversion for the memory of Hunter, one of his schoolmasters, who, he said, once was a brutal fellow, "*so brutal*," added he, "*that no man who had been educated by him ever sent his son to the same school.*" I have, however, heard him acknowledge his scholarship to be very great. His next master he despised, as knowing less than himself, I found, but the name of that gentleman has slipped my memory. Mr. Johnson was himself exceedingly disposed to the general indulgence of children, and was even scrupulously and ceremoniously attentive not to offend them; he had strongly persuaded himself of the difficulty people always find to erase early impressions either of kindness or resentment, and said "*he should never have so loved his mother when a man had she not given him coffee she could ill afford, to gratify his appetite when a boy.*" "*If you had had children, sir*," said I, "*would you have taught them anything?*" "*I hope*," replied he, "*that I should have willingly lived on bread and water to obtain instruction for them; but I would not have set their future friendship to hazard for the sake of thrusting into their heads knowledge of things for which they might not perhaps have either taste or necessity. You teach your daughters the diameters of the planets, and wonder when you have done that they do not delight in your company. No science can be communicated by mortal creatures without attention from the scholar; no attention can be obtained from children without the infliction of pain, and pain is never remembered without resentment.*"

That something should be learned was, however, so certainly his opinion that I have heard him say how education had been often compared to agriculture, yet that it resembled it chiefly in this: "*That if nothing is sown, no crop*," says he, "*can be obtained.*" His contempt of the lady who fancied her son could be eminent without study, because Shakespeare was found wanting in scholastic learning, was expressed in terms so gross and so well known, I will not repeat them here. To recollect, however, and to repeat the sayings of Dr. Johnson, is almost all that can be done by the writers of his life, as his life, at least since my acquaintance with him, consisted in little else than talking, when he was not absolutely employed in some serious piece of work; and whatever work he did seemed so much below his powers of performance that he appeared the idlest of all human beings, ever musing till he was called out to converse, and conversing till the fatigue of his friends, or the promptitude of his own temper to take offence, consigned him back again to silent meditation.

The remembrance of what had passed in his own childhood made Mr. Johnson very solicitous to preserve the felicity of children: and when he had persuaded Dr. Sumner to remit the tasks usually given to fill up boys' time during the holidays, he rejoiced exceedingly in the success of his negotiation, and told me that he had never ceased representing to all the eminent schoolmasters in England the absurd tyranny of poisoning the hour of permitted pleasure by keeping future misery before the children's eyes, and tempting them by bribery or falsehood to evade it. *"Bob Sumner,"* said he, *"however, I have at length prevailed upon. I know not, indeed, whether his tenderness was persuaded, or his reason convinced, but the effect will always be the same. Poor Dr. Sumner died, however, before the next vacation."* Mr. Johnson was of opinion, too, that young people should have positive, not general, rules given for their direction. *"My mother,"* said he, *"was always telling me that I did not behave myself properly, that I should endeavour to learn behaviour, and such cant; but when I replied that she ought to tell me what to do, and what to avoid, her admonitions were commonly, for that time at least, at an end."* This I fear was, however, at best a momentary refuge found out by perverseness.

No man knew better than Johnson in how many nameless and numberless actions behaviour consists—actions which can scarcely be reduced to rule, and which come under no description. Of these he retained so many very strange ones, that I suppose no one who saw his odd manner of gesticulating much blamed or wondered at the good lady's solicitude concerning her son's behaviour. Though he was attentive to the peace of children in general, no man had a stronger contempt than he for such parents as openly profess that they cannot govern their children. *"How,"* says he, *"is an army governed? Such people, for the most part, multiply prohibitions till obedience becomes impossible, and authority appears absurd, and never suspect that they tease their family, their friends, and themselves, only because conversation runs low, and something must be said."* Of parental authority, indeed, few people thought with a lower degree of estimation. I one day mentioned the resignation of Cyrus to his father's will, as related by Xenophon, when, after all his conquests, he requested the consent of Cambyses to his marriage with a neighbouring princess, and I added Rollin's applause and recommendation of the example. *"Do you not perceive, then,"* says Johnson, *"that Xenophon on this occasion commends like a pedant, and Pere Rollin applauds like a slave? If Cyrus by his conquests had not purchased emancipation, he had conquered to little purpose indeed. Can you forbear to see the folly of a fellow who has in his care the lives of thousands, when he begs his papa permission to be married, and confesses his inability to decide in a matter which concerns no man's happiness but his own?"*

Mr. Johnson caught me another time reprimanding the daughter of my housekeeper for having sat down unpermitted in her mother's presence. *"Why, she gets her living, does she not,"* said he, *"without her mother's help? Let the wench alone,"* continued he. And when we were again out of the women's sight who was concerned in the dispute: *"Poor people's children, dear lady,"* said he, *"never respect them. I did not respect my own mother, though I loved her. And one day, when in anger she called me a puppy, I asked her if she knew what they called a puppy's mother."*

We were talking of a young fellow who used to come often to the house; he was about fifteen years old, or less, if I remember right, and had a manner at once sullen and sheepish. *"That lad,"* says Mr. Johnson, *"looks like the son of a schoolmaster, which,"* added he, *"is one of the very worst conditions of childhood. Such a boy has no father, or worse than none; he never can reflect on his parent but the reflection brings to his mind some idea of pain inflicted, or of sorrow suffered."* I will relate one thing more that Dr. Johnson said about babyhood before I quit the subject; it was this: *"That little people should be encouraged always to tell whatever they hear particularly striking to some brother, sister, or servant immediately, before the impression is erased by the intervention of newer occurrences. He perfectly remembered the first time he ever heard of Heaven and Hell,"* he said, *"because when his mother had made out such a description of both places as she thought likely to seize the attention of her infant auditor, who was then in bed with her, she got up, and dressing him before the usual time, sent him directly to call a favourite workman in the house, to whom he knew he would communicate the conversation while it was yet impressed upon his mind. The event was what she wished, and it was to that method chiefly that he owed his uncommon felicity of remembering distant occurrences and long past conversations."*

At the age of eighteen Dr. Johnson quitted school, and escaped from the tuition of those he hated or those he despised. I have heard him relate very few college adventures. He used to say that our best accounts of his behaviour there would be gathered from Dr. Adams and Dr. Taylor, and that he was sure they would always tell the truth. He told me, however, one day how, when he was first entered at the University, he passed a morning, in compliance with the customs of the place, at his tutor's chambers; but, finding him no scholar, went no more. In about ten days after, meeting the same gentleman, Mr. Jordan, in the street, he offered to pass by without saluting him; but the tutor stopped, and inquired, not roughly neither, what he had been doing? *"Sliding on the ice,"* was the reply, and so turned away with disdain. He laughed very heartily at the recollection of his own insolence, and said they endured it from him with wonderful acquiescence, and a gentleness that, whenever he thought of it, astonished himself.

He told me, too, that when he made his first declamation, he wrote over but one copy, and that coarsely; and having given it into the hand of the tutor, who stood to receive it as he passed, was obliged to begin by chance and continue on how he could, for he had got but little of it by heart; so fairly trusting to his present powers for immediate supply, he finished by adding astonishment to the applause of all who knew how little was owing to study. A prodigious risk, however, said some one. *"Not at all!"* exclaims Johnson. *"No man, I suppose, leaps at once into deep water who does not know how to swim."* I doubt not but this story will be told by many of his biographers, and said so to him when he told it me on the 18th of July, 1773. "*And who will be my biographer,*" said he, "*do you think?*" "*Goldsmith, no doubt,*" replied I, "*and he will do it the best among us.*" "*The dog would write it best, to be sure,*" replied he; "*but his particular malice towards me, and general disregard for truth, would make the book useless to all, and injurious to my character.*" "*Oh! as to that,*" said I, "*we should all fasten upon him, and force him to do you justice; but the worst is, the Doctor does not know your life; nor can I tell indeed who does, except Dr. Taylor of Ashbourne.*" "*Why, Taylor,*" said he, "*is better acquainted with my heart than any man or woman now alive; and the history of my Oxford exploits lies all between him and Adams; but Dr. James knows my very early days better than he. After my coming to London to drive the world about a little, you must all go to Jack Hawkesworth for anecdotes. I lived in great familiarity with him (though I think there was not much affection) from the year 1753 till the time Mr. Thrale and you took me up. I intend, however, to disappoint the rogues, and either make you write the life, with Taylor's intelligence, or, which is better, do it myself, after outliving you all. I am now,*" added he, "*keeping a diary, in hopes of using it for that purpose some time.*"

Here the conversation stopped, from my accidentally looking in an old magazine of the year 1768, where I saw the following lines with his name to them, and asked if they were his:— Verses said to be written by Dr. Samuel Johnson, at the request of a gentleman to whom a lady had given a sprig of myrtle.

"*What hopes, what terrors, does thy gift create,*
Ambiguous emblem of uncertain fate;
The myrtle, ensign of supreme command,
Consigned by Venus to Melissa's hand:
Not less capricious than a reigning fair,
Now grants, and now rejects a lover's prayer.
In myrtle shades oft sings the happy swain,
In myrtle shades despairing ghosts complain:
The myrtle crowns the happy lovers' heads,
The unhappy lover's grave the myrtle spreads:
Oh, then, the meaning of thy gift impart,

And ease the throbbings of an anxious heart!
Soon must this bough, as you shall fix his doom,
Adorn Philander's head, or grace his tomb."

"Why, now, do but see how the world is gaping for a wonder!" cries Mr. Johnson. *"I think it is now just forty years ago that a young fellow had a sprig of myrtle given him by a girl he courted, and asked me to write him some verses that he might present her in return. I promised, but forgot; and when he called for his lines at the time agreed on—'Sit still a moment,' says I, 'dear Mund, and I'll fetch them thee,' so stepped aside for five minutes, and wrote the nonsense you now keep such a stir about."*

Upon revising these anecdotes, it is impossible not to be struck with shame and regret that one treasured no more of them up; but no experience is sufficient to cure the vice of negligence. Whatever one sees constantly, or might see constantly, becomes uninteresting; and we suffer every trivial occupation, every slight amusement, to hinder us from writing down what, indeed, we cannot choose but remember, but what we should wish to recollect with pleasure, unpoisoned by remorse for not remembering more. While I write this, I neglect impressing my mind with the wonders of art and beauties of nature that now surround me; and shall one day, perhaps, think on the hours I might have profitably passed in the Florentine Gallery, and reflecting on Raphael's St. John at that time, as upon Johnson's conversation in this moment, may justly exclaim of the months spent by me most delightfully in Italy— *"That I prized every hour that passed by, Beyond all that had pleased me before; But now they are past, and I sigh And I grieve that I prized them no more."* Shenstone.

Dr. Johnson delighted in his own partiality for Oxford; and one day, at my house, entertained five members of the other University with various instances of the superiority of Oxford, enumerating the gigantic names of many men whom it had produced, with apparent triumph. At last I said to him, *"Why, there happens to be no less than five Cambridge men in the room now." "I did not,"* said he, *"think of that till you told me; but the wolf don't count the sheep."* When the company were retired, we happened to be talking of Dr. Barnard, the Provost of Eton, who died about that time; and after a long and just eulogium on his wit, his learning, and his goodness of heart, "*He was the only man, too,*" says Mr. Johnson, quite seriously, "*that did justice to my good breeding; and you may observe that I am well-bred to a degree of needless scrupulosity. No man,*" continued he, not observing the amazement of his hearers, "*no man is so cautious not to interrupt another; no man thinks it so necessary to appear attentive when others are speaking; no man so steadily refuses preference to himself, or so willingly bestows it on another, as I do; nobody holds so strongly as I do the necessity of ceremony, and the ill effects which follow the breach of it, yet people think me rude; but Barnard did me justice.*" "*'Tis pity,*" said I, laughing, "*that he had not heard you compliment the Cambridge men after dinner to-day.*" "*Why,*" replied he, "*I was inclined to down them sure enough; but then a fellow deserves to be of Oxford that talks so.*"

I have heard him at other times relate how he used so sit in some coffee-house there, and turn M——'s "*C-r-ct-c-s*" into ridicule for the diversion of himself and of chance comers-in. "*The 'Elf-da,'*" says he, "*was too exquisitely pretty; I could make no fun out of that.*" When upon some occasions he would express his astonishment that he should have an enemy in the world, while he had been doing nothing but good to his neighbours, I used to make him recollect these circumstances. "*Why, child,*" said he, "*what harm could that do the fellow? I always thought very well of M——n for a Cambridge man; he is, I believe, a mighty blameless character.*"

Such tricks were, however, the more unpardonable in Mr. Johnson, because no one could harangue like him about the difficulty always found in forgiving petty injuries, or in provoking by needless offence. Mr. Jordan, his tutor, had much of his affection, though he despised his want of scholastic learning. "*That creature would,*" said he, "*defend his pupils to the last: no young lad under his care should suffer for committing slight improprieties, while he had breath to defend, or power to protect them. If I had had sons to send to College,*" added he, "*Jordan should have been their tutor.*"

Sir William Browne, the physician, who lived to a very extraordinary age, and was in other respects an odd mortal, with more genius than understanding, and more self sufficiency than wit, was the only person who ventured to oppose Mr. Johnson when he had a mind to shine by exalting his favourite university, and to express his contempt of the Whiggish notions which prevail at Cambridge. He did it once, however, with surprising felicity. His antagonist having repeated with an air of triumph the famous epigram written by Dr. Trapp— *"Our royal master saw, with heedful eyes, The wants of his two universities: Troops he to Oxford sent, as knowing why That learned body wanted loyalty: But books to Cambridge gave, as well discerning That that right loyal body wanted learning."* Which, says Sir William, might well be answered thus:— *"The King to Oxford sent his troop of horse, For Tories own no argument but force; With equal care to Cambridge books he sent, For Whigs allow no force but argument."* Mr. Johnson did him the justice to say it was one of the happiest extemporaneous productions he ever met with, though he once comically confessed that he hated to repeat the wit of a Whig urged in support of Whiggism. Says Garrick to him one day, *"Why did not you make me a Tory, when we lived so much together? You love to make people Tories." "Why,"* says Johnson, pulling a heap of halfpence from his pocket, *"did not the king make these guineas?"*

Of Mr. Johnson's Toryism the world has long been witness, and the political pamphlets written by him in defence of his party are vigorous and elegant. He often delighted his imagination with the thoughts of having destroyed Junius, an anonymous writer who flourished in the years 1769 and 1770, and who kept himself so ingeniously concealed from every endeavour to detect him that no probable guess was, I believe, ever formed concerning the author's name, though at that time the subject of general conversation. Mr. Johnson made us all laugh one day, because I had received a remarkably fine Stilton cheese as a present from some person who had packed and directed it carefully, but without mentioning whence it came. Mr. Thrale, desirous to know who we were obliged to, asked every friend as they came in, but nobody owned it. *"Depend upon it, sir,"* says Johnson, *"it was sent by Junius ."*

The "False Alarm," his first and favourite pamphlet, was

written at our house between eight o'clock on Wednesday night and twelve o'clock on Thursday night. We read it to Mr. Thrale when he came very late home from the House of Commons; the other political tracts followed in their order. I have forgotten which contains the stroke at Junius, but shall for ever remember the pleasure it gave him to have written it. It was, however, in the year 1775 that Mr. Edmund Burke made the famous speech in Parliament that struck even foes with admiration, and friends with delight. Among the nameless thousands who are contented to echo those praises they have not skill to invent, _I_ ventured, before Dr. Johnson himself, to applaud with rapture the beautiful passage in it concerning Lord Bathurst and the Angel, which, said our Doctor, had I been in the house, I would have answered thus:— *"Suppose, Mr. Speaker, that to Wharton or to Marlborough, or to any of the eminent Whigs of the last age, the devil had, not with any great impropriety, consented to appear, he would, perhaps, in somewhat like these words, have commenced the conversation: "'You seem, my lord, to be concerned at the judicious apprehension that while you are sapping the foundations of royalty at home, and propagating here the dangerous doctrine of resistance, the distance of America may secure its inhabitants from your arts, though active. But I will unfold to you the gay prospects of futurity. This people, now so innocent and harmless, shall draw the sword against their mother country, and bathe its point in the blood of their benefactors; this people, now contented with a little, shall then refuse to spare what they themselves confess they could not miss; and these men, now so honest and so grateful, shall, in return for peace and for protection, see their vile agents in the House of Parliament, there to sow the seeds of sedition, and propagate confusion, perplexity, and pain. Be not dispirited, then, at the contemplation of their present happy state: I promise you that anarchy, poverty, and death shall, by my care, be carried even across the spacious Atlantic, and settle in America itself, the sure consequences of our beloved Whiggism.'"*

This I thought a thing so very particular that I begged his leave to write it down directly, before anything could intervene that might make me forget the force of the expressions. A trick which I have, however, seen played on common occasions, of sitting steadily down at the other end of the room to write at the moment what should be said in company, either by Dr. Johnson or to him, I never practised myself, nor approved of in another. There is something so ill-bred, and so inclining to treachery in this conduct, that were it commonly adopted all confidence would soon be exiled from society, and a conversation assembly-room would become tremendous as a court of justice. A set of acquaintance joined in familiar chat may say a thousand things which, as the phrase is, pass well enough at the time, though they cannot stand the test of critical examination; and as all talk beyond that which is necessary to the purposes of actual business is a kind of game, there will be ever found ways of playing fairly or unfairly at it, which distinguish the gentleman from the juggler.

Dr. Johnson, as well as many of my acquaintance, knew that I kept a common-place book, and he one day said to me good-humouredly that he would give me something to write in my repository. "*I warrant,*" said he, "*there is a great deal about me in it. You shall have at least one thing worth your pains, so if you will get the pen and ink I will repeat to you Anacreon's 'Dove' directly; but tell at the same time that as I never was struck with anything in the Greek language till I read that, so I never read anything in the same language since that pleased me as much. I hope my translation,*" continued he, "*is not worse than that of Frank Fawkes.*" Seeing me disposed to laugh, "*Nay, nay,*" said he, "*Frank Fawkes has done them very finely.*"

"Lovely courier of the sky,
Whence and whither dost thou fly?
Scatt'ring, as thy pinions play,
Liquid fragrance all the way.
Is it business? is it love?
Tell me, tell me, gentle Dove.
'Soft Anacreon's vows I bear,
Vows to Myrtale the fair;
Graced with all that charms the heart,
Blushing nature, smiling art.
Venus, courted by an ode,
On the bard her Dove bestowed.

Vested with a master's right
Now Anacreon rules my flight;
His the letters that you see,
Weighty charge consigned to me;
Think not yet my service hard,
Joyless task without reward;
Smiling at my master's gates,
Freedom my return awaits.
But the liberal grant in vain
Tempts me to be wild again.
Can a prudent Dove decline
Blissful bondage such as mine?
Over hills and fields to roam,
Fortune's guest without a home;
Under leaves to hide one's head,
Slightly sheltered, coarsely fed;
Now my better lot bestows
Sweet repast, and soft repose;
Now the generous bowl I sip
As it leaves Anacreon's lip;
Void of care, and free from dread,
From his fingers snatch his bread,
Then with luscious plenty gay,
Round his chamber dance and play;
Or from wine, as courage springs,
O'er his face extend my wings;
And when feast and frolic tire,
Drop asleep upon his lyre.
This is all, be quick and go,
More than all thou canst not know;
Let me now my pinions ply,
I have chattered like a pie.'"

When I had finished, "*But you must remember to add,*" says Mr. Johnson, "*that though these verses were planned, and even begun, when I was sixteen years old, I never could find time to make an end of them before I was sixty-eight.*" This facility of writing, and this dilatoriness ever to write, Mr. Johnson always retained, from the days that he lay abed and dictated his first publication to Mr. Hector, who acted as his amanuensis, to the moment he made me copy out those variations in Pope's "Homer" which are printed in the "Poets' Lives." "*And now,*" said he, when I had finished it for him, "*I fear not Mr. Nicholson of a pin.*" The fine 'Rambler,' on the subject of Procrastination, was hastily composed, as I have heard, in Sir Joshua Reynolds's parlour, while the boy waited to carry it to press; and numberless are the instances of his writing under immediate pressure of importunity or distress. He told me that the character of Sobre in the 'Idler' was by himself intended as his own portrait, and that he had his own outset into life in his eye when he wrote the Eastern story of "Gelaleddin."

Of the allegorical papers in the 'Rambler,' Labour and Rest was his favourite; but Scrotinus, the man who returns late in life to receive honours in his native country, and meets with mortification instead of respect, was by him considered as a masterpiece in the science of life and manners. The character of Prospero in the fourth volume Garrick took to be his; and I have heard the author say that he never forgave the offence. Sophron was likewise a picture drawn from reality, and by Gelidus, the philosopher, he meant to represent Mr. Coulson, a mathematician, who formerly lived at Rochester. The man immortalised for purring like a cat was, as he told me, one Busby, a proctor in the Commons. He who barked so ingeniously, and then called the drawer to drive away the dog, was father to Dr. Salter, of the Charterhouse. He who sang a song, and by correspondent motions of his arm chalked out a giant on the wall, was one Richardson, an attorney. The letter signed "Sunday" was written by Miss Talbot; and he fancied the billets in the first volume of the 'Rambler' were sent him by Miss Mulso, now Mrs. Chapone. The papers contributed by Mrs. Carter had much of his esteem, though he always blamed me for preferring the letter signed "Chariessa" to the allegory, where religion and superstition are indeed most masterly delineated.

When Dr. Johnson read his own satire, in which the life of a scholar is painted, with the various obstructions thrown in his way to fortune and to fame, he burst into a passion of tears one day. The family and Mr. Scott only were present, who, in a jocose way, clapped him on the back, and said, *"What's all this, my dear sir? Why, you and I and hercules, you know, were all troubled with melancholy."* As there are many gentlemen of the same name, I should say, perhaps, that it was a Mr. Scott who married Miss Robinson, and that I think I have heard Mr. Thrale call him George Lowis, or George Augustus, I have forgot which. He was a very large man, however, and made out the triumvirate with Johnson and Hercules comically enough. The Doctor was so delighted at his odd sally that he suddenly embraced him, and the subject was immediately changed. I never saw Mr. Scott but that once in my life. Dr. Johnson was liberal enough in granting literary assistance to others, I think; and innumerable are the prefaces, sermons, lectures, and dedications which he used to make for people who begged of him.

Mr. Murphy related in his and my hearing one day, and he did not deny it, that when Murphy joked him the week before for having been so diligent of late between Dodd's sermon and Kelly's prologue, Dr. Johnson replied, *"Why, sir, when they come to me with a dead staymaker and a dying parson, what can a man do?"* He said, however, that *"he hated to give away literary performances, or even to sell them too cheaply. The next generation shall not accuse me,"* added he, *"of beating down the price of literature. One hates, besides, ever to give that which one has been accustomed to sell. Would not you, sir,"* turning to Mr. Thrale, *"rather give away money than porter?"*

Mr. Johnson had never, by his own account, been a close student, and used to advise young people never to be without a book in their pocket, to be read at bye-times when they had nothing else to do. *"It has been by that means,"* said he to a boy at our house one day, *"that all my knowledge has been gained, except what I have picked up by running about the world with my wits ready to observe, and my tongue ready to talk. A man is seldom in a humour to unlock his bookcase, set his desk in order, and betake himself to serious study; but a retentive memory will do something, and a fellow shall have strange credit given him, if he can but recollect striking passages from different books, keep the authors separate in his head, and bring his stock of knowledge artfully into play. How else,"* added he, *"do the gamesters manage when they play for more money than they are worth?"*

His Dictionary, however, could not, one would think, have been written by running up and down; but he really did not consider it as a great performance; and used to say *"that he might have done it easily in two years had not his health received several shocks during the time."* When Mr. Thrale, in consequence of this declaration, teased him in the year 1768 to give a new edition of it, because, said he, there are four or five gross faults: *"Alas! sir,"* replied Johnson, *"there are four or five hundred faults instead of four or five; but you do not consider that it would take me up three whole months' labour, and when the time was expired the work would not be done."* When the booksellers set him about it, however, some years after, he went cheerfully to the business, said he was well paid, and that they deserved to have it done carefully. His reply to the person who complimented him on its coming out first, mentioning the ill success of the French in a similar attempt, is well known, and, I trust, has been often recorded. *"Why, what would you expect, dear sir,"* said he, *"from fellows that eat frogs?"*

I have, however, often thought Dr. Johnson more free than prudent in professing so loudly his little skill in the Greek language; for though he considered it as a proof of a narrow mind to be too careful of literary reputation, yet no man could be more enraged than he if an enemy, taking advantage of this confession, twitted him with his ignorance; and I remember when the King of Denmark was in England one of his noblemen was brought by Mr. Colman to see Dr. Johnson at our country house, and having heard, he said, that he was not famous for Greek literature, attacked him on the weak side, politely adding that he chose that conversation on purpose to favour himself.

Our Doctor, however, displayed so copious, so compendious a knowledge of authors, books, and every branch of learning in that language, that the gentleman appeared astonished. When he was gone home, says Johnson, *"Now, for all this triumph I may thank Thrale's Xenophon here, as I think, excepting that one, I have not looked in a Greek book these ten years; but see what haste my dear friends were all in,"* continued he, *"to tell this poor innocent foreigner that I know nothing of Greek! Oh, no, he knows nothing of Greek!"* with a loud burst of laughing. When Davies printed the "Fugitive Pieces" without his knowledge or consent, *"How,"* said I, *"would Pope have raved, had he been served so!" "We should never,"* replied he, *"have heard the last on't, to be sure; but then Pope was a narrow man. I will, however,"* added he, *"storm and bluster myself a little this time,"* so went to London in all the wrath he could muster up. At his return I asked how the affair ended. *"Why,"* said he, *"I was a fierce fellow, and pretended to be very angry; and Thomas was a good-natured fellow, and pretended to be very sorry; so there the matter ended. I believe the dog loves me dearly. Mr. Thrale,"* turning to my husband, *"what shall you and I do that is good for Tom Davies? We will do something for him, to be sure."*

Of Pope as a writer he had the highest opinion, and once when a lady at our house talked of his preface to Shakespeare as superior to Pope's, *"I fear not, madam,"* said he, *"the little fellow has done wonders."*

His superior reverence of Dryden, notwithstanding, still appeared in his talk as in his writings; and when some one mentioned the ridicule thrown on him in the 'Rehearsal,' as having hurt his general character as an author, *"On the contrary,"* says Mr. Johnson, *"the greatness of Dryden's reputation is now the only principle of vitality which keeps the Duke of Buckingham's play from putrefaction."*

It was not very easy, however, for people not quite intimate with Dr. Johnson to get exactly his opinion of a writer's merit, as he would now and then divert himself by confounding those who thought themselves obliged to say to-morrow what he had said yesterday; and even Garrick, who ought to have been better acquainted with his tricks, professed himself mortified that one time when he was extolling Dryden in a rapture that I suppose disgusted his friend, Mr. Johnson suddenly challenged him to produce twenty lines in a series that would not disgrace the poet and his admirer. Garrick produced a passage that he had once heard the Doctor commend, in which he now found, if I remember rightly, sixteen faults, and made Garrick look silly at his own table.

When I told Mr. Johnson the story, "*Why, what a monkey was David now,*" says he, "*to tell of his own disgrace!*" And in the course of that hour's chat he told me how he used to tease Garrick by commendations of the tomb-scene in Congreve's 'Mourning Bride,' protesting, that Shakespeare had in the same line of excellence nothing as good. "*All which is strictly true,*" said he; "*but that is no reason for supposing Congreve is to stand in competition with Shakespeare: these fellows know not how to blame, nor how to commend.*"

I forced him one day, in a similar humour, to prefer Young's description of " Night" to the so much admired ones of Dryden and Shakespeare, as more forcible and more general. Every reader is not either a lover or a tyrant, but every reader is interested when he hears that "*Creation sleeps; 'tis as the general pulse Of life stood still, and nature made a pause; An awful pause—prophetic of its end.*" "*This,*" said he, "*is true; but remember that, taking the compositions of Young in general, they are but like bright stepping-stones over a miry road. Young froths and foams, and bubbles sometimes very vigorously; but we must not compare the noise made by your tea-kettle here with the roaring of the ocean.*"

Somebody was praising Corneille one day in opposition to Shakespeare. "*Corneille is to Shakespeare,*" replied Mr. Johnson, "*as a clipped hedge is to a forest.*" When we talked of Steele's Essays, "*They are too thin,*" says our critic, "*for an Englishman's taste: mere superficial observations on life and manners, without erudition enough to make them keep, like the light French wines, which turn sour with standing awhile for want of body, as we call it.*" Of a much-admired poem, when extolled as beautiful, he replied, "*That it had indeed the beauty of a bubble. The colours are gay,*" said he, "*but the substance slight.*"

Of James Harris's Dedication to his "*Hermes,*" I have heard him observe that, though but fourteen lines long, there were six grammatical faults in it. A friend was praising the style of Dr. Swift; Mr. Johnson did not find himself in the humour to agree with him: the critic was driven from one of his performances to the other. At length, "*You must allow me,*" said the gentleman, *"that there are strong facts in the account of 'The Four Last Years of Queen Anne.'" "Yes, surely, sir,"* replies Johnson, *"and so there are in the Ordinary of Newgate's account."*

This was like the story which Mr. Murphy tells, and Johnson always acknowledged: how Mr. Rose of Hammersmith, contending for the preference of Scotch writers over the English, after having set up his authors like ninepins, while the Doctor kept bowling them down again; at last, to make sure of victory, he named Ferguson upon *"Civil Society,"* and praised the book for being written in a new manner. *"I do not,"* says Johnson, *"perceive the value of this new manner; it is only like Buckinger, who had no hands, and so wrote with his feet."* Of a modern Martial, when it came out: *"There are in these verses,"* says Dr. Johnson, *"too much folly for madness, I think, and too much madness for folly."*

If, however, Mr. Johnson lamented that the nearer he approached to his own times, the more enemies he should make, by telling biographical truths in his "Lives of the Later Poets," what may I not apprehend, who, if I relate anecdotes of Mr. Johnson, am obliged to repeat expressions of severity, and sentences of contempt? Let me at least soften them a little by saying that he did not hate the persons he treated with roughness, or despise them whom he drove from him by apparent scorn. He really loved and respected many whom he would not suffer to love him. And when he related to me a short dialogue that passed between himself and a writer of the first eminence in the world, when he was in Scotland, I was shocked to think how he must have disgusted him. *"Dr. — — asked me,"* said he, *"why I did not join in their public worship when among them? for,"* said he, *"I went to your churches often when in England." "So,"* replied Johnson, *"I have read that the Siamese sent ambassadors to Louis Quatorze, but I never heard that the King of France thought it worth his while to send ambassadors from his court to that of Siam."*

He was no gentler with myself, or those for whom I had the greatest regard. When I one day lamented the loss of a first cousin killed in America, *"Prithee, my dear,"* said he, *"have done with canting. How would the world be worse for it, I may ask, if all your relations were at once spitted like larks, and roasted for Presto's supper?"* Presto was the dog that lay under the table while we talked.

When we went into Wales together, and spent some time at Sir Robert Cotton's, at Lleweny, one day at dinner I meant to please Mr. Johnson particularly with a dish of very young peas. "*Are not they charming?*" said I to him, while he was eating them. "*Perhaps,*" said he, "*they would be so—to a pig.*" I only instance these replies, to excuse my mentioning those he made to others.

When a well-known author published his poems in the year 1777: "*Such a one's verses are come out,*" said I. "*Yes,*" replied Johnson, "*and this frost has struck them in again. Here are some lines I have written to ridicule them; but remember that I love the fellow dearly now, for all I laugh at him:—*

'Wheresoe'er I turn my view,
All is strange, yet nothing new;
Endless labour all along,
Endless labour to be wrong;
Phrase that Time has flung away;
Uncouth words in disarray,
Tricked in antique ruff and bonnet,
Ode, and elegy, and sonnet.'"

When he parodied the verses of another eminent writer, it was done with more provocation, I believe, and with some merry malice. A serious translation of the same lines, which I think are from Euripides, may be found in Burney's "History of Music." Here are the burlesque ones:—

"Err shall they not, who resolute explore
Time's gloomy backward with judicious eyes;
And scanning right the practices of yore,
Shall deem our hoar progenitors unwise.
"They to the dome where smoke with curling play
Announced the dinner to the regions round,
Summoned the singer blithe, and harper gay,
And aided wine with dulcet streaming sound.
"The better use of notes, or sweet or shrill,
By quivering string, or modulated wind;

Trumpet or lyre—to their harsh bosoms chill,
Admission ne'er had sought, or could not find.
"Oh! send them to the sullen mansions dun,
Her baleful eyes where Sorrow rolls around;
Where gloom-enamoured Mischief loves to dwell,
And Murder, all blood-boltered, schemes the wound.
"When cates luxuriant pile the spacious dish,
And purple nectar glads the festive hour;
The guest, without a want, without a wish,
Can yield no room to Music's soothing power."

Some of the old legendary stories put in verse by modern writers provoked him to caricature them thus one day at Streatham; but they are already well known, I am sure.

"The tender infant, meek and mild,
Fell down upon the stone;
The nurse took up the squealing child,
But still the child squealed on."

A famous ballad also, beginning 'Rio verde, Rio verde,' when I commended the translation of it, he said he could do it better himself—as thus:

"Glassy water, glassy water,
Down whose current clear and strong,
Chiefs confused in mutual slaughter,
Moor and Christian roll along."

"But, sir," said I, *"this is not ridiculous at all." "Why, no,"* replied he, *"why should I always write ridiculously? Perhaps because I made these verses to imitate such a one,"* naming him:

"'Hermit hoar, in solemn cell
Wearing out life's evening grey;
Strike thy bosom, sage! and tell
What is bliss, and which the way?'
"Thus I spoke, and speaking sighed,
Scarce repressed the starting tear,
When the hoary sage replied,
'Come, my lad, and drink some beer.'"

I could give another comical instance of caricatura imitation. Recollecting some day, when praising these verses of Lopez de Vega—

"Se acquien los leones vence,
Vence una muger hermosa,
O el de flaco averguence,
O ella di ser mas furiosa,"

more than he thought they deserved, Mr. Johnson instantly observed *"that they were founded on a trivial conceit, and that conceit ill-explained and ill-expressed besides. The lady, we all know, does not conquer in the same manner as the lion does. 'Tis a mere play of words,"* added he, *"and you might as well say that*

"'If the man who turnips cries,
Cry not when his father dies,
'Tis a proof that he had rather
Have a turnip than his father.'"

And this humour is of the same sort with which he answered the friend who commended the following line:—"Who rules o'er freemen should himself be free." *"To be sure,"* said Dr. Johnson— *"'Who drives fat oxen should himself be fat.'"* This readiness of finding a parallel, or making one, was shown by him perpetually in the course of conversation.

When the French verses of a certain pantomime were quoted thus:

"Je suis Cassandre descendue des cieux,
Pour vous faire entendre, mesdames et messieurs,
Que je suis Cassandre descendue des cieux,"

he cried out gaily and suddenly, almost in a moment—

"I am Cassandra come down from the sky,
To tell each bystander what none can deny,
That I am Cassandra come down from the sky."

The pretty Italian verses, too, at the end of Baretti's book called "Easy Phraseology," he did all' improviso, in the same manner:

"Viva! viva la padrona!
Tutta bella, e tutta buona,
La padrona e un angiolella
Tutta buona e tutta bella;
Tutta bella e tutta buona;
Viva! viva la padrona!"

"Long may live my lovely Hetty!

Always young and always pretty,
Always pretty, always young,
Live my lovely Hetty long!
Always young and always pretty!
Long may live my lovely Hetty!"

The famous distich, too, of an Italian improvisatore, when the Duke of Modena ran away from the comet in the year 1742 or 1743:

"Se al venir vestro i principi sen' vanno,
Deh venga ogni di — durate un anno;"
"which," said he, *"would do just as well in our language thus:*
"'If at your coming princes disappear,
Comets! come every day—and stay a year.'"

When some one in company commended the verses of M. de Benserade a son Lit:

"Theatre des ris et des pleurs,
Lit! on je nais, et ou je meurs,
Tu nous fais voir comment voisins
Sont nos plaisirs et nos chagrins."
To which he replied without hesitating—
"'In bed we laugh, in bed we cry,
And born in bed, in bed we die;
The near approach a bed may show
Of human bliss to human woe.'"

The inscription on the collar of Sir Joseph Banks's goat, which had been on two of his adventurous expeditions with him, and was then, by the humanity of her amiable master, turned out to graze in Kent as a recompense for her utility and faithful service, was given me by Johnson in the year 1777, I think, and I have never yet seen it printed: "Perpetui, ambita, bis terra, premia lactis, Haec habet altrici Capra secunda Jovis." The epigram written at Lord Anson's house many years ago, *"where,"* says Mr. Johnson, *"I was well received and kindly treated, and with the true gratitude of a wit ridiculed the master of the house before I had left it an hour,"* has been falsely printed in many papers since his death.

I wrote it down from his own lips one evening in August, 1772, not neglecting the little preface accusing himself of making so graceless a return for the civilities shown him. He had, among other elegancies about the park and gardens, been made to observe a temple to the winds, when this thought naturally presented itself to a wit:

"Gratum animum laudo;
Qui debuit omnia ventis,
Quam bene ventorum,
surgere templa jubet!"

A translation of Dryden's epigram, too, I used to fancy I had to myself: *"Quos laudet vates, Graius, Romanus, et Anglus, Tres tria temporibus secla dedere suis: Sublime ingenium, Graius,— Romanus habebat Carmen grande sonans, Anglus utrumque tulit. Nil majus natura capit: clarare priores Quae potuere duos, tertius unus habet:"* from the famous lines written under Milton's picture:

"Three poets in three distant ages born,
Greece, Italy, and England did adorn;
The first in loftiness of thought surpassed,
The next in majesty; in both the last.
The force of Nature could no further go,
To make a third she joined the former two."

One evening in the oratorio season of the year 1771 Mr. Johnson went with me to Covent Garden Theatre, and though he was for the most part an exceedingly bad playhouse companion, as his person drew people's eyes upon the box, and the loudness of his voice made it difficult for me to hear anybody but himself, he sat surprisingly quiet, and I flattered myself that he was listening to the music. When we were got home, however, he repeated these verses, which he said he had made at the oratorio, and he bade me translate them: in theatro

"Tertii verso quater orbe lustri
Quid theatrales tibi crispe pompae!
Quam decet canos male literatos Sera voluptas!
"Tene mulceri fidibus canoris?
Tene cantorum modulis stupere?
Tene per pictas oculo elegante Currere formas?
"Inter equales sine felle liber,

Codices veri studiosus inter Rectius vives,
sua quisque carpat Gaudia gratus.
"Lusibus gaudet puer otiosis
Luxus oblectat juvenem theatri,
At seni fluxo sapienter uti Tempore restat."

I gave him the following lines in imitation, which he liked well enough, I think:

"When threescore years have chilled thee quite,
Still can theatric scenes delight?
Ill suits this place with learned wight,
May Bates or Coulson cry.
"The scholar's pride can Brent disarm?
His heart can soft Guadagni warm?
Or scenes with sweet delusion charm
The climacteric eye?
"The social club, the lonely tower,
Far better suit thy midnight hour;
Let each according to his power
In worth or wisdom shine!
"And while play pleases idle boys,
And wanton mirth fond youth employs,
To fix the soul, and free from toys,
That useful task be thine."

The copy of verses in Latin hexameters, as well as I remember, which he wrote to Dr. Lawrence, I forgot to keep a copy of; and he obliged me to resign his translation of the song beginning, "*Busy, curious, thirsty fly,*" for him to give Mr. Langton, with a promise not to retain a copy. I concluded he knew why, so never inquired the reason. He had the greatest possible value for Mr. Langton, of Langton Hall, Lincoln, of whose virtue and learning he delighted to talk in very exalted terms; and poor Dr. Lawrence had long been his friend and confident. The conversation I saw them hold together in Essex Street one day, in the year 1781 or 1782, was a melancholy one, and made a singular impression on my mind. He was himself exceedingly ill, and I accompanied him thither for advice. The physician was, however, in some respects more to be pitied than the patient. Johnson was panting under an asthma and dropsy, but Lawrence had been brought home that very morning struck with the palsy, from which he had, two hours before we came, strove to awaken himself by blisters. They were both deaf, and scarce able to speak besides: one from difficulty of breathing, the other from paralytic debility. To give and receive medical counsel, therefore, they fairly sat down on each side a table in the doctor's gloomy apartment, adorned with skeletons, preserved monsters, etc., and agreed to write Latin billets to each other. Such a scene did I never see. "*You,*" said Johnson, "*are timide and gelide,*" finding that his friend had prescribed palliative, not drastic, remedies. "*It is not me,*" replies poor Lawrence, in an interrupted voice, "'*tis nature that is gelide and timide.*"

In fact, he lived but few months after, I believe, and retained his faculties still a shorter time. He was a man of strict piety and profound learning, but little skilled in the knowledge of life or manners, and died without having ever enjoyed the reputation he so justly deserved. Mr. Johnson's health had been always extremely bad since I first knew him, and his over-anxious care to retain without blemish the perfect sanity of his mind contributed much to disturb it. He had studied medicine diligently in all its branches, but had given particular attention to the diseases of the imagination, which he watched in himself with a solicitude destructive of his own peace, and intolerable to those he trusted. Dr. Lawrence told him one day that if he would come and beat him once a week he would bear it, but to hear his complaints was more than man could support. 'Twas therefore that he tried, I suppose, and in eighteen years contrived to weary the patience of a woman.

When Mr. Johnson felt his fancy, or fancied he felt it, disordered, his constant recurrence was to the study of arithmetic, and one day that he was totally confined to his chamber, and I inquired what he had been doing to divert himself, he showed me a calculation which I could scarce be made to understand, so vast was the plan of it, and so very intricate were the figures: no other, indeed, than that the national debt, computing it at one hundred and eighty millions sterling, would, if converted into silver, serve to make a meridian of that metal, I forgot how broad, for the globe of the whole earth, the real globe.

On a similar occasion I asked him, knowing what subject he would like best to talk upon, how his opinion stood towards the question between Paschal and Soame Jennings about number and numeration? as the French philosopher observes that infinity, though on all sides astonishing, appears most so when the idea is connected with the idea of number; for the notion of infinite number—and infinite number we know there is—stretches one's capacity still more than the idea of infinite space. "*Such a notion, indeed,*" adds he, "can scarcely find room in the human mind." *Our English author, on the other hand, exclaims, let no man give himself leave to talk about infinite number, for infinite number is a contradiction in terms; whatever is once numbered, we all see, cannot be infinite. "I think,"* said Mr. Johnson, after a pause, "*we must settle the matter thus: numeration is certainly infinite, for eternity might be employed in adding unit to unit; but every number is in itself finite, as the possibility of doubling it easily proves; besides, stop at what point you will, you find yourself as far from infinitude as ever.*" These passages I wrote down as soon as I had heard them, and repent that I did not take the same method with a dissertation he made one other day that he was very ill, concerning the peculiar properties of the number sixteen, which I afterwards tried, but in vain, to make him repeat.

As ethics or figures, or metaphysical reasoning, was the sort of talk he most delighted in, so no kind of conversation pleased him less, I think, than when the subject was historical fact or general polity. "*What shall we learn from that stuff?*" said he. "*Let us not fancy, like Swift, that we are exalting a woman's character by telling how she "'Could name the ancient heroes round, Explain for what they were renowned,' etc.*" I must not, however, lead my readers to suppose that he meant to reserve such talk for men's company as a proof of pre-eminence. "*He never,*" as he expressed it, "*desired to hear of the Punic War while he lived; such conversation was lost time,*" he said, "*and carried one away from common life, leaving no ideas behind which could serve living wight as warning or direction.*" "*How I should act is not the case,*

But how would Brutus in my place." "*And now*," cries Mr. Johnson, laughing with obstreperous violence, "*if these two foolish lines can be equalled in folly, except by the two succeeding ones—show them me.*"

I asked him once concerning the conversation powers of a gentleman with whom I was myself unacquainted. "*He talked to me at club one day*," replies our Doctor, "*concerning Catiline's conspiracy, so I withdrew my attention, and thought about Tom Thumb.*"

Modern politics fared no better. I was one time extolling the character of a statesman, and expatiating on the skill required to direct the different currents, reconcile the jarring interests, etc. "*Thus*," replies he, "*a mill is a complicated piece of mechanism enough, but the water is no part of the workmanship.*" On another occasion, when some one lamented the weakness of a then present Minister, and complained that he was dull and tardy, and knew little of affairs: "*You may as well complain, sir*," says Johnson, "*that the accounts of time are kept by the clock; for he certainly does stand still upon the stair-head—and we all know that he is no great chronologer.*"

In the year 1777, or thereabouts, when all the talk was of an invasion, he said most pathetically one afternoon, "*Alas! alas! how this unmeaning stuff spoils all my comfort in my friends' conversation! Will the people have done with it; and shall I never hear a sentence again without the French in it? Here is no invasion coming, and you know there is none. Let the vexatious and frivolous talk alone, or suffer it at least to teach you one truth; and learn by this perpetual echo of even unapprehended distress how historians magnify events expected or calamities endured; when you know they are at this very moment collecting all the big words they can find, in which to describe a consternation never felt, for a misfortune which never happened. Among all your lamentations, who eats the less—who sleeps the worse, for one general's ill-success, or another's capitulation? Oh, pray let us hear no more of it!*"

No man, however, was more zealously attached to his party; he not only loved a Tory himself, but he loved a man the better if he heard he hated a Whig. "*Dear Bathurst*," said he to me one day, "*was a man to my very heart's content: he hated a fool, and he hated a rogue, and he hated a whig; he was a very good hater.*" Some one mentioned a gentleman of that party for having behaved oddly on an occasion where faction was not concerned: "*Is he not a citizen of London, a native of North America, and a Whig?*" says Johnson. "*Let him be absurd, I beg you of you; when a monkey is too like a man, it shocks one.*"

Severity towards the poor was, in Dr. Johnson's opinion (as is visible in his "Life of Addison" particularly), an undoubted and constant attendant or consequence upon Whiggism; and he was not contented with giving them relief, he wished to add also indulgence. He loved the poor as I never yet saw any one else do, with an earnest desire to make them happy. "*What signifies,*" says some one, "*giving halfpence to common beggars? they only lay it out in gin or tobacco.*" "*And why should they be denied such sweeteners of their existence?*" says Johnson; "*it is surely very savage to refuse them every possible avenue to pleasure, reckoned too coarse for our own acceptance. Life is a pill which none of us can bear to swallow without gilding; yet for the poor we delight in stripping it still barer, and are not ashamed to show even visible displeasure if ever the bitter taste is taken from their mouths.*"

In consequence of these principles he nursed whole nests of people in his house, where the lame, the blind, the sick, and the sorrowful found a sure retreat from all the evils whence his little income could secure them: and commonly spending the middle of the week at our house, he kept his numerous family in Fleet Street upon a settled allowance; but returned to them every Saturday, to give them three good dinners, and his company, before he came back to us on the Monday night—treating them with the same, or perhaps more ceremonious civility than he would have done by as many people of fashion—making the Holy Scriptures thus the rule of his conduct, and only expecting salvation as he was able to obey its precepts.

While Dr. Johnson possessed, however, the strongest compassion for poverty or illness, he did not even pretend to feel for those who lamented the loss of a child, a parent, or a friend. "*These are the distresses of sentiment,*" he would reply, *"which a man who is really to be pitied has no leisure to feel. The sight of people who want food and raiment is so common in great cities, that a surly fellow like me has no compassion to spare for wounds given only to vanity or softness."* No man, therefore, who smarted from the ingratitude of his friends, found any sympathy from our philosopher. *"Let him do good on higher motives next time,"* *would be the answer; "he will then be sure of his reward."* It is easy to observe that the justice of such sentences made them offensive; but we must be careful how we condemn a man for saying what we know to be true, only because it is so. I hope that the reason our hearts rebelled a little against his severity was chiefly because it came from a living mouth.

Books were invented to take off the odium of immediate superiority, and soften the rigour of duties prescribed by the teachers and censors of human kind— setting at least those who are acknowledged wiser than ourselves at a distance. When we recollect, however, that for this very reason they are seldom consulted and little obeyed, how much cause shall his contemporaries have to rejoice that their living Johnson forced them to feel there proofs due to vice and folly, while Seneca and Tillotson were no longer able to make impression—except on our shelves!

Few things, indeed, which pass well enough with others would do with him: he had been a great reader of Mandeville, and was ever on the watch to spy out those stains of original corruption so easily discovered by a penetrating observer even in the purest minds. I mentioned an event, which if it had happened would greatly have injured Mr. Thrale and his family—*"and then, dear sir,"* said I, *"how sorry you would have been!"* *"I hope"* replied he, after a long pause, *"I should have been very sorry; but remember Rochefoucault's maxim."* *"I would rather,"* answered I, *"remember Prior's verses, and ask— 'What need of books these truths to tell, Which folks perceive that cannot spell? And must we spectacles apply, To see what hurts our naked eye?' Will anybody's mind bear this eternal microscope that you place upon your own so?"* *"I never,"* replied he, *"saw one that would, except that of my dear Miss Reynolds—and hers is very near to purity itself.*" Of slighter evils, and friends more distant than our own household, he spoke less cautiously.

An acquaintance lost the almost certain hope of a good estate that had been long expected. "*Such a one will grieve,*" said I, "*at her friend's disappointment.*" "*She will suffer as much, perhaps,*" said he, "*as your horse did when your cow miscarried.*" I professed myself sincerely grieved when accumulated distresses crushed Sir George Colebrook's family; and I was so. "*Your own prosperity,*" said he, "*may possibly have so far increased the natural tenderness of your heart, that for aught I know you may be a little sorry; but it is sufficient for a plain man if he does not laugh when he sees a fine new house tumble down all on a sudden, and a snug cottage stand by ready to receive the owner, whose birth entitled him to nothing better, and whose limbs are left him to go to work again with.*" I tried to tell him in jest that his morality was easily contented, and when I have said something as if the wickedness of the world gave me concern, he would cry out aloud against canting, and protest that he thought there was very little gross wickedness in the world, and still less of extraordinary virtue.

Nothing, indeed, more surely disgusted Dr. Johnson than hyperbole; he loved not to be told of sallies of excellence, which he said were seldom valuable, and seldom true. "*Heroic virtues,*" said he, "*are the bons mots of life; they do not appear often, and when they do appear are too much prized, I think, like the aloe-tree, which shoots and flowers once in a hundred years. But life is made up of little things; and that character is the best which does little but repeated acts of beneficence; as that conversation is the best which consists in elegant and pleasing thoughts expressed in natural and pleasing terms. With regard to my own notions of moral virtue,*" continued he, "*I hope I have not lost my sensibility of wrong; but I hope, likewise, that I have lived long enough in the world to prevent me from expecting to find any action of which both the original motive and all the parts were good.*"

The piety of Dr. Johnson was exemplary and edifying; he was punctiliously exact to perform every public duty enjoined by the Church, and his spirit of devotion had an energy that affected all who ever saw him pray in private. The coldest and most languid hearer of the Word must have felt themselves animated by his manner of reading the Holy Scriptures; and to pray by his sick-bed required strength of body as well as of mind, so vehement were his manners, and his tones of voice so pathetic. I have many times made it my request to Heaven that I might be spared the sight of his death; and I was spared it. Mr. Johnson, though in general a gross feeder, kept fast in Lent, particularly the Holy Week, with a rigour very dangerous to his general health; but though he had left off wine (for religious motives, as I always believed, though he did not own it), yet he did not hold the commutation of offences by voluntary penance, or encourage others to practise severity upon themselves. He even once said "that he thought it an error to endeavour at pleasing God by taking the rod of reproof out of His hands." And when we talked of convents, and the hardships suffered in them: "*Remember always,*" said he, "*that a convent is an idle place, and where there is nothing to be done something must be endured: mustard has a bad taste per se, you may observe, but very insipid food cannot be eaten without it.*"

His respect, however, for places of religious retirement was carried to the greatest degree of earthly veneration; the Benedictine convent at Paris paid him all possible honours in return, and the Prior and he parted with tears of tenderness. Two of that college being sent to England on the mission some years after, spent much of their time with him at Bolt Court, I know, and he was ever earnest to retain their friendship; but though beloved by all his Roman Catholic acquaintance, particularly Dr. Nugent, for whose esteem he had a singular value, yet was Mr. Johnson a most unshaken Church of England man; and I think, or at least I once did think, that a letter written by him to Mr. Barnard, the King's Librarian, when he was in Italy collecting books, contained some very particular advice to his friend to be on his guard against the seductions of the Church of Rome.

The settled aversion Dr. Johnson felt towards an infidel he expressed to all ranks, and at all times, without the smallest reserve; for though on common occasions he paid great deference to birth or title, yet his regard for truth and virtue never gave way to meaner considerations. We talked of a dead wit one evening, and somebody praised him. *"Let us never praise talents so ill employed, sir; we foul our mouths by commending such infidels,"* said he. *"Allow him the lumieres at least,"* entreated one of the company. *"I do allow him, sir,"* replied Johnson, *"just enough to light him to hell."* Of a Jamaica gentleman, then lately dead: *"He will not, whither he is now gone,"* said Johnson, *"find much difference, I believe, either in the climate or the company."*

The Abbe Reynal probably remembers that, being at the house of a common friend in London, the master of it approached Johnson with that gentleman so much celebrated in his hand, and this speech in his mouth: *"Will you permit me, sir, to present to you the Abbe Reynal?" "No sir,"* replied the Doctor very loud, and suddenly turned away from them both. Though Mr. Johnson had but little reverence either for talents or fortune when he found them unsupported by virtue, yet it was sufficient to tell him a man was very pious, or very charitable, and he would at least begin with him on good terms, however the conversation might end. He would sometimes, too, good-naturedly enter into a long chat for the instruction or entertainment of people he despised. I perfectly recollect his condescending to delight my daughter's dancing-master with a long argument about his art, which the man protested, at the close of the discourse, the Doctor knew more of than himself, who remained astonished, enlightened, and amused by the talk of a person little likely to make a good disquisition upon dancing.

I have sometimes, indeed, been rather pleased than vexed when Mr. Johnson has given a rough answer to a man who perhaps deserved one only half as rough, because I knew he would repent of his hasty reproof, and make us all amends by some conversation at once instructive and entertaining, as in the following cases. A young fellow asked him abruptly one day, *"Pray, sir, what and where is Palmyra? I heard somebody talk last night of the ruins of Palmyra." "'Tis a hill in Ireland,"* replies Johnson, *"with palms growing on the top, and a bog at the bottom, and so they call it palm-mira."* Seeing, however, that the lad thought him serious, and thanked him for the information, he undeceived him very gently indeed: told him the history, geography, and chronology of Tadmor in the wilderness, with every incident that literature could furnish, I think, or eloquence express, from the building of Solomon's palace to the voyage of Dawkins and Wood!

On another occasion, when he was musing over the fire in our drawing-room at Streatham, a young gentleman called to him suddenly, and I suppose he thought disrespectfully, in these words: "*Mr. Johnson, would you advise me to marry?*" "*I would advise no man to marry, sir,*" returns for answer in a very angry tone Dr. Johnson, "*who is not likely to propagate understanding,*" and so left the room. Our companion looked confounded, and I believe had scarce recovered the consciousness of his own existence, when Johnson came back, and drawing his chair among us, with altered looks and a softened voice, joined in the general chat, insensibly led the conversation to the subject of marriage, where he laid himself out in a dissertation so useful, so elegant, so founded on the true knowledge of human life, and so adorned with beauty of sentiment, that no one ever recollected the offence, except to rejoice in its consequences.

He repented just as certainly, however, if he had been led to praise any person or thing by accident more than he thought it deserved; and was on such occasions comically earnest to destroy the praise or pleasure he had unintentionally given. Sir Joshua Reynolds mentioned some picture as excellent. "*It has often grieved me, sir,*" said Mr. Johnson, "*to see so much mind as the science of painting requires laid out upon such perishable materials. Why do not you oftener make use of copper? I could wish your superiority in the art you profess to be preserved in stuff more durable than canvas.*" Sir Joshua urged the difficulty of procuring a plate large enough for historical subjects, and was going to raise further observations. "*What foppish obstacles are these!*" exclaims on a sudden Dr. Johnson. "*Here is Thrale has a thousand tun of copper; you may paint it all round if you will, I suppose; it will serve him to brew in afterwards. Will it not, sir?*" (to my husband, who sat by). Indeed, Dr. Johnson's utter scorn of painting was such that I have heard him say that he should sit very quietly in a room hung round with the works of the greatest masters, and never feel the slightest disposition to turn them if their backs were outermost, unless it might be for the sake of telling Sir Joshua that he had turned them.

Such speeches may appear offensive to many, but those who knew he was too blind to discern the perfections of an art which applies itself immediately to our eyesight must acknowledge he was not in the wrong. He delighted no more in music than in painting; he was almost as deaf as he was blind; travelling with Dr. Johnson was for these reasons tiresome enough. Mr. Thrale loved prospects, and was mortified that his friend could not enjoy the sight of those different dispositions of wood and water, hill and valley, that travelling through England and France affords a man. But when he wished to point them out to his companion: "*Never heed such nonsense,*" would be the reply; "*a blade of grass is always a blade of grass, whether in one country or another. Let us, if we do talk, talk about something; men and women are my subjects of inquiry; let us see how these differ from those we have left behind.*"

When we were at Rouen together, he took a great fancy to the Abbe Roffette, with whom he conversed about the destruction of the order of Jesuits, and condemned it loudly as a blow to the general power of the Church, and likely to be followed with many and dangerous innovations, which might at length become fatal to religion itself, and shake even the foundation of Christianity. The gentleman seemed to wonder and delight in his conversation. The talk was all in Latin, which both spoke fluently, and Mr. Johnson pronounced a long eulogium upon Milton with so much ardour, eloquence, and ingenuity, that the Abbe rose from his seat and embraced him. My husband, seeing them apparently so charmed with the company of each other, politely invited the Abbe to England, intending to oblige his friend, who, instead of thanking, reprimanded him severely before the man for such a sudden burst of tenderness towards a person he could know nothing at all of, and thus put a sudden finish to all his own and Mr. Thrale's entertainment from the company of the Abbe Roffette.

When at Versailles the people showed us the theatre. As

we stood on the stage looking at some machinery for playhouse purposes: "*Now we are here, what shall we act, Mr. Johnson—The Englishman at Paris?*" "*No, no,*" replied he, "*we will try to act Harry the Fifth.*" His dislike to the French was well known to both nations, I believe; but he applauded the number of their books and the graces of their style. "*They have few sentiments,*" said he, "*but they express them neatly; they have little meat, too, but they dress it well.*"

Johnson's own notions about eating, however, were nothing less than delicate: a leg of pork boiled till it dropped from the bone, a veal pie with plums and sugar, or the outside cut of a salt buttock of beef, were his favourite dainties. With regard to drink, his liking was for the strongest, as it was not the flavour, but the effect, he sought for, and professed to desire; and when I first knew him, he used to pour capillaire into his port wine. For the last twelve years, however, he left off all fermented liquors. To make himself some amends, indeed, he took his chocolate liberally, pouring in large quantities of cream, or even melted butter; and was so fond of fruit, that though he usually ate seven or eight large peaches of a morning before breakfast began, and treated them with proportionate attention after dinner again, yet I have heard him protest that he never had quite as much as he wished of wall-fruit, except once in his life, and that was when we were all together at Ombersley, the seat of my Lord Sandys.

I was saying to a friend one day, that I did not like goose; "*one smells it so while it is roasting,*" said I. "*But you, madam,*" replies the Doctor, "*have been at all times a fortunate woman, having always had your hunger so forestalled by indulgence, that you never experienced the delight of smelling your dinner beforehand.*" "*Which pleasure,*" answered I pertly, "*is to be enjoyed in perfection by such as have the happiness to pass through Porridge Island of a morning.*" "*Come, come,*" says he, gravely, "*let's have no sneering at what is serious to so many. Hundreds of your fellow-creatures, dear lady, turn another way, that they may not be tempted by the luxuries of Porridge Island to wish for gratifications they are not able to obtain. You are certainly not better than all of them; give God thanks that you are happier.*"

I received on another occasion as just a rebuke from Mr. Johnson, for an offence of the same nature, and hope I took care never to provoke a third; for after a very long summer, particularly hot and dry, I was wishing naturally but thoughtlessly for some rain to lay the dust as we drove along the Surrey roads. "*I cannot bear,*" replied he, with much asperity and an altered look, "*when I know how many poor families will perish next winter for want of that bread which the present drought will deny them, to hear ladies sighing for rain, only that their complexions may not suffer from the heat, or their clothes be incommoded by the dust. For shame! leave off such foppish lamentations, and study to relieve those whose distresses are real.*"

With advising others to be charitable, however, Dr. Johnson did not content himself. He gave away all he had, and all he ever had gotten, except the two thousand pounds he left behind; and the very small portion of his income which he spent on himself, with all our calculation, we never could make more than seventy, or at most four-score pounds a year, and he pretended to allow himself a hundred. He had numberless dependents out of doors as well as in, who, as he expressed it, "*did not like to see him latterly unless he brought 'em money.*"

For those people he used frequently to raise contributions on his richer friends; "*and this,*" says he, "*is one of the thousand reasons which ought to restrain a man from drony solitude and useless retirement. Solitude,*" added he one day, "*is dangerous to reason, without being favourable to virtue: pleasures of some sort are necessary to the intellectual as to the corporeal health; and those who resist gaiety will be likely for the most part to fall a sacrifice to appetite; for the solicitations of sense are always at hand, and a dram to a vacant and solitary person is a speedy and seducing relief. Remember,*" concluded he, "*that the solitary mortal is certainly luxurious, probably superstitious, and possibly mad: the mind stagnates for want of employment, grows morbid, and is extinguished like a candle in foul air.*"

It was on this principle that Johnson encouraged parents to carry their daughters early and much into company: "*for what harm can be done before so many witnesses? Solitude is the surest nurse of all prurient passions, and a girl in the hurry of preparation, or tumult of gaiety, has neither inclination nor leisure to let tender expressions soften or sink into her heart. The ball, the show, are not the dangerous places: no, it is the private friend, the kind consoler, the companion of the easy, vacant hour, whose compliance with her opinions can flatter her vanity, and whose conversation can just soothe, without ever stretching her mind, that is the lover to be feared. He who buzzes in her ear at court or at the opera must be contented to buzz in vain."* These notions Dr. Johnson carried so very far, that I have heard him say, "*If you shut up any man with any woman, so as to make them derive their whole pleasure from each other, they would inevitably fall in love, as it is called, with each other; but at six months' end, if you would throw them both into public life, where they might change partners at pleasure, each would soon forget that fondness which mutual dependence and the paucity of general amusement alone had caused, and each would separately feel delighted by their release.*"

In these opinions Rousseau apparently concurs with him exactly; and Mr. Whitehead's poem, called "Variety," is written solely to elucidate this simple proposition. Prior likewise advises the husband to send his wife abroad, and let her see the world as it really stands:— "*Powder, and pocket-glass, and beau.*" Mr. Johnson was indeed unjustly supposed to be a lover of singularity. Few people had a more settled reverence for the world than he, or was less captivated by new modes of behaviour introduced, or innovations on the long-received customs of common life.

He hated the way of leaving a company without taking notice to the lady of the house that he was going, and did not much like any of the contrivances by which ease had lately been introduced into society instead of ceremony, which had more of his approbation. Cards, dress, and dancing, however, all found their advocate in Dr. Johnson, who inculcated, upon principle, the cultivation of those arts which many a moralist thinks himself bound to reject, and many a Christian holds unfit to be practised. "*No person,*" said he one day, "*goes under-dressed till he thinks himself of consequence enough to forbear carrying the badge of his rank upon his back.*"

And in answer to the arguments urged by Puritans, Quakers, etc., against showy decorations of the human figure, I once heard him exclaim, "*Oh, let us not be found, when our Master calls us, ripping the lace off our waistcoats, but the spirit of contention from our souls and tongues! Let us all conform in outward customs, which are of no consequence, to the manners of those whom we live among, and despise such paltry distinctions. Alas, sir!*" continued he, "*a man who cannot get to heaven in a green coat, will not find his way thither sooner in a grey one.*"

On an occasion of less consequence, when he turned his back on Lord Bolingbroke in the rooms at Brighthelmstone, he made this excuse, "*I am not obliged, sir,*" said he to Mr. Thrale, who stood fretting, "*to find reasons for respecting the rank of him who will not condescend to declare it by his dress or some other visible mark. What are stars and other signs of superiority made for?*" The next evening, however, he made us comical amends, by sitting by the same nobleman, and haranguing very loudly about the nature and use and abuse of divorces. Many people gathered round them to hear what was said, and when my husband called him away, and told him to whom he had been talking, received an answer which I will not write down. Though no man, perhaps, made such rough replies as Dr. Johnson, yet nobody had a more just aversion to general satire; he always hated and censured Swift for his unprovoked bitterness against the professors of medicine, and used to challenge his friends, when they lamented the exorbitancy of physicians' fees, to produce him one instance of an estate raised by physic in England.

When an acquaintance, too, was one day exclaiming against the tediousness of the law and its partiality: "*Let us hear, sir,*" said Johnson, "*no general abuse; the law is the last result of human wisdom acting upon human experience for the benefit of the public.*" As the mind of Dr. Johnson was greatly expanded, so his first care was for general, not particular or petty morality; and those teachers had more of his blame than praise, I think, who seek to oppress life with unnecessary scruples. "*Scruples would,*" as he observed, "*certainly make men miserable, and seldom make them good. Let us ever,*" he said, "*studiously fly from those instructors against whom our Saviour denounces heavy judgments, for having bound up burdens grievous to be borne, and laid them on the shoulders of mortal men."*

No one had, however, higher notions of the hard task of true Christianity than Johnson, whose daily terror lest he had not done enough, originated in piety, but ended in little less than disease. Reasonable with regard to others, he had formed vain hopes of performing impossibilities himself; and finding his good works ever below his desires and intent, filled his imagination with fears that he should never obtain forgiveness for omissions of duty and criminal waste of time. These ideas kept him in constant anxiety concerning his salvation; and the vehement petitions he perpetually made for a longer continuance on earth, were doubtless the cause of his so prolonged existence: for when I carried Dr. Pepys to him in the year 1782, it appeared wholly impossible for any skill of the physician or any strength of the patient to save him. He was saved that time, however, by Sir Lucas's prescriptions; and less skill on one side, or less strength on the other, I am morally certain, would not have been enough.

He had, however, possessed an athletic constitution, as he said the man who dipped people in the sea at Brighthelmstone acknowledged; for seeing Mr. Johnson swim, in the year 1766, "*Why, sir,*" says the dipper, "*you must have been a stout-hearted gentleman forty years ago.*" Mr. Thrale and he used to laugh about that story very often: but Garrick told a better, for he said that in their young days, when some strolling players came to Lichfield, our friend had fixed his place upon the stage, and got himself a chair accordingly; which leaving for a few minutes, he found a man in it at his return, who refused to give it back at the first entreaty. Mr. Johnson, however, who did not think it worth his while to make a second, took chair and man and all together, and threw them all at once into the pit. I asked the Doctor if this was a fact. "Garrick has not spoiled it in the telling," said he, "it is very near true, to be sure."

Mr. Beauclerc, too, related one day how on some occasion he ordered two large mastiffs into his parlour, to show a friend who was conversant in canine beauty and excellence how the dogs quarrelled, and fastening on each other, alarmed all the company except Johnson, who seizing one in one hand by the cuff of the neck, the other in the other hand, said gravely, "*Come, gentlemen! where's your difficulty? put one dog out at the door, and I will show this fierce gentleman the way out of the window:*" which, lifting up the mastiff and the sash, he contrived to do very expeditiously, and much to the satisfaction of the affrighted company. We inquired as to the truth of this curious recital. "*The dogs have been somewhat magnified, I believe, sir,*" was the reply: "*they were, as I remember, two stout young pointers; but the story has gained but little.*"

One reason why Mr. Johnson's memory was so particularly exact, might be derived from his rigid attention to veracity; being always resolved to relate every fact as it stood, he looked even on the smaller parts of life with minute attention, and remembered such passages as escape cursory and common observers. "*A story,*" says he, "*is a specimen of human manners, and derives its sole value from its truth. When Foote has told me something, I dismiss it from my mind like a passing shadow: when Reynolds tells me something, I consider myself as possessed of an idea the more.*" Mr. Johnson liked a frolic or a jest well enough, though he had strange serious rules about it too: and very angry was he if anybody offered to be merry when he was disposed to be grave. "*You have an ill-founded notion,*" said he, "*that it is clever to turn matters off with a joke (as the phrase is); whereas nothing produces enmity so certain as one persons showing a disposition to be merry when another is inclined to be either serious or displeased.*"

One may gather from this how he felt when his Irish friend Grierson, hearing him enumerate the qualities necessary to the formation of a poet, began a comical parody upon his ornamented harangue in praise of a cook, concluding with this observation, that he who dressed a good dinner was a more excellent and a more useful member of society than he who wrote a good poem. "*And in this opinion,*" said Mr. Johnson in reply, "*all the dogs in the town will join you.*" Of this Mr. Grierson I have heard him relate many droll stories, much to his advantage as a wit, together with some facts more difficult to be accounted for; as avarice never was reckoned among the vices of the laughing world. But Johnson's various life, and spirit of vigilance to learn and treasure up every peculiarity of manner, sentiment, or general conduct, made his company, when he chose to relate anecdotes of people he had formerly known, exquisitely amusing and comical. It is indeed inconceivable what strange occurrences he had seen, and what surprising things he could tell when in a communicative humour. It is by no means my business to relate memoirs of his acquaintance; but it will serve to show the character of Johnson himself, when I inform those who never knew him that no man told a story with so good a grace, or knew so well what would make an effect upon his auditors.

When he raised contributions for some distressed author, or wit in want, he often made us all more than amends by diverting descriptions of the lives they were then passing in corners unseen by anybody but himself; and that odd old surgeon whom he kept in his house to tend the out-pensioners, and of whom he said most truly and sublimely that—

"In misery's darkest caverns known,
His useful care was ever nigh,
Where hopeless anguish pours her groan,
And lonely want retires to die."

I have forgotten the year, but it could scarcely I think be later than 1765 or 1766, that he was called abruptly from our house after dinner, and returning in about three hours, said he had been with an enraged author, whose landlady pressed him for payment within doors, while the bailiffs beset him without; that he was drinking himself drunk with Madeira to drown care, and fretting over a novel which, when finished, was to be his whole fortune; but he could not get it done for distraction, nor could he step out of doors to offer it to sale. Mr. Johnson therefore set away the bottle, and went to the bookseller, recommending the performance, and desiring some immediate relief; which when he brought back to the writer, he called the woman of the house directly to partake of punch, and pass their time in merriment. It was not till ten years after,

I dare say, that something in Dr. Goldsmith's behaviour struck me with an idea that he was the very man, and then Johnson confessed it was so; the novel was the charming " Vicar of Wakefield."

There was a Mr. Boyce, too, who wrote some very elegant verses printed in the magazines of five-and-twenty years ago, of whose ingenuity and distress I have heard Dr. Johnson tell some curious anecdotes, particularly that when he was almost perishing with hunger, and some money was produced to purchase him a dinner, he got a piece of roast beef, but could not eat it without ketchup, and laid out the last half-guinea he possessed in truffles and mushrooms, eating them in bed, too, for want of clothes, or even a shirt to sit up in.

Another man, for whom he often begged, made as wild use of his friend's beneficence as these, spending in punch the solitary guinea which had been brought him one morning; when resolving to add another claimant to a share of the bowl, besides a woman who always lived with him, and a footman who used to carry out petitions for charity, he borrowed a chairman's watch, and pawning it for half-a-crown, paid a clergyman to marry him to a fellow-lodger in the wretched house they all inhabited, and got so drunk over the guinea bowl of punch the evening of his wedding-day, that having many years lost the use of one leg, he now contrived to fall from the top of the stairs to the bottom, and break his arm, in which condition his companions left him to call Mr. Johnson, who, relating the series of his tragi-comical distresses obtained from the Literary Club a seasonable relief

Of that respectable society I have heard him speak in the highest terms, and with a magnificent panegyric on each member, when it consisted only of a dozen or fourteen friends; but as soon as the necessity of enlarging it brought in new faces, and took off from his confidence in the company, he grew less fond of the meeting, and loudly proclaimed his carelessness Who might be admitted, when it was become a mere dinner club. I think the original names, when I first heard him talk with fervour of every member's peculiar powers of instructing or delighting mankind, were Sir John Hawkins, Mr.

Burke, Mr. Langton, Mr. Beauclerc, Dr. Percy, Dr. Nugent, Dr. Goldsmith, Sir Robert Chambers, Mr. Dyer, and Sir Joshua Reynolds, whom he called their Romulus, or said somebody else of the company called him so, which was more likely: but this was, I believe, in the year 1775 or 1776. It was a supper meeting then, and I fancy Dr. Nugent ordered an omelet sometimes on a Friday or Saturday night; for I remember Mr. Johnson felt very painful sensations at the sight of that dish soon after his death, and cried, "*Ah, my poor dear friend! I shall never eat omelet with thee again!*" quite in an agony.

The truth is, nobody suffered more from pungent sorrow at a friend's death than Johnson, though he would suffer no one else to complain of their losses in the same way; "*for,*" says he, "*we must either outlive our friends, you know, or our friends must outlive us; and I see no man that would hesitate about the choice.*" Mr. Johnson loved late hours extremely, or more properly hated early ones. Nothing was more terrifying to him than the idea of retiring to bed, which he never would call going to rest, or suffer another to call so. "*I lie down,*" said he, "*that my acquaintance may sleep; but I lie down to endure oppressive misery, and soon rise again to pass the night in anxiety and pain.*" By this pathetic manner, which no one ever possessed in so eminent a degree, he used to shock me from quitting his company, till I hurt my own health not a little by sitting up with him when I was myself far from well; nor was it an easy matter to oblige him even by compliance, for he always maintained that no one forbore their own gratifications for the sake of pleasing another, and if one did sit up it was probably to amuse oneself.

Some right, however, he certainly had to say so, as he made his company exceedingly entertaining when he had once forced one, by his vehement lamentations and piercing reproofs, not to quit the room, but to sit quietly and make tea for him, as I often did in London till four o'clock in the morning. At Streatham, indeed, I managed better, having always some friend who was kind enough to engage him in talk, and favour my retreat. The first time I ever saw this extraordinary man was in the year 1764, when Mr. Murphy, who had been long the friend and confidential intimate of Mr. Thrale, persuaded him to wish for Johnson's conversation, extolling it in terms which that of no other person could have deserved, till we were only in doubt how to obtain his company, and find an excuse for the invitation.

The celebrity of Mr. Woodhouse, a shoemaker, whose verses were at that time the subject of common discourse, soon afforded a pretence, and Mr. Murphy brought Johnson to meet him, giving me general cautions not to be surprised at his figure, dress, or behaviour. What I recollect best of the day's talk was his earnestly recommending Addison's works to Mr. Woodhouse as a model for imitation. *"Give nights and days, sir,"* said he, *"to the study of Addison, if you mean either to be a good writer, or what is more worth, an honest man."* When I saw something like the same expression in his criticism on that author, lately published, I put him in mind of his past injunctions to the young poet, to which he replied, *"that he wished the shoemaker might have remembered them as well."*

Mr. Johnson liked his new acquaintance so much, however, that, from that time he dined with us every Thursday through the winter, and in the autumn of the next year he followed us to Brighthelmstone, whence we were gone before his arrival; so he was disappointed and enraged, and wrote us a letter expressive of anger, which we were very desirous to pacify, and to obtain his company again, if possible. Mr. Murphy brought him back to us again very kindly, and from that time his visits grew more frequent, till in the year 1766 his health, which he had always complained of, grew so exceedingly bad, that he could not stir out of his room in the court he inhabited for many weeks together- -I think months.

Mr. Thrale's attentions and my own now became so acceptable to him, that he often lamented to us the horrible condition of his mind, which he said was nearly distracted; and though he charged us to make him odd solemn promises of secrecy on so strange a subject, yet when we waited on him one morning, and heard him, in the most pathetic terms, beg the prayers of Dr. Delap, who had left him as we came in, I felt excessively affected with grief, and well remember my husband involuntarily lifted up one hand to shut his mouth, from provocation at hearing a man so wildly proclaim what he could at last persuade no one to believe, and what, if true, would have been so very unfit to reveal.

Mr. Thrale went away soon after, leaving me with him, and bidding me prevail on him to quit his close habitation in the court and come with us to Streatham, where I undertook the care of his health, and had the honour and happiness of contributing to its restoration. This task, though distressing enough sometimes, would have been less so had not my mother and he disliked one another extremely, and teased me often with perverse opposition, petty contentions, and mutual complaints. Her superfluous attention to such accounts of the foreign politics as are transmitted to us by the daily prints, and her willingness to talk on subjects he could not endure, began the aversion; and when, by the peculiarity of his style, she found out that he teased her by writing in the newspapers concerning battles and plots which had no existence, only to feed her with new accounts of the division of Poland, perhaps, or the disputes between the States of Russia and Turkey, she was exceedingly angry, to be sure, and scarcely, I think, forgave the offence till the domestic distresses of the year 1772 reconciled them to and taught them the true value of each other, excellent as they both were, far beyond the excellence of any other man and woman I ever yet saw.

As her conduct, too, extorted his truest esteem, her cruel illness excited all his tenderness, nor was the sight of beauty, scarce to be subdued by disease, and wit, flashing through the apprehension of evil, a scene which Dr. Johnson could see without sensibility. He acknowledged himself improved by her piety, and astonished at her fortitude, and hung over her bed with the affection of a parent, and the reverence of a son. Nor did it give me less pleasure to see her sweet mind cleared of all its latent prejudices, and left at liberty to admire and applaud that force of thought and versatility of genius, that comprehensive soul and benevolent heart, which attracted and commanded veneration from all, but inspired peculiar sensations of delight mixed with reverence in those who, like her, had the opportunity to observe these qualities stimulated by gratitude, and actuated by friendship.

When Mr. Thrale's perplexities disturbed his peace, dear Dr. Johnson left him scarce a moment, and tried every artifice to amuse as well as every argument to console him: nor is it more possible to describe than to forget his prudent, his pious attentions towards the man who had some years before certainly saved his valuable life, perhaps his reason, by half obliging him to change the foul air of Fleet Street for the wholesome breezes of the Sussex Downs.

The epitaph engraved on my mother's monument shows how deserving she was of general applause. I asked Johnson why he named her person before her mind. He said it was *"because everybody could judge of the one, and but few of the other."* Juxta sepulta est HESTERA MARIA Thomae Cotton de Combermere baronetti Cestriensis filia, Johannis Salusbury armigeri Flintiensis uxor. Forma felix, felix ingenio: Omnibus jucunda, suorum amantissima. Linguis artibusque ita exculta Ut loquenti nunquam deessent Sermonis nitor, sententiarum flosculi, Sapientiae gravitas, leporum gratia: Modum servandi adeo perita, Ut domestica inter negotia literis oblectaretur. Literarum inter delicias, rem familiarem sedulo curaret, Multis illi multos annos precantibus diri carcinomatis veneno contabuit, nexibusque vitae paulatim resolutis, e terris—meliora sperans—emigravit. Nata 1707. Nupta 1739. Obiit 1773.

Mr. Murphy, who admired her talents and delighted in her company, did me the favour to paraphrase this elegant inscription in verses which I fancy have never yet been published. His fame has long been out of my power to increase as a poet: as a man of sensibility perhaps these lines may set him higher than he now stands. I remember with gratitude the friendly tears which prevented him from speaking as he put them into my hand. Near this place Are deposited the remains of HESTER MARIA, The daughter of Sir Thomas Cotton of Combermere, in the county of Cheshire, Bart., the wife of John Salusbury, of the county of Flint, Esquire. She was born in the year 1707, married in 1739, and died in 1773.

A pleasing form, where every grace combined,
With genius blest, a pure enlightened mind;
Benevolence on all that smiles bestowed,
A heart that for her friends with love o'erflowed:
In language skilled, by science formed to please,
Her mirth was wit, her gravity was ease.
Graceful in all, the happy mien she knew,
Which even to virtue gives the limits due;
Whate'er employed her, that she seemed to choose,
Her house, her friends, her business, or the muse.
Admired and loved, the theme of general praise,
All to such virtue wished a length of days.
But sad reverse! with slow-consuming pains,
Th' envenomed cancer revelled in her veins;
Preyed on her spirits—stole each power away;
Gradual she sank, yet smiling in decay;
She smiled in hope, by sore affliction tried,
And in that hope the pious Christian died.

The following epitaph on Mr. Thrale, who has now a monument close by hers in Streatham Church, I have seen printed and commended in Maty's Review for April, 1784; and a friend has favoured me with the translation:—

Hic conditur quod reliquum est HENRICI THRALE, Qui res seu civiles, seu domesticas, ita egit, Ut vitam illi longiorem multi optarent; Ita sacras, Ut quam brevem esset habiturus praescire videretur. Simplex, apertus, sibique semper similis, Nihil ostentavit aut arte fictum aut cura Elaboratum. In senatu, regi patriaeque Fideliter studuit; Vulgi obstrepentis contemptor animosus, Domi inter mille mercaturae negotia Literarum elegantiam minime neglexit.

Amicis quocunque modo laborantibus, Conciliis, auctoritate, muneribus adfuit. Inter familiares, comites, convivas, hospites, Tam facili fuit morum suavitate Ut omnium animos ad se alliceret; Tam felici sermonis libertate Ut nulli adulatus, omnibus placeret. Natus 1724. Ob. 1781. Consortes tumuli habet Rodolphum patrem, strenuum fortemque virum, et Henricum filium unicum, quem spei parentum mors inopina decennem praeripuit. Ita Domus felix et opulenta, quam erexit

Avus, auxitque pater, cum nepote decidit. Abi viator! Et vicibus rerum humanarum perspectis, AEternitatem cogita!

Here are deposited the remains of HENRY THRALE, Who managed all his concerns in the present world, public and private, in such a manner as to leave many wishing he had continued longer in it; And all that related to a future world, as if he had been sensible how short a time he was to continue in this. Simple, open, and uniform in his manners, his conduct was without either art or affectation. In the senate steadily attentive to the true interests of his king and country, He looked down with contempt on the clamours of the multitude: Though engaged in a very extensive business, He found some time to apply to polite literature And was ever ready to assist his friends labouring under any difficulties, with his advice, his influence, and his purse. To his friends, acquaintance, and guests, he behaved with such sweetness of manners as to attach them all to his person: So happy in his conversation with them, as to please all, though he flattered none. He was born in the year 1724, and died in 1781. In the same tomb lie interred his father, Ralph Thrale, a man of vigour and activity, And his only son Henry, who died before his father, Aged ten years. Thus a happy and opulent family, Raised by the grandfather, and augmented by the father, became extinguished with the grandson. Go, Reader! And reflecting on the vicissitudes of all human affairs, Meditate on eternity.

I never recollect to have heard that Dr. Johnson wrote inscriptions for any sepulchral stones except Dr. Goldsmith's, in Westminster Abbey, and these two in Streatham Church. He made four lines once on the death of poor Hogarth, which were equally true and pleasing. I know not why Garrick's were preferred to them. "*The hand of him here torpid lies, That drew th' essential form of grace; Here clos'd in death th' attentive eyes, That saw the manners in the face.*" Mr. Hogarth, among the variety of kindnesses shown to me when I was too young to have a proper sense of them, was used to be very earnest that I should obtain the acquaintance, and if possible the friendship, of Dr. Johnson, whose conversation was, to the talk of other men, "*like Titian's painting compared to Hudson's,*" he said: "*but don't you tell people, now, that I say so,"* continued he, *"for the connoisseurs and I are at war, you know; and because I hate them, they think I hate Titian—and let them!"*

Many were indeed the lectures I used to have in my very early days from dear Mr. Hogarth, whose regard for my father induced him, perhaps, to take notice of his little girl, and give her some odd particular directions about dress, dancing, and many other matters, interesting now only because they were his. As he made all his talents, however, subservient to the great purposes of morality, and the earnest desire he had to mend mankind, his discourse commonly ended in an ethical dissertation, and a serious charge to me, never to forget his picture of the "Lady's Last Stake."

Of Dr. Johnson, when my father and he were talking together about him one day, *"That man,"* says Hogarth, *"is not contented with believing the Bible, but he fairly resolves, I think, to believe nothing but the Bible. Johnson,"* added he, *"though so wise a fellow, is more like King David than King Solomon; for he says in his haste that 'all men are liars.'"* This charge, as I afterwards came to know, was but too well founded.

Mr. Johnson's incredulity amounted almost to disease, and I have seen it mortify his companions exceedingly. But the truth is, Mr. Thrale had a very powerful influence over the Doctor, and could make him suppress many rough answers. He could likewise prevail on him to change his shirt, his coat, or his plate, almost before it came indispensably necessary to the comfort of his friends. But as I never had any ascendency at all over Mr. Johnson, except just in the things that concerned his health, it grew extremely perplexing and difficult to live in the house with him when the master of it was no more; the worse, indeed, because his dislikes grew capricious; and he could scarce bear to have anybody come to the house whom it was absolutely necessary for me to see.

Two gentlemen, I perfectly well remember, dining with us at Streatham in the summer, 1782, when Elliot's brave defence of Gibraltar was a subject of common discourse, one of these men naturally enough began some talk about red-hot balls thrown with surprising dexterity and effect, which Dr.

Johnson having listened some time to, *"I would advise you, sir,"* said he, with a cold sneer, *"never to relate this story again; you really can scarce imagine how very poor a figure you make in the telling of it."* Our guest being bred a Quaker, and, I believe, a man of an extremely gentle disposition, needed no more reproofs for the same folly; so if he ever did speak again, it was in a low voice to the friend who came with him. The check was given before dinner, and after coffee I left the room. When in the evening, however, our companions were returned to London, and Mr. Johnson and myself were left alone, with only our usual family about us, *"I did not quarrel with those Quaker fellows,"* said he, very seriously. *"You did perfectly right,"* replied I, *"for they gave you no cause of offence." "No offence!"* returned he, with an altered voice; *"and is it nothing, then, to sit whispering together when _I_ am present, without ever directing their discourse towards me, or offering me a share in the conversation?" "That was because you frighted him who spoke first about those hot balls." "Why, madam, if a creature is neither capable of giving dignity to falsehood, nor willing to remain contented with the truth, he deserves no better treatment."*

Mr. Johnson's fixed incredulity of everything he heard, and his little care to conceal that incredulity, was teasing enough, to be sure; and I saw Mr. Sharp was pained exceedingly when relating the history of a hurricane that happened about that time in the West Indies, where, for aught I know, he had himself lost some friends too, he observed Dr. Johnson believed not a syllable of the account. *"For 'tis so easy,"* says he, *"for a man to fill his mouth with a wonder, and run about telling the lie before it can be detected, that I have no heart to believe hurricanes easily raised by the first inventor, and blown forwards by thousands more."* I asked him once if he believed the story of the destruction of Lisbon by an earthquake when it first happened. *"Oh! not for six months,"* said he, *"at least. I did think that story too dreadful to be credited, and can hardly yet persuade myself that it was true to the full extent we all of us have heard."*

Among the numberless people, however, whom I heard him grossly and flatly contradict, I never yet saw any one who did not take it patiently excepting Dr. Burney, from whose habitual softness of manners I little expected such an exertion of spirit; the event was as little to be expected. Mr. Johnson asked his pardon generously and genteelly, and when he left the room, rose up to shake hands with him, that they might part in peace. On another occasion, when he had violently provoked Mr. Pepys, in a different but perhaps not a less offensive manner, till something much too like a quarrel was grown up between them, the moment he was gone, "*Now,*" says Dr. Johnson, "*is Pepys gone home hating me, who love him better than I did before. He spoke in defence of his dead friend; but though I hope _I_ spoke better who spoke against him, yet all my eloquence will gain me nothing but an honest man for my enemy!*" He did not, however, cordially love Mr. Pepys, though he respected his abilities. "*I know the dog was a scholar,*" said he when they had been disputing about the classics for three hours together one morning at Streatham, "*but that he had so much taste and so much knowledge I did not believe. I might have taken Barnard's word though, for Barnard would not lie.*"

We had got a little French print among us at Brighthelmstone, in November, 1782, of some people skating, with these lines written under:—

"Sur un mince chrystal l'hyver conduit leurs pas,
Le precipice est sous la glace;
Telle est de nos plaisirs la legere surface,
Glissez mortels; n'appayez pas."

And I begged translation from everybody. Dr. Johnson gave me this:—

"O'er ice the rapid skater flies,
With sport above and death below;
Where mischief lurks in gay disguise,
Thus lightly touch and quickly go."

He was, however, most exceedingly enraged when he knew that in the course of the season I had asked half-a-dozen acquaintance to do the same thing; and said, "*it was a piece of treachery, and done to make everybody else look little when compared to my favourite friends the Pepyses, whose translations were unquestionably the best.*" I will insert them, because he did say so. This is the distich given me by Sir Lucas, to whom I owe more solid obligations, no less than the power of thanking him for the life he saved, and whose least valuable praise is the correctness of his taste:—

"O'er the ice as o'er pleasure you lightly should glide,
Both have gulfs which their flattering surfaces hide."

This other more serious one was written by his brother:—

"Swift o'er the level how the skaters slide,
And skim the glitt'ring surface as they go:
Thus o'er life's specious pleasures lightly glide,
But pause not, press not on the gulf below."

Dr. Johnson seeing this last, and thinking a moment, repeated:—

"O'er crackling ice, o'er gulfs profound,
With nimble glide the skaters play;
O'er treacherous pleasure's flow'ry ground
Thus lightly skim, and haste away."

Though thus uncommonly ready both to give and take offence, Mr. Johnson had many rigid maxims concerning the necessity of continued softness and compliance of disposition: and when I once mentioned Shenstone's idea that some little quarrel among lovers, relations, and friends was useful, and contributed to their general happiness upon the whole, by making the soul feel her elastic force, and return to the beloved object with renewed delight: "*Why, what a pernicious maxim is this now,*" cries Johnson, "*All quarrels ought to be avoided studiously, particularly conjugal ones, as no one can possibly tell where they may end; besides that lasting dislike is often the consequence of occasional disgust, and that the cup of life is surely bitter enough without squeezing in the hateful rind of resentment.*"

It was upon something like the same principle, and from his general hatred of refinement, that when I told him how Dr. Collier, in order to keep the servants in humour with his favourite dog, by seeming rough with the animal himself on many occasions, and crying out, "*Why will nobody knock this cur's brains out?*" meant to conciliate their tenderness towards Pompey; he returned me for answer, "*that the maxim was evidently false, and founded on ignorance of human life: that the servants would kick the dog sooner for having obtained such a sanction to their severity. And I once,"* added he, *"chid my wife for beating the cat before the maid, who will now,"* said I, *"treat puss with cruelty, perhaps, and plead her mistress's example."*

I asked him upon this if he ever disputed with his wife? (I had heard that he loved her passionately.) *"Perpetually,"* said he: *"my wife had a particular reverence for cleanliness, and desired the praise of neatness in her dress and furniture, as many ladies do, till they become troublesome to their best friends, slaves to their own besoms, and only sigh for the hour of sweeping their husbands out of the house as dirt and useless lumber. 'A clean floor is so comfortable,' she would say sometimes, by way of twitting; till at last I told her that I thought we had had talk enough about the floor, we would now have a touch at the ceiling."*

On another occasion I have heard him blame her for a fault many people have, of setting the miseries of their neighbours half unintentionally, half wantonly before their eyes, showing them the bad side of their profession, situation, etc. He said, *"She would lament the dependence of pupilage to a young heir, etc., and once told a waterman who rowed her along the Thames in a wherry, that he was no happier than a galley-slave, one being chained to the oar by authority, the other by want. I had, however,"* said he, laughing, *"the wit to get her daughter on my side always before we began the dispute. She read comedy better than anybody he ever heard,"* he said; *"in tragedy she mouthed too much."* Garrick told Mr. Thrale, however, that she was a little painted puppet, of no value at all, and quite disguised with affectation, full of odd airs of rural elegance; and he made out some comical scenes, by mimicking her in a dialogue he pretended to have overheard. I do not know whether he meant such stuff to be believed or no, it was so comical; nor did I indeed ever see him represent her ridiculously, though my husband did.

The intelligence I gained of her from old Levett was only perpetual illness and perpetual opium. The picture I found of her at Lichfield was very pretty, and her daughter, Mrs. Lucy Porter, said it was like. Mr. Johnson has told me that her hair was eminently beautiful, quite blonde, like that of a baby; but that she fretted about the colour, and was always desirous to dye it black, which he very judiciously hindered her from doing. His account of their wedding we used to think ludicrous enough. "*I was riding to church,*" says Johnson, "*and she following on another single horse. She hung back, however, and I turned about to see whether she could get her steed along, or what was the matter. I had, however, soon occasion to see it was only coquetry, and that I despised, so quickening my pace a little, she mended hers; but I believe there was a tear or two—pretty dear creature!*"

Johnson loved his dinner exceedingly, and has often said in my hearing, perhaps for my edification, "*that wherever the dinner is ill got there is poverty or there is avarice, or there is stupidity; in short, the family is somehow grossly wrong: for,*" continued he, "*a man seldom thinks with more earnestness of anything than he does of his dinner, and if he cannot get that well dressed, he should be suspected of inaccuracy in other things.*" One day, when he was speaking upon the subject, I asked him if he ever huffed his wife about his dinner? "*So often,*" replied he, "*that at last she called to me, and said, 'Nay, hold, Mr. Johnson, and do not make a farce of thanking God for a dinner which in a few minutes you will protest not eatable.'*"

When any disputes arose between our married acquaintance, however, Mr. Johnson always sided with the husband, "*whom,*" he said, "*the woman had probably provoked so often, she scarce knew when or how she had disobliged him first. Women,*" says Dr. Johnson, "*give great offence by a contemptuous spirit of non-compliance on petty occasions. The man calls his wife to walk with him in the shade, and she feels a strange desire just at that moment to sit in the sun: he offers to read her a play, or sing her a song, and she calls the children in to disturb them, or advises him to seize that opportunity of settling the family accounts. Twenty such tricks will the faithfullest wife in the world not refuse to play, and then look astonished when the fellow fetches in a mistress.*

Boarding-schools were established," continued he, "*for the conjugal quiet of the parents. The two partners cannot agree which child to fondle, nor how to fondle them, so they put the young ones to school, and remove the cause of contention. The little girl pokes her head, the mother reproves her sharply. 'Do not mind your mamma,' says the father, 'my dear, but do your own way.' The mother complains to me of this. 'Madam,' said I, 'your husband is right all the while; he is with you but two hours of the day, perhaps, and then you tease him by making the child cry. Are not ten hours enough for tuition? and are the hours of pleasure so frequent in life, that when a man gets a couple of quiet ones to spend in familiar chat with his wife, they must be poisoned by petty mortifications? Put missy to school; she will learn to hold her head like her neighbours, and you will no longer torment your family for want of other talk.'"*.

The vacuity of life had at some early period of his life struck so forcibly on the mind of Mr. Johnson, that it became by repeated impression his favourite hypothesis, and the general tenor of his reasonings commonly ended there, wherever they might begin. Such things, therefore, as other philosophers often attribute to various and contradictory causes, appeared to him uniform enough; all was done to fill up the time, upon his principle. I used to tell him that it was like the clown's answer in As You Like It, of "*Oh, lord, sir!*" for that it suited every occasion. One man, for example, was profligate and wild, as we call it, followed the girls, or sat still at the gaming-table. "*Why, life must be filled up,*" says Johnson, "*and the man who is not capable of intellectual pleasures must content himself with such as his senses can afford.*" Another was a hoarder. "*Why, a fellow must do something; and what, so easy to a narrow mind as hoarding halfpence till they turn into sixpences.*"

Avarice was a vice against which, however, I never much heard Mr. Johnson declaim, till one represented it to him connected with cruelty, or some such disgraceful companion. "*Do not,*" said he, "*discourage your children from hoarding if they have a taste to it: whoever lays up his penny rather than part with it for a cake, at least is not the slave of gross appetite, and shows besides a preference always to be esteemed, of the future to the present moment. Such a mind may be made a good one; but the natural spendthrift, who grasps his pleasures greedily and coarsely, and cares for nothing but immediate indulgence, is very little to be valued above a negro.*"

We talked of Lady Tavistock, who grieved herself to death for the loss of her husband—"*She was rich, and wanted employment,*" says Johnson, "*so she cried till she lost all power of restraining her tears: other women are forced to outlive their husbands, who were just as much beloved, depend on it; but they have no time for grief: and I doubt not, if we had put my Lady Tavistock into a small chandler's shop, and given her a nurse-child to tend, her life would have been saved. The poor and the busy have no leisure for sentimental sorrow."*

We were speaking of a gentleman who loved his friend—"*Make him Prime Minister,*" says Johnson, "*and see how long his friend will be remembered.*"

But he had a rougher answer for me, when I commended a sermon preached by an intimate acquaintance of our own at the trading end of the town. "*What was the subject, madam?*" says Dr. Johnson. "*Friendship, sir,*" replied I. "*Why, now, is it not strange that a wise man, like our dear little Evans, should take it in his head to preach on such a subject, in a place where no one can be thinking of it?*" "*Why, what are they thinking upon, sir?*" said I. "*Why, the men are thinking on their money, I suppose, and the women are thinking of their mops.*"

Dr. Johnson's knowledge and esteem of what we call low or coarse life was indeed prodigious; and he did not like that the upper ranks should be dignified with the name of the world. Sir Joshua Reynolds said one day that nobody wore laced coats now; and that once everybody wore them. "*See, now,*" says Johnson, "*how absurd that is; as if the bulk of mankind consisted of fine gentlemen that came to him to sit for their pictures. If every man who wears a laced coat (that he can pay for) was extirpated, who would miss them?*"

With all this haughty contempt of gentility, no praise was more welcome to Dr. Johnson than that which said he had the notions or manners of a gentleman: which character I have heard him define with accuracy, and describe with elegance. "*Officers,*" he said, "*were falsely supposed to have the carriage of gentlemen; whereas no profession left a stronger brand behind it than that of a soldier; and it was the essence of a gentleman's character to bear the visible mark of no profession whatever.*" He once named Mr. Berenger as the standard of true elegance; but some one objecting that he too much resembled the gentleman in Congreve's comedies, Mr. Johnson said, "*We must fix them upon the famous Thomas Hervey, whose manners were polished even to acuteness and brilliancy, though he lost but little in solid power of reasoning, and in genuine force of mind."*

Mr. Johnson had, however, an avowed and scarcely limited partiality for all who bore the name or boasted the alliance of an Aston or a Hervey; and when Mr. Thrale once asked him which had been the happiest period of his past life? he replied, *"It was that year in which he spent one whole evening with Molly Aston. That, indeed,"* said he, *"was not happiness, it was rapture; but the thoughts of it sweetened the whole year."* I must add that the evening alluded to was not passed tete-a-tete, but in a select company, of which the present Lord Killmorey was one. *"Molly,"* says Dr. Johnson, *"was a beauty and a scholar, and a wit and a Whig; and she talked all in praise of liberty: and so I made this epigram upon her. She was the loveliest creature I ever saw!!!*

"'Liber ut esse velim, suasisti pulchra Maria,
Ut maneam liber— pulchra Maria, vale!'"

"Will it do this way in English, sir?" said I.

*"Persuasions to freedom fall oddly from you;
If freedom we seek—fair Maria, adieu!"*

"It will do well enough," replied he, *"but it is translated by a lady, and the ladies never loved Molly Aston."* I asked him what his wife thought of this attachment? *"She was jealous, to be sure,"* said he, *"and teased me sometimes when I would let her; and one day, as a fortune-telling gipsy passed us when we were walking out in company with two or three friends in the country, she made the wench look at my hand, but soon repented her curiosity; 'for,' says the gipsy, 'your heart is divided, sir, between a Betty and a Molly: Betty loves you best, but you take most delight in Molly's company.' When I turned about to laugh, I saw my wife was crying. Pretty charmer! she had no reason!"*

It was, I believe, long after the currents of life had driven him to a great distance from this lady, that he spent much of his time with Mrs. F-tzh—b—t, of whom he always spoke with esteem and tenderness, and with a veneration very difficult to deserve. *"That woman,"* said he, *"loved her husband as we hope and desire to be loved by our guardian angel. F-tzh—b- -t was a gay, good-humoured fellow, generous of his money and of his meat, and desirous of nothing but cheerful society among people distinguished in some way, in any way, I think; for Rousseau and St. Austin would have been equally welcome to his table and to his kindness.*

The lady, however, was of another way of thinking: her first care was to preserve her husband's soul from corruption; her second, to keep his estate entire for their children: and I owed my good reception in the family to the idea she had entertained, that I was fit company for F-tzh—b—t, whom I loved extremely. 'They dare not,' said she, 'swear, and take other conversation-liberties before you.'" I asked if her husband returned her regard? "*He felt her influence too powerfully,*" replied Mr. Johnson; "*no man will be fond of what forces him daily to feel himself inferior. She stood at the door of her paradise in Derbyshire, like the angel with a flaming sword, to keep the devil at a distance. But she was not immortal, poor dear! she died, and her husband felt at once afflicted and released.*" I inquired if she was handsome? "*She would have been handsome for a queen,*" replied the panegyrist; "*her beauty had more in it of majesty than of attraction, more of the dignity of virtue than the vivacity of wit.*"

The friend of this lady, Miss B—thby, succeeded her in the management of Mr. F-tzh—b—t's family, and in the esteem of Dr. Johnson, though he told me she pushed her piety to bigotry, her devotion to enthusiasm, that she somewhat disqualified herself for the duties of this life, by her perpetual aspirations after the next. Such was, however, the purity of her mind, he said, and such the graces of her manner, that Lord Lyttelton and he used to strive for her preference with an emulation that occasioned hourly disgust, and ended in lasting animosity. "*You may see,*" said he to me, when the "Poets' Lives" were printed, "*that dear B—thby is at my heart still. She would delight in that fellow Lyttelton's company though, all that I could do; and I cannot forgive even his memory the preference given by a mind like hers.*" I have heard Baretti say that when this lady died, Dr. Johnson was almost distracted with his grief, and that the friends about him had much ado to calm the violence of his emotion.

Dr. Taylor, too, related once to Mr. Thrale and me, that

when he lost his wife, the negro Francis ran away, though in the middle of the night, to Westminster, to fetch Dr. Taylor to his master, who was all but wild with excess of sorrow, and scarce knew him when he arrived. After some minutes, however, the Doctor proposed their going to prayers, as the only rational method of calming the disorder this misfortune had occasioned in both their spirits. Time, and resignation to the will of God, cured every breach in his heart before I made acquaintance with him, though he always persisted in saying he never rightly recovered the loss of his wife. It is in allusion to her that he records the observation of a female critic, as he calls her, in Gray's "Life;" and the lady of great beauty and elegance, mentioned in the criticisms upon Pope's epitaphs, was Miss Molly Aston. The person spoken of in his strictures upon Young's poetry is the writer of these anecdotes, to whom he likewise addressed the following verses when he was in the Isle of Skye with Mr. Boswell.

The letters written in his journey, I used to tell him, were better than the printed book; and he was not displeased at my having taken the pains to copy them all over. Here is the Latin ode:—

"Permeo terras, ubi nuda rupes
Saxeas miscet nebulis ruinas,
Torva ubi rident steriles coloni Rura labores.
"Pervagor gentes, hominum ferorum
Vita ubi nullo decorata cultu,
Squallet informis, tigurique fumis Faeda latescit.
"Inter erroris salebrosa longi,
Inter ignotae strepitus loquelae,
Quot modis mecum, quid agat requiro Thralia dulcis?
"Seu viri curas pia nupta mulcet,
Seu fovet mater sobolem benigna,
Sive cum libris novitate pascit Sedula mentem:
"Sit memor nostri, fideique merces,
Stet fides constans, meritoque blandum
Thraliae discant resonare nomen Littora Skiae."

On another occasion I can boast verses from Dr. Johnson. As I went into his room the morning of my birthday once, and said to him, *"Nobody sends me any verses now, because I am five-and-thirty years old, and Stella was fed with them till forty-six, I remember."* My being just recovered from illness and confinement will account for the manner in which he burst out, suddenly, for so he did without the least previous hesitation whatsoever, and without having entertained the smallest intention towards it half a minute before:

"Oft in danger, yet alive, We are come to thirty-five;
Long may better years arrive, Better years than thirty-five.
Could philosophers contrive Life to stop at thirty-five,
Time his hours should never drive O'er the bounds of thirty-five.
High to soar, and deep to dive, Nature gives at thirty-five.
Ladies, stock and tend your hive, Trifle not at thirty-five:
For howe'er we boast and strive, Life declines from thirty-five.
He that ever hopes to thrive Must begin by thirty-five;
And all who wisely wish to wive Must look on Thrale at thirty-five."

"And now," said he, as I was writing them down, *"you may see what it is to come for poetry to a dictionary-maker; you may observe that the rhymes run in alphabetical order exactly."* And so they do. Mr. Johnson did indeed possess an almost Tuscan power of improvisation. When he called to my daughter, who was consulting with a friend about a new gown and dressed hat she thought of wearing to an assembly, thus suddenly, while she hoped he was not listening to their conversation—

"Wear the gown and wear the hat,
Snatch thy pleasures while they last;
Hadst thou nine lives like a cat,
Soon those nine lives would be past."

It is impossible to deny to such little sallies the power of the Florentines, who do not permit their verses to be ever written down, though they often deserve it, because, as they express it, Cosi se perde-rebbe la poca gloria.

As for translations, we used to make him sometimes run off with one or two in a good humour. He was praising this song of Metastasio:—

"Deh, se piacermi vuoi,

Lascia i sospetti tuoi,
Non mi turbar conquesto
Molesto dubitar:
Chi ciecamente crede,
Impegna a serbar fede:
Chi sempre inganno aspetta,
Alletta ad ingannar."
"Should you like it in English," said he, "thus?"
"Would you hope to gain my heart,
Bid your teasing doubts depart;
He who blindly trusts,
will find Faith from every generous mind:
He who still expects deceit,
Only teaches how to cheat."

Mr. Baretti coaxed him likewise one day at Streatham out of a translation of Emirena's speech to the false courtier Aquileius, and it is probably printed before now, as I think two or three people took copies; but perhaps it has slipped their memories.

"Ah! tu in corte invecchiasti, e giurerei Che fra i pochi non sei tenace ancora Dell' antica onesta: quando bisogna,Saprai sereno in volto Vezzeggiare un nemico: accio vi cada, Aprirgli innanzi un precipizio, e poi Piangerne la caduta. Offrirti a tutti E non esser che tuo; di false lodi Vestir le accuse, ed aggravar le colpe Nel farne la difesa, ognor dal trono I buoni allontanar; d'ogni castigo Lasciar Vodio allo seettro, c d'ogni dono Il merito usurpar: tener nascosto Sotto un zelo apparente un empio fine, Ne fabbricar che sulle altrui rouine."

"Grown old in courts, thou art not surely one
Who keeps the rigid rules of ancient honour;
Well skilled to soothe a foe with looks of kindness,
To sink the fatal precipice before him,
And then lament his fall with seeming friendship:
Open to all, true only to thyself,
Thou know'st those arts which blast with envious praise,
Which aggravate a fault with feigned excuses,
And drive discountenanced virtue from the throne;
That leave blame of rigour to the prince,

And of his every gift usurp the merit;
That hide in seeming zeal a wicked purpose,
And only build upon another's ruin."

These characters Dr. Johnson, however, did not delight in reading, or in hearing of: he always maintained that the world was not half so wicked as it was represented; and he might very well continue in that opinion, as he resolutely drove from him every story that could make him change it; and when Mr. Bickerstaff's flight confirmed the report of his guilt, and my husband said, in answer to Johnson's astonishment, that he had long been a suspected man: "*By those who look close to the ground, dirt will be seen, sir,*" was the lofty reply. "*I hope I see things from a greater distance.*"

His desire to go abroad, particularly to see Italy, was very great; and he had a longing wish, too, to leave some Latin verses at the Grand Chartreux. He loved, indeed, the very act of travelling, and I cannot tell how far one might have taken him in a carriage before he would have wished for refreshment. He was therefore in some respects an admirable companion on the road, as he piqued himself upon feeling no inconvenience, and on despising no accommodations. On the other hand, however, he expected no one else to feel any, and felt exceedingly inflamed with anger if any one complained of the rain, the sun, or the dust. "*How,*" said he, "*do other people bear them?*" As for general uneasiness, or complaints of lone confinement in a carriage, he considered all lamentations on their account as proofs of an empty head, and a tongue desirous to talk without materials of conversation. "*A mill that goes without grist,*" said he, "*is as good a companion as such creatures.*"

I pitied a friend before him, who had a whining wife that found everything painful to her, and nothing pleasing. "*He does not know that she whimpers,*" says Johnson; "*when a door has creaked for a fortnight together, you may observe—the master will scarcely give sixpence to get it oiled.*" Of another lady, more insipid than offensive, I once heard him say, "*She has some softness indeed, but so has a pillow.*" And when one observed, in reply, that her husband's fidelity and attachment were exemplary, notwithstanding this low account at which her perfections were rated—"*Why, sir,*" cries the Doctor, "*being married to those sleepy-souled women is just like playing at cards for nothing: no passion is excited, and the time is filled up. I do not, however, envy a fellow one of those honeysuckle wives for my part, as they are but creepers at best, and commonly destroy the tree they so tenderly cling about.*"

For a lady of quality, since dead, who received us at her husband's seat in Wales with less attention than he had long been accustomed to, he had a rougher denunciation. "*That woman,*" cries Johnson, "*is like sour small-beer, the beverage of her table, and produce of the wretched country she lives in: like that, she could never have been a good thing, and even that bad thing is spoiled.*" This was in the same vein of asperity, and I believe with something like the same provocation, that he observed of a Scotch lady, "*that she resembled a dead nettle; were she alive,*" said he, "*she would sting.*"

Mr. Johnson's hatred of the Scotch is so well known, and so many of his bons mots expressive of that hatred have been already repeated in so many books and pamphlets, that 'tis perhaps scarcely worth while to write down the conversation between him and a friend of that nation who always resides in London, and who at his return from the Hebrides asked him, with a firm tone of voice, "*What he thought of his country?*" "*That it is a very vile country, to be sure, sir,*" returned for answer Dr. Johnson. "*Well, sir!*" replies the other, somewhat mortified, "*God made it.*" "*Certainly He did,*" answers Mr. Johnson again, "*but we must always remember that He made it for Scotchmen, and comparisons are odious, Mr. S——; but God made hell.*"

Dr. Johnson did not, I think, much delight in that kind of conversation which consists in telling stories. "*Everybody,*" said he, "*tells stories of me, and I tell stories of nobody. I do not recollect,*" added he, "*that I have ever told you, that have been always favourites, above three stories; but I hope I do not play the Old Fool, and force people to hear uninteresting narratives, only because I once was diverted with them myself.*" He was, however, no enemy to that sort of talk from the famous Mr. Foote, "*whose happiness of manner in relating was such,*" he said, "*as subdued arrogance and roused stupidity. His stories were truly like those of Biron in Love's Labour's Lost, so very attractive— 'That aged ears played truant with his tales, And younger hearings were quite ravished, So sweet and voluble was his discourse.'*

Of all conversers, however," added he, "*the late Hawkins Browne was the most delightful with whom I ever was in company: his talk was at once so elegant, so apparently artless, so pure, so pleasing, it seemed a perpetual stream of sentiment, enlivened by gaiety, and sparkling with images.*" When I asked Dr. Johnson who was the best man he had ever known? "*Psalmanazar,*" was the unexpected reply.

He said, likewise, "*that though a native of France, as his friend imagined, he possessed more of the English language than any one of the other foreigners who had separately fallen in his way.*" Though there was much esteem, however, there was, I believe, but little confidence between them; they conversed merely about general topics, religion and learning, of which both were undoubtedly stupendous examples; and, with regard to true Christian perfection, I have heard Johnson say, "*That George Psalmanazar's piety, penitence, and virtue exceeded almost what we read as wonderful even in the lives of saints.*"

I forget in what year it was this extraordinary person lived and died at a house in Old Street, where Mr. Johnson was witness to his talents and virtues, and to his final preference of the Church of England, after having studied, disgraced, and adorned so many modes of worship. The name he went by was not supposed by his friend to be that of his family, but all inquiries were vain.

His reasons for concealing his original were penitentiary; he deserved no other name than that of the impostor, he said. That portion of the Universal History which was written by him does not seem to me to be composed with peculiar spirit, but all traces of the wit and the wanderer were probably worn out before he undertook the work. His pious and patient endurance of a tedious illness, ending in an exemplary death, confirmed the strong impression his merit had made upon the mind of Mr. Johnson. "*It is so very difficult,*" said he, always, "*for a sick man not to be a scoundrel. Oh! set the pillows soft, here is*

Mr. Grumbler a-coming. Ah! let no air in for the world, Mr. Grumbler will be here presently."

This perpetual preference is so offensive, where the privileges of sickness are, besides, supported by wealth, and nourished by dependence, that one cannot much wonder that a rough mind is revolted by them. It was, however, at once comical and touchant (as the French call it), to observe Mr. Johnson so habitually watchful against this sort of behaviour, that he was often ready to suspect himself of it; and when one asked him gently, how he did?—"*Ready to become a scoundrel, madam,*" would commonly be the answer; "*with a little more spoiling you will, I think, make me a complete rascal!*"

His desire of doing good was not, however, lessened by his aversion to a sick chamber. He would have made an ill man well by any expense or fatigue of his own, sooner than any of the canters. Canter, indeed, was he none: he would forget to ask people after the health of their nearest relations, and say in excuse, "*That he knew they did not care: why should they?*" says he; "*every one in this world has as much as they can do in caring for themselves, and few have leisure really to think of their neighbours' distresses, however they may delight their tongues with talking of them.*"

The natural depravity of mankind and remains of original sin were so fixed in Mr. Johnson's opinion, that he was indeed a most acute observer of their effects; and used to say sometimes, half in jest, half in earnest, that they were the remains of his old tutor Mandeville's instructions. As a book, however, he took care always loudly to condemn the "Fable of the Bees," but not without adding, "*that it was the work of a thinking man.*" I have in former days heard Dr. Collier of the Commons loudly condemned for uttering sentiments, which twenty years after I have heard as loudly applauded from the lips of Dr. Johnson, concerning the well-known writer of that celebrated work: but if people will live long enough in this capricious world, such instances of partiality will shock them less and less by frequent repetition.

Mr. Johnson knew mankind, and wished to mend them: he therefore, to the piety and pure religion, the untainted integrity, and scrupulous morals of my earliest and most disinterested friend, judiciously contrived to join a cautious attention to the capacity of his hearers, and a prudent resolution not to lessen the influence of his learning and virtue, by casual freaks of humour and irregular starts of ill-managed merriment. He did not wish to confound, but to inform his auditors; and though he did not appear to solicit benevolence, he always wished to retain authority, and leave his company impressed with the idea that it was his to teach in this world, and theirs to learn. What wonder, then, that all should receive with docility from Johnson those doctrines, which, propagated by Collier, they drove away from them with shouts!

Dr. Johnson was not grave, however, because he knew not how to be merry. No man loved laughing better, and his vein of humour was rich and apparently inexhaustible; though Dr. Goldsmith said once to him, "*We should change companions oftener, we exhaust one another, and shall soon be both of us worn out.*" Poor Goldsmith was to him, indeed, like the earthen pot to the iron one in Fontaine's fables; it had been better for him, perhaps, that they had changed companions oftener; yet no experience of his antagonist's strength hindered him from continuing the contest. He used to remind me always of that verse in Berni—

"*Il pover uomo che non sen' era accorto,*
Andava combattendo—ed era morto."

Mr. Johnson made him a comical answer one day, when seeming to repine at the success of Beattie's "Essay on Truth"—"*Here's such a stir,*" said he, "*about a fellow that has written one book, and I have written many.*" "*Ah, Doctor,*" says his friend, "*there go two-and-forty sixpences, you know, to one guinea.*" They had spent an evening with Eaton Graham, too, I remember hearing it was at some tavern; his heart was open, and he began inviting away; told what he could do to make his college agreeable, and begged the visit might not be delayed. Goldsmith thanked him, and proposed setting out with Mr. Johnson for Buckinghamshire in a fortnight. "*Nay, hold, Dr. Minor,*" says the other, "*I did not invite you.*"

Many such mortifications arose in the course of their

intimacy, to be sure, but few more laughable than when the newspapers had tacked them together as the pedant and his flatterer in Love's Labour's Lost. Dr. Goldsmith came to his friend, fretting and foaming, and vowing vengeance against the printer, etc., till Mr. Johnson, tired of the bustle, and desirous to think of something else, cried out at last, "*Why, what would'st thou have, dear Doctor! who the plague is hurt with all this nonsense? and how is a man the worse, I wonder, in his health, purse, or character, for being called Holofernes?*" "*I do not know,*" replies the other, "*how you may relish being called Holofernes, but I do not like at least to play Goodman Dull.*"

Dr. Johnson was indeed famous for disregarding public abuse. When the people criticised and answered his pamphlets, papers, etc., "*Why, now, these fellows are only advertising my book,*" he would say; "*it is surely better a man should be abused than forgotten.*" When Churchill nettled him, however, it is certain he felt the sting, or that poet's works would hardly have been left out of the edition. Of that, however, I have no right to decide; the booksellers, perhaps, did not put Churchill on their list. I know Mr. Johnson was exceedingly zealous to declare how very little he had to do with the selection. Churchill's works, too, might possibly be rejected by him upon a higher principle; the highest, indeed, if he was inspired by the same laudable motive which made him reject every authority for a word in his dictionary that could only be gleaned from writers dangerous to religion or morality. "*I would not,*" said he, "*send people to look for words in a book, that by such a casual seizure of the mind might chance to mislead it for ever.*"

In consequence of this delicacy, Mrs. Montague once observed, "*That were an angel to give the imprimatur, Dr. Johnson's works were among those very few which would not be lessened by a line.*" That such praise from such a lady should delight him, is not strange; insensibility in a case like that must have been the result alone of arrogance acting on stupidity. Mr. Johnson had indeed no dislike to the commendations which he knew he deserved. "*What signifies protesting so against flattery!*" would he cry; "*when a person speaks well of one, it must be either true or false, you know; if true, let us rejoice in his good opinion; if he lies, it is a proof at least that he loves more to please me than to sit silent when he need say nothing."* That natural roughness of his manner so often mentioned would, notwithstanding the regularity of his notions, burst through them all from time to time; and he once bade a very celebrated lady, who praised him with too much zeal, perhaps, or perhaps too strong an emphasis (which always offended him), *"Consider what her flattery was worth before she choked him with it."*

A few more winters passed in the talking world showed him the value of that friend's commendations, however; and he was very sorry for the disgusting speech he made her. I used to think Mr. Johnson's determined preference of a cold, monotonous talker over an emphatical and violent one would make him quite a favourite among the men of ton, whose insensibility, or affectation of perpetual calmness, certainly did not give to him the offence it does to many. He loved *"conversation without effort,"* he said; and the encomiums I have heard him so often pronounce on the manners of Topham Beaucler in society constantly ended in that peculiar praise, that *"it was without effort."* We were talking of Richardson, who wrote "Clarissa." *"You think I love flattery,"* says Dr. Johnson, *"and so I do; but a little too much always disgusts me. That fellow Richardson, on the contrary, could not be contented to sail quietly down the stream of reputation without longing to taste the froth from every stroke of the oar."*

With regard to slight insults from newspaper abuse, I have already declared his notions. *"They sting one,"* says he, *"but as a fly stings a horse; and the eagle will not catch flies."* He once told me, however, that Cummyns, the famous Quaker, whose friendship he valued very highly, fell a sacrifice to their insults, having declared on his death-bed to Dr. Johnson that the pain of an anonymous letter, written in some of the common prints of the day, fastened on his heart, and threw him into the slow fever of which he died. Nor was Cummyns the only valuable member so lost to society. Hawkesworth, the pious, the virtuous, and the wise, for want of that fortitude which casts a shield before the merits of his friend, fell a lamented sacrifice to wanton malice and cruelty, I know not how provoked; but all in turn feel the lash of censure in a country where, as every baby is allowed to carry a whip, no person can escape except by chance. The unpublished crimes, unknown distresses, and even death itself, however, daily occurring in less liberal governments and less free nations, soon teach one to content oneself with such petty grievances, and make one acknowledge that the undistinguishing severity of newspaper abuse may in some measure diminish the diffusion of vice and folly in Great Britain, and while they fright delicate minds into forced refinements and affected insipidity, they are useful to the great causes of virtue in the soul and liberty in the State; and though sensibility often sinks under the roughness of their prescriptions, it would be no good policy to take away their licence.

Knowing the state of Mr. Johnson's nerves, and how easily they were affected, I forbore reading in a new magazine, one day, the death of a Samuel Johnson who expired that month; but my companion snatching up the book, saw it himself, and contrary to my expectation, "*Oh!*" said he, "*I hope Death will now be glutted with Sam Johnsons, and let me alone for some time to come; I read of another namesake's departure last week.*" Though Mr. Johnson was commonly affected even to agony at the thoughts of a friend's dying, he troubled himself very little with the complaints they might make to him about ill-health. "*Dear Doctor,*" said he one day to a common acquaintance, who lamented the tender state of his inside, "*do not be like the spider, man, and spin conversation thus incessantly out of thy own bowels.*" I told him of another friend who suffered grievously with the gout. "*He will live a vast many years for all that,*" replied he, "*and then what signifies how much he suffers! But he will die at last, poor fellow; there's the misery; gout seldom takes the fort by a coup-de-main, but turning the siege into a blockade, obliges it to surrender at discretion.*"

A lady he thought well of was disordered in her health. "*What help has she called in?*" inquired Johnson. "*Dr. James, sir,*" was the reply. "*What is her disease?*" "*Oh, nothing positive; rather a gradual and gentle decline.*" "*She will die, then, pretty dear!*"

answered he. "*When Death's pale horse runs away with a person on full speed, an active physician may possibly give them a turn; but if he carries them on an even, slow pace, down-hill, too! no care nor skill can save them!*"

When Garrick was on his last sick-bed, no arguments, or recitals of such facts as I had heard, would persuade Mr. Johnson of his danger. He had prepossessed himself with a notion, that to say a man was sick was very near wishing him so: and few things offended him more than prognosticating even the death of an ordinary acquaintance. "*Ay, ay,*" said he, "*Swift knew the world pretty well when he said that— 'Some dire misfortune to portend, No enemy can match a friend.'*"

The danger, then, of Mr. Garrick, or of Mr. Thrale, whom he loved better, was an image which no one durst present before his view; he always persisted in the possibility and hope of their recovering disorders from which no human creatures by human means alone ever did recover. His distress for their loss was for that very reason poignant to excess. But his fears of his own salvation were excessive. His truly tolerant spirit and Christian charity, which hopeth all things, and believeth all things, made him rely securely on the safety of his friends; while his earnest aspiration after a blessed immortality made him cautious of his own steps, and timorous concerning their consequences.

He knew how much had been given, and filled his mind with fancies of how much would be required, till his impressed imagination was often disturbed by them, and his health suffered from the sensibility of his too tender conscience. A real Christian is so apt to find his talk above his power of performance! Mr. Johnson did not, however, give in to ridiculous refinements either of speculation or practice, or suffer himself to be deluded by specious appearances. "*I have had dust thrown in my eyes too often,*" would he say, "*to be blinded so. Let us never confound matters of belief with matters of opinion.*" Some one urged in his presence the preference of hope to possession; and as I remember produced an Italian sonnet on the subject. "*Let us not,*" cries Johnson, "*amuse ourselves with subtleties and sonnets, when speaking about hope, which is the follower of faith and the precursor of eternity; but if you only mean those air-built hopes which to-day excite and to-morrow will destroy, let us talk away, and remember that we only talk of the pleasures of hope; we feel those of possession, and no man in his senses would change the last for the first. Such hope is a mere bubble, that by a gentle breath may be blown to what size you will almost, but a rough blast bursts it at once. Hope is an amusement rather than a good, and adapted to none but very tranquil minds."*

The truth is, Mr. Johnson hated what he called unprofitable chat; and to a gentleman who had disserted some time about the natural history of the mouse—"*I wonder what such a one would have said,*" cried Johnson, "*if he had ever had the luck to see a lion!*" I well remember that at Brighthelmstone once, when he was not present, Mr. Beauclerc asserted that he was afraid of spirits; and I, who was secretly offended at the charge, asked him, the first opportunity I could find, "*what ground he had ever given to the world for such a report?*" "*I can,*" replied he, "*recollect nothing nearer it than my telling Dr. Lawrence, many years ago, that a long time after my poor mother's death I heard her voice call 'Sam!'*" "*What answer did the Doctor make to your story, sir?*" said I. "*None in the world,*" replied he, and suddenly changed the conversation.

Now, as Mr. Johnson had a most unshaken faith, without any mixture of credulity, this story must either have been strictly true, or his persuasion of its truth the effect of disordered spirits. I relate the anecdote precisely as he told it me, but could not prevail on him to draw out the talk into length for further satisfaction of my curiosity. As Johnson was the firmest of believers, without being credulous, so he was the most charitable of mortals, without being what we call an active friend. Admirable at giving counsel, no man saw his way so clearly; but he would not stir a finger for the assistance of those to whom he was willing enough to give advice: besides that, he had principles of laziness, and could be indolent by rule. To hinder your death, or procure you a dinner, I mean if really in want of one; his earnestness, his exertions could not be prevented, though health and purse and ease were all destroyed by their violence.

If you wanted a slight favour, you must apply to people of other dispositions; for not a step would Johnson move to obtain a man a vote in a society, to repay a compliment which might be useful or pleasing, to write a letter of request, or to obtain a hundred pounds a year more for a friend, who perhaps had already two or three. No force could urge him to diligence, no importunity could conquer his resolution of standing still. "*What good are we doing with all this ado?*" would he say; "*dearest lady, let's hear no more of it!*"

I have, however, more than once in my life forced him on such services, but with extreme difficulty. We parted at his door one evening when I had teased him for many weeks to write a recommendatory letter of a little boy to his schoolmaster; and after he had faithfully promised to do this prodigious feat before we met again—"*Do not forget dear Dick, sir,*" said I, as he went out of the coach. He turned back, stood still two minutes on the carriage-step—"*When I have written my letter for Dick, I may hang myself, mayn't I?*" and turned away in a very ill humour indeed. Though apt enough to take sudden likings or aversions to people he occasionally met, he would never hastily pronounce upon their character; and when, seeing him justly delighted with Solander's conversation, I observed once that he was a man of great parts who talked from a full mind- -"*It may be so,*" said Mr. Johnson, "*but you cannot know it yet, nor I neither: the pump works well, to be sure! but how, I wonder, are we to decide in so very short an acquaintance, whether it is supplied by a spring or a reservoir?*"

He always made a great difference in his esteem between talents and erudition; and when he saw a person eminent for literature, though wholly unconversible, it fretted him. "*Teaching such tonies,*" said he to me one day, "*is like setting a lady's diamonds in lead, which only obscures the lustre of the stone, and makes the possessor ashamed on't.*" Useful and what we call everyday knowledge had the most of his just praise. "*Let your boy learn arithmetic, dear madam,*" was his advice to the mother of a rich young heir: "*he will not then be a prey to every rascal which this town swarms with. Teach him the value of money, and how to reckon it; ignorance to a wealthy lad of one-and-twenty is only so much fat to a sick sheep: it just serves to call the rooks about him.*" "*And all that prey in vice or folly Joy to see their quarry fly; Here the gamester light and jolly, There the lender grave and sly.*"

These improviso lines, making part of a long copy of verses which my regard for the youth on whose birthday they were written obliges me to suppress, lest they should give him pain, show a mind of surprising activity and warmth; the more so as he was past seventy years of age when he composed them; but nothing more certainly offended Mr. Johnson than the idea of a man's faculties (mental ones, I mean) decaying by time. "*It is not true, sir,*" would he say; "*what a man could once do, he would always do, unless, indeed, by dint of vicious indolence, and compliance with the nephews and the nieces who crowd round an old fellow, and help to tuck him in, till he, contented with the exchange of fame for ease, e'en resolves to let them set the pillows at his back, and gives no further proof of his existence than just to suck the jelly that prolongs it.*"

For such a life or such a death Dr. Johnson was indeed never intended by Providence: his mind was like a warm climate, which brings everything to perfection suddenly and vigorously, not like the alembicated productions of artificial fire, which always betray the difficulty of bringing them forth when their size is disproportionate to their flavour. "*Je ferois un Roman tout comme un autre, mais la vie n'est point un Roman,*" says a famous French writer; and this was so certainly the opinion of the author of the "Rambler," that all his conversation precepts tended towards the dispersion of romantic ideas, and were chiefly intended to promote the cultivation of "*That which before thee lies in daily life.*" Milton.

And when he talked of authors, his praise went spontaneously to such passages as are sure in his own phrase to leave something behind them useful on common occasions, or observant of common manners. For example, it was not the two last, but the two first volumes of "Clarissa" that he prized; "*for give me a sick-bed and a dying lady,*" said he, "*and I'll be pathetic myself. But Richardson had picked the kernel of life,*" he said, "*while Fielding was contented with the husk.*" It was not King Lear cursing his daughters, or deprecating the storm, that I remember his commendations of; but Iago's ingenious malice and subtle revenge; or Prince Hal's gay compliance with the vices of Falstaff, whom he all along despised. Those plays had indeed no rivals in Johnson's favour: "*No man but Shakespeare*," he said, "*could have drawn Sir John*."

His manner of criticising and commending Addison's prose was the same in conversation as we read it in the printed strictures, and many of the expressions used have been heard to fall from him on common occasions. It was notwithstanding observable enough (or I fancied so) that he did never like, though he always thought fit to praise it; and his praises resembled those of a man who extols the superior elegance of high painted porcelain, while he himself always chooses to eat off plate. I told him so one day, and he neither denied it nor appeared displeased. Of the pathetic in poetry he never liked to speak, and the only passage I ever heard him applaud as particularly tender in any common book was Jane Shore's exclamation in the last act— "Forgive me! but forgive me!"

It was not, however, from the want of a susceptible heart that he hated to cite tender expressions, for he was more strongly and more violently affected by the force of words representing ideas capable of affecting him at all than any other man in the world, I believe: and when he would try to repeat the celebrated Prosa Ecclesiastica pro Mortuis, as it is called, beginning "Dies irae, Dies illa," he could never pass the stanza ending thus, "Tantus labour non sit cassus," without bursting into a flood of tears; which sensibility I used to quote against him when he would inveigh against devotional poetry, and protest that all religious verses were cold and feeble, and unworthy the subject, which ought to be treated with higher reverence, he said, than either poets or painters could presume to excite or bestow.

Nor can anything be a stronger proof of Dr. Johnson's piety than such an expression; for his idea of poetry was magnificent indeed, and very fully was he persuaded of its superiority over every other talent bestowed by heaven on man. His chapter upon that particular subject in his " Rasselas" is really written from the fulness of his heart, and quite in his best manner, I think. I am not so sure that this is the proper place to mention his writing that surprising little volume in a week or ten days' time, in order to obtain money for his journey to Lichfield when his mother lay upon her last sick-bed.

Promptitude of thought, indeed, and quickness of expression, were among the peculiar felicities of Johnson; his notions rose up like the dragon's teeth sowed by Cadmus all ready clothed, and in bright armour too, fit for immediate battle. He was therefore (as somebody is said to have expressed it) a tremendous converser, and few people ventured to try their skill against an antagonist with whom contention was so hopeless. One gentleman, however, who dined at a nobleman's house in his company, and that of Mr. Thrale, to whom I was obliged for the anecdote, was willing to enter the lists in defence of King William's character, and having opposed and contradicted Johnson two or three times petulantly enough, the master of the house began to feel uneasy, and expect disagreeable consequences; to avoid which he said, loud enough for the Doctor to hear, "*Our friend here has no meaning now in all this, except just to relate at club to-morrow how he teased Johnson at dinner to-day—this is all to do himself honour.*" "*No, upon my word,*" replied the other, "*I see no honour in it, whatever you may do.*" "*Well, sir!*" returned Mr. Johnson, sternly, "*if you do not see the honour, I am sure I feel the disgrace.*"

A young fellow, less confident of his own abilities, lamenting one day that he had lost all his Greek—"*I believe it happened at the same time, sir,*" said Johnson, "*that I lost all my large estate in Yorkshire.*" But however roughly he might be suddenly provoked to treat a harmless exertion of vanity, he did not wish to inflict the pain he gave, and was sometimes very sorry when he perceived the people to smart more than they deserved. "*How harshly you treated that man today,*" said I once, "who harangued us so about gardening." "*I am sorry,*" said he, "*if I vexed the creature, for there is certainly no harm in a fellow's rattling a rattle-box, only don't let him think that he thunders.*" The Lincolnshire lady who showed him a grotto she had been making, came off no better, as I remember. "*Would it not be a pretty cool habitation in summer,"* said she, *"Mr. Johnson?" "I think it would, madam,"* replied he, *"for a toad."*

All desire of distinction, indeed, had a sure enemy in Mr. Johnson. We met a friend driving six very small ponies, and stopped to admire them. *"Why does nobody,"* said our Doctor, *"begin the fashion of driving six spavined horses, all spavined of the same leg? It would have a mighty pretty effect, and produce the distinction of doing something worse than the common way."* When Mr. Johnson had a mind to compliment any one he did it with more dignity to himself, and better effect upon the company, than any man. I can recollect but few instances, indeed, though perhaps that may be more my fault than his. When Sir Joshua Reynolds left the room one day, he said, *"There goes a man not to be spoilt by prosperity."*

And when Mrs. Montague showed him some China plates which had once belonged to Queen Elizabeth, he told her *"that they had no reason to be ashamed of their present possessor, who was so little inferior to the first."* I likewise remember that he pronounced one day at my house a most lofty panegyric upon Jones the Orientalist, who seemed little pleased with the praise, for what cause I know not. He was not at all offended when, comparing all our acquaintance to some animal or other, we pitched upon the elephant for his resemblance, adding that the proboscis of that creature was like his mind most exactly, strong to buffet even the tiger, and pliable to pick up even the pin.

The truth is, Mr. Johnson was often good humouredly willing to join in childish amusements, and hated to be left out of any innocent merriment that was going forward. Mr. Murphy always said he was incomparable at buffoonery; and I verily think, if he had had good eyes, and a form less inflexible, he would have made an admirable mimic. He certainly rode on Mr. Thrale's old hunter with a good firmness, and though he would follow the hounds fifty miles on end sometimes, would never own himself either tired or amused. *"I have now learned,"* said he, *"by hunting, to perceive that it is no diversion at all, nor ever takes a man out of himself for a moment: the dogs have less sagacity than I could have prevailed on myself to suppose; and the gentlemen often call to me not to ride over them. It is very strange, and very melancholy, that the paucity of human pleasure should persuade us ever to call hunting one of them."*

He was, however, proud to be amongst the sportsmen; and I think no praise ever went so close to his heart as when Mr. Hamilton called out one day upon Brighthelmstone Downs, *"Why, Johnson rides as well, for aught I see, as the most illiterate fellow in England."* Though Dr. Johnson owed his very life to air and exercise, given him when his organs of respiration could scarcely play, in the year 1766, yet he ever persisted in the notion that neither of them had anything to do with health. *"People live as long,"* said he, *"in Pepper Alley as on Salisbury Plain; and they live so much happier, that an inhabitant of the first would, if he turned cottager, starve his understanding for want of conversation, and perish in a state of mental inferiority."*

Mr. Johnson, indeed, as he was a very talking man himself, had an idea that nothing promoted happiness so much as conversation. A friend's erudition was commended one day as equally deep and strong. *"He will not talk, sir,"* was the reply, *"so his learning does no good, and his wit, if he has it, gives us no pleasure. Out of all his boasted stores I never heard him force but one word, and that word was Richard."* With a contempt not inferior he received the praises of a pretty lady's face and behaviour. *"She says nothing, sir,"* answers Johnson; *"a talking blackamoor were better than a white creature who adds nothing to life, and by sitting down before one thus desperately silent, takes away the confidence one should have in the company of her chair if she were once out of it."*

No one was, however, less willing to begin any discourse than himself. His friend, Mr. Thomas Tyers, said he was like the ghosts, who never speak till they are spoken to: and he liked the expression so well, that he often repeated it. He had, indeed, no necessity to lead the stream of chat to a favourite channel, that his fulness on the subject might be shown more clearly whatever was the topic; and he usually left the choice to others. His information best enlightened, his argument strengthened, and his wit made it ever remembered. Of him it might have been said, as he often delighted to say of Edmund

Burke, "*that you could not stand five minutes with that man beneath a shed while it rained, but you must be convinced you had been standing with the greatest man you had ever yet seen.*"

As we had been saying, one day, that no subject failed of receiving dignity from the manner in which Mr. Johnson treated it, a lady at my house said she would make him talk about love, and took her measures accordingly, deriding the novels of the day because they treated about love. "*It is not,*" replied our philosopher, "*because they treat, as you call it, about love, but because they treat of nothing, that they are despicable. We must not ridicule a passion which he who never felt never was happy, and he who laughs at never deserves to feel—a passion which has caused the change of empires and the loss of worlds—a passion which has inspired heroism and subdued avarice.*"

He thought he had already said too much. "*A passion, in short,*" added he, with an altered tone, "*that consumes me away for my pretty Fanny here, and she is very cruel,*" speaking of another lady in the room. He told us, however, in the course of the same chat, how his negro Francis had been eminent for his success among the girls. Seeing us all laugh, "*I must have you know, ladies,*" said he, "*that Frank has carried the empire of Cupid further than most men. When I was in Lincolnshire so many years ago he attended me thither; and when we returned home together, I found that a female haymaker had followed him to London for love.*"

Francis was indeed no small favourite with his master, who retained, however, a prodigious influence over his most violent passions. On the birthday of our eldest daughter, and that of our friend Dr. Johnson, the 17th and the 18th of September, we every year made up a little dance and supper, to divert our servants and their friends, putting the summer-house into their hands for the two evenings, to fill with acquaintance and merriment. Francis and his white wife were invited, of course. She was eminently pretty, and he was jealous, as my maids told me. On the first of these days' amusements (I know not what year) Frank took offence at some attentions paid his Desdemona, and walked away next morning to London in wrath. His master and I driving the same road an hour after, overtook him. *"What is the matter, child,"* says Dr. Johnson, *"that you leave Streatham to-day. Art sick?" "He is jealous,"* whispered I. *"Are you jealous of your wife, you stupid blockhead?"* cries out his master in another tone. The fellow hesitated, and, "to be sure, Sir, I don't quite approve, Sir," was the stammering reply. *"Why, what do they do to her, man? Do the footmen kiss her?" "No, sir, no! Kiss my wife, sir! I hope not, sir." "Why, what do they do to her, my lad?" "Why, nothing, sir, I'm sure, sir." "Why, then go back directly and dance, you dog, do; and let's hear no more of such empty lamentations."*

I believe, however, that Francis was scarcely as much the object of Mr. Johnson's personal kindness as the representative of Dr. Bathurst, for whose sake he would have loved anybody or anything. When he spoke of negroes, he always appeared to think them of a race naturally inferior, and made few exceptions in favour of his own; yet whenever disputes arose in his household among the many odd inhabitants of which it consisted, he always sided with Francis against the others, whom he suspected (not unjustly, I believe) of greater malignity. It seems at once vexatious and comical to reflect that the dissensions those people chose to live constantly in distressed and mortified him exceedingly.

He really was oftentimes afraid of going home, because he was so sure to be met at the door with numberless complaints; and he used to lament pathetically to me, and to Mr. Sastres, the Italian master, who was much his favourite, that they made his life miserable from the impossibility he found of making theirs happy, when every favour he bestowed on one was wormwood to the rest If, however, I ventured to blame their ingratitude, and condemn their conduct, he would instantly set about softening the one and justifying the other; and finished commonly by telling me, that I knew not how to make allowances for situations I never experienced. *"To thee no reason who know'st only good, But evil hast not tried."* Milton.

Dr. Johnson knew how to be merry with mean people, too, as well as to be sad with them; he loved the lower ranks of humanity with a real affection: and though his talents and learning kept him always in the sphere of upper life, yet he never lost sight of the time when he and they shared pain and pleasure in common. A borough election once showed me his toleration of boisterous mirth, and his content in the company of people whom one would have thought at first sight little calculated for his society. A rough fellow one day on such an occasion, a hatter by trade, seeing Mr. Johnson's beaver in a state of decay, seized it suddenly with one hand, and clapping him on the back with the other, "*Ah, Master Johnson,*" says he, "*this is no time to be thinking about hats.*" "*No, no, sir,*" replied our Doctor in a cheerful tone, "*hats are of no use now, as you say, except to throw up in the air and huzza with,*" accompanying his words with a true election halloo.

But it was never against people of coarse life that his contempt was expressed, while poverty of sentiment in men who considered themselves to be company for the parlour, as he called it, was what he could not bear. A very ignorant young fellow, who had plagued us all for nine or ten months, died at last consumptive. "*I think,*" said Mr. Johnson, when he heard the news, "*I am afraid I should have been more concerned for the death of the dog; but—*" (hesitating a while) "*I am not wrong now in all this, for the dog acted up to his character on every occasion that we know; but that dunce of a fellow helped forward the general disgrace of humanity.*" "*Why, dear sir,*" said I, "*how odd you are! you have often said the lad was not capable of receiving further instruction.*" "*He was,*" replied the Doctor, "*like a corked bottle, with a drop of dirty water in it, to be sure; one might pump upon it for ever without the smallest effect; but when every method to open and clean it had been tried, you would not have me grieve that the bottle was broke at last.*"

This was the same youth who told us he had been reading "Lucius Florus;" Florus Delphini was the phrase. "*And my mother,*" said he, "*thought it had something to do with Delphos; but of that I know nothing.*" "*Who founded Rome, then ?*" inquired Mr. Thrale. The lad replied, "*Romulus.*" "*And who succeeded Romulus?*" said I. A long pause, and apparently distressful hesitation, followed the difficult question. "*Why will you ask him in terms that he does not comprehend?*" said Mr. Johnson, enraged. "*You might as well bid him tell you who phlebotomised*

Romulus. This fellow's dulness is elastic," continued he, *"and all we do is but like kicking at a woolsack."* The pains he took, however, to obtain the young man more patient instructors were many, and oftentimes repeated. He was put under the care of a clergyman in a distant province; and Mr. Johnson used both to write and talk to his friends concerning his education.

It was on that occasion that I remember his saying, *"A boy should never be sent to Eton or Westminster School before he is twelve years old at least; for if in his years of babyhood he escapes that general and transcendent knowledge without which life is perpetually put to a stand, he will never get it at a public school, where, if he does not learn Latin and Greek, he learns nothing."* Mr. Johnson often said, *"that there was too much stress laid upon literature as indispensably necessary: there is surely no need that everybody should be a scholar, no call that every one should square the circle. Our manner of teaching,"* said he, *"cramps and warps many a mind, which if left more at liberty would have been respectable in some way, though perhaps not in that. We lop our trees, and prune them, and pinch them about,"* he would say, *"and nail them tight up to the wall, while a good standard is at last the only thing for bearing healthy fruit, though it commonly begins later. Let the people learn necessary knowledge; let them learn to count their fingers, and to count their money, before they are caring for the classics; for,"* says Mr. Johnson, *"though I do not quite agree with the proverb, that Nullum numen abest si sit prudentia, yet we may very well say, that Nullum numen adest—ni sit prudentia."*

We had been visiting at a lady's house, whom as we returned some of the company ridiculed for her ignorance. *"She is not ignorant,"* said he, *"I believe, of anything she has been taught, or of anything she is desirous to know: and I suppose if one wanted a little run tea, she might be a proper person enough to apply to."* When I relate these various instances of contemptuous behaviour shown to a variety of people, I am aware that those who till now have heard little of Mr. Johnson will here cry out against his pride and his severity; yet I have been as careful as I could to tell them that all he did was gentle, if all he said was rough. Had I given anecdotes of his actions instead of his words, we should, I am sure, have had nothing on record but acts of virtue differently modified, as different occasions called that virtue forth: and among all the nine biographical essays or performances which I have heard will at last be written about dear Dr. Johnson, no mean or wretched, no wicked or even slightly culpable action will, I trust, be found, to produce and put in the scale against a life of seventy years, spent in the uniform practice of every moral excellence and every Christian perfection, save humility alone, says a critic, but that I think must be excepted.

He was not, however, wanting even in that to a degree seldom attained by man, when the duties of piety or charity called it forth. Lowly towards God, and docile towards the Church; implicit in his belief of the Gospel, and ever respectful towards the people appointed to preach it; tender of the unhappy, and affectionate to the poor, let no one hastily condemn as proud a character which may perhaps somewhat justly be censured as arrogant. It must, however, be remembered again, that even this arrogance was never shown without some intention, immediate or remote, of mending some fault or conveying some instruction. Had I meant to make a panegyric on Mr. Johnson's well-known excellences, I should have told his deeds only, not his words—sincerely protesting, that as I never saw him once do a wrong thing, so we had accustomed ourselves to look upon him almost as an excepted being: and I should as much have expected injustice from Socrates, or impiety from Paschal, as the slightest deviation from truth and goodness in any transaction one might be engaged in with Samuel Johnson.

His attention to veracity was without equal or example: and when I mentioned Clarissa as a perfect character; "*On the contrary,*" said he, "*you may observe there is always something which she prefers to truth. Fielding's Amelia was the most pleasing heroine of all the romances,*" he said, "*but that vile broken nose, never cured, ruined the sale of perhaps the only book, which being printed off betimes one morning, a new edition was called for before night.*" Mr. Johnson's knowledge of literary history was extensive and surprising. He knew every adventure of every book you could name almost, and was exceedingly pleased with the opportunity which writing the "Poets' Lives" gave him to display it. He loved to be set at work, and was sorry when he came to the end of the business he was about. I do not feel so myself with regard to these sheets: a fever which has preyed on me while I wrote them over for the press, will perhaps lessen my power of doing well the first, and probably the last work I should ever have thought of presenting to the public. I could doubtless wish so to conclude it, as at least to show my zeal for my friend, whose life, as I once had the honour and happiness of being useful to, I should wish to record a few particular traits of, that those who read should emulate his goodness; but feeling the necessity of making even virtue and learning such as his agreeable, that all should be warned against such coarseness of manners, as drove even from him those who loved, honoured, and esteemed him.

His wife's daughter, Mrs. Lucy Porter, of Lichfield, whose veneration for his person and character has ever been the greatest possible, being opposed one day in conversation by a clergyman who came often to her house, and feeling somewhat offended, cried out sudden, "*Why, Mr. Pearson,*" said she, "*you are just like Dr. Johnson, I think: I do not mean that you are a man of the greatest capacity in all the world like Dr. Johnson, but that you contradict one every word one speaks, just like him.*" Mr. Johnson told me the story: he was present at the giving of the reproof. It was, however, observable, that with all his odd severity, he could not keep even indifferent people from teasing him with unaccountable confessions of silly conduct, which one would think they would scarcely have had inclination to reveal even to their tenderest and most intimate companions; and it was from these unaccountable volunteers in sincerity that he learned to warn the world against follies little known, and seldom thought on by other moralists.

Much of his eloquence, and much of his logic, have I heard him use to prevent men from making vows on trivial occasions; and when he saw a person oddly perplexed about a slight difficulty, "*Let the man alone,*" he would say, "*and torment him no more about it; there is a vow in the case, I am convinced; but is it not very strange that people should be neither afraid nor ashamed of bringing in God Almighty thus at every turn between themselves and their dinner?"* When I asked what ground he had for such imaginations, he informed me, "*That a young lady once told him in confidence that she could never persuade herself to be dressed against the bell rung for dinner, till she had made a vow to heaven that she would never more be absent from the family meals.*"

The strangest applications in the world were certainly made from time to time towards Mr. Johnson, who by that means had an inexhaustible fund of ancecdote, and could, if he pleased, tell the most astonishing stories of human folly and human weakness that ever were confided to any man not a confessor by profession. One day, when he was in a humour to record some of them, he told us the following tale:—"*A person,*" said he, "*had for these last five weeks often called at my door, but would not leave his name or other message, but that he wished to speak with me. At last we met, and he told me that he was oppressed by scruples of conscience. I blamed him gently for not applying, as the rules of our Church direct, to his parish priest or other discreet clergyman; when, after some compliments on his part, he told me that he was clerk to a very eminent trader, at whose warehouses much business consisted in packing goods in order to go abroad; that he was often tempted to take paper and packthread enough for his own use, and that he had indeed done so so often, that he could recollect no time when he ever had bought any for himself. 'But probably,' said I, 'your master was wholly indifferent with regard to such trivial emoluments. You had better ask for it at once, and so take your trifles with content.' 'Oh, sir!' replies the visitor, 'my master bid me have as much as I pleased, and was half angry when I talked to him about it.' 'Then pray, sir,' said I, 'tease me no more about such airy nothings,' and was going on to be very angry, when I recollected that the fellow might be mad, perhaps; so I asked him, 'When he left the counting-house of an evening?' 'At seven o'clock, sir.' 'And when do you go to bed, sir?' 'At twelve o'clock.' 'Then,' replied I, 'I have at least learnt thus much by my new acquaintance—that five hours of the four-and-twenty unemployed are enough for a man to go mad in; so I would advise you, sir, to study algebra, if you are not an adept already in it. Your head would get less muddy, and you will leave off tormenting your neighbours about paper and packthread, while we all live together in a world that is bursting with sin and sorrow.' It is perhaps needless to add that this visitor came no more."*

Mr. Johnson had, indeed, a real abhorrence of a person that had ever before him treated a little thing like a great one; and he quoted this scrupulous gentleman with his packthread very often, in ridicule of a friend who, looking out on Streatham Common from our windows, one day, lamented the enormous wickedness of the times because some bird-catchers were busy there one fine Sunday morning. "*While half the Christian world is permitted,*" said he, "*to dance and sing and celebrate Sunday as a day of festivity, how comes your Puritanical spirit so offended with frivolous and empty deviations from exactness? Whoever loads life with unnecessary scruples, sir,*" continued he, "*provokes the attention of others on his conduct, and incurs the censure of singularity without reaping the reward of superior virtue.*"

I must not, among the anecdotes of Dr. Johnson's life, omit to relate a thing that happened to him one day, which he told me of himself. As he was walking along the Strand a gentleman stepped out of some neighbouring tavern, with his napkin in his hand, and no hat, and stopping him as civilly as he could, "*I beg your pardon, sir, but you are Dr. Johnson, I believe?*" "*Yes, sir.*" "*We have a wager depending on your reply. Pray, sir, is it irr_e_parable or irrep_air_able that one should say?*" "*The last, I think, sir,*" answered Dr. Johnson, "*for the adverb ought to follow the verb; but you had better consult my 'Dictionary' than me, for that was the result of more thought than you will now give me time for.*" "*No, no,*" replied the gentleman, gaily, "*the book I have no certainty at all of, but here is the author, to whom I referred. Is he not, sir?*"—to a friend with him. "*I have won my twenty guineas quite fairly, and am much obliged to you, sir;*" and so shaking Mr. Johnson kindly by the hand, he went back to finish his dinner or dessert.

Another strange thing he told me once which there was no danger of forgetting; how a young gentleman called on him one morning, and told him that his father having, just before his death, dropped suddenly into the enjoyment of an ample fortune, he (the son) was willing to qualify himself for genteel society by adding some literature to his other endowments, and wished to be put in an easy way of obtaining it. Dr. Johnson recommended the university, *"for you read Latin, sir, with facility?" " I read it a little, to be sure, sir." " But do you read it with facility, I say?" "Upon my word, sir, I do not very well know, but I rather believe not."*

Mr. Johnson now began to recommend other branches of science, when he found languages at such an immeasurable distance, and advising him to study natural history, there arose some talk about animals, and their divisions into oviparous and viviparous. *"And the cat here, sir,"* said the youth, who wished for instruction; *"pray in what class is she?"* Our Doctor's patience and desire of doing good began now to give way to the natural roughness of his temper. *"You would do well,"* said he, *"to look for some person to be always about you, sir, who is capable of explaining such matters, and not come to us"*—there were some literary friends present, as I recollect—*"to know whether the cat lays eggs or not. Get a discreet man to keep you company: there are so many who would be glad of your table and fifty pounds a year."*

The young gentleman retired, and in less than a week informed his friends that he had fixed on a preceptor to whom no objections could be made; but when he named as such one of the most distinguished characters in our age or nation, Mr. Johnson fairly gave himself up to an honest burst of laughter; and seeing this youth at such a surprising distance from common knowledge of the world, or of anything in it, desired to see his visitor no more. He had not much better luck with two boys that he used to tell of, to whom he had taught the classics, *"so that,"* he said, *"they were no incompetent or mean scholars."* It was necessary, however, that something more familiar should be known, and he bid them read the History of England. After a few months had elapsed he asked them, *"If they could recollect who first destroyed the monasteries in our island?"* One modestly replied that he did not know; the other said Jesus Christ!

Of the truth of stories which ran currently about the town concerning Dr. Johnson it was impossible to be certain, unless one asked him himself, and what he told, or suffered to be told, before his face without contradicting, has every public mark, I think, of real and genuine authenticity. I made, one day, very minute inquiries about the tale of his knocking down the famous Tom Osborne with his own "Dictionary" in the man's own house. "*And how was that affair? In earnest? Do tell me, Mr. Johnson?*" "*There is nothing to tell, dearest lady, but that he was insolent, and I beat him, and that he was a blockhead, and told of it, which I should never have done. So the blows have been multiplying and the wonder thickening for all these years, as Thomas was never a favourite with the public. I have beat many a fellow, but the rest had the wit to hold their tongues.*"

I have heard Mr. Murphy relate a very singular story, while he was present, greatly to the credit of his uncommon skill and knowledge of life and manners. When first the "Ramblers" came out in separate numbers, as they were the objects of attention to multitudes of people, they happened, as it seems, particularly to attract the notice of a society who met every Saturday evening during the summer at Romford in Essex, and were known by the name of the Bowling-Green Club. These men seeing one day the character of Leviculus, the fortune-hunter, or Tetrica, the old maid: another day some account of a person who spent his life in hoping for a legacy, or of him who is always prying into other folks' affairs, began sure enough to think they were betrayed, and that some of the coterie sate down to divert himself by giving to the public the portrait of all the rest.

Filled with wrath against the traitor of Romford, one of them resolved to write to the printer, and inquire the author's name. Samuel Johnson, was the reply. No more was necessary; Samuel Johnson was the name of the curate, and soon did each begin to load him with reproaches for turning his friends into ridicule in a manner so cruel and unprovoked. In vain did the guiltless curate protest his innocence; one was sure that Aligu meant Mr. Twigg, and that Cupidus was but another name for neighbour Baggs, till the poor parson, unable to contend any longer, rode to London, and brought them full satisfaction concerning the writer, who, from his own knowledge of general manners, quickened by a vigorous and warm imagination, had happily delineated, though unknown to himself, the members of the Bowling-Green Club.

Mr. Murphy likewise used to tell before Dr. Johnson, of the first time they met, and the occasion of their meeting, which he related thus. That being in those days engaged in a periodical paper, he found himself at a friend's house out of town; and not being disposed to lose pleasure for the sake of business, wished rather to content his bookseller by sending some unstudied essay to London by the servant, than deny himself the company of his acquaintance, and drive away to his chambers for the purpose of writing something more correct. He therefore took up a French Journal Litteraire that lay about the room, and translating something he liked from it, sent it away without further examination. Time, however, discovered that he had translated from the French a "Rambler" of Johnson's, which had been but a month before taken from the English; and thinking it right to make him his personal excuses, he went next day, and found our friend all covered with soot like a chimney-sweeper, in a little room, with an intolerable heat and strange smell, as if he had been acting Lungs in the 'Alchymist,' making aether. "*Come, come,*" says Dr. Johnson, "*dear Mur, the story is black enough now; and it was a very happy day for me that brought you first to my house, and a very happy mistake about the 'Ramblers.'*"

Dr. Johnson was always exceeding fond of chemistry; and we made up a sort of laboratory at Streatham one summer, and diverted ourselves with drawing essences and colouring liquors. But the danger Mr. Thrale found his friend in one day when I was driven to London, and he had got the children and servants round him to see some experiments performed, put an end to all our entertainment, so well was the master of the house persuaded that his short sight would have been his destruction in a moment, by bringing him close to a fierce and violent flame. Indeed, it was a perpetual miracle that he did not set himself on fire reading a-bed, as was his constant custom, when exceedingly unable even to keep clear of mischief with our best help; and accordingly the fore-top of all his wigs were burned by the candle down to the very net work. Mr. Thrale's valet de chambre [Mr Henderson], for that reason, kept one always in his own hands, with which he met him at the parlour-door when the bell had called him down to dinner, and as he went upstairs to sleep in the afternoon, the same man constantly followed him with another. Future experiments in chemistry, however, were too dangerous, and Mr. Thrale insisted that we should do no more towards finding the Philosopher's Stone.

Mr. Johnson's amusements were thus reduced to the pleasures of conversation merely. And what wonder that he should have an avidity for the sole delight he was able to enjoy? No man conversed so well as he on every subject; no man so acutely discerned the reason of every fact, the motive of every action, the end of every design. He was indeed often pained by the ignorance or causeless wonder of those who knew less than himself, though he seldom drove them away with apparent scorn, unless he thought they added presumption to stupidity. And it was impossible not to laugh at the patience he showed, when a Welsh parson of mean abilities, though a good heart, struck with reverence at the sight of Dr. Johnson, whom he had heard of as the greatest man living, could not find any words to answer his inquiries concerning a motto round somebody's arms which adorned a tombstone in Ruabon churchyard. If I remember right the words were— *"Heb Dw, Heb Dym, Dw o' diggon."* And though of no very difficult construction, the gentleman seemed wholly confounded, and unable to explain them; till Mr. Johnson, having picked out the meaning by little and little, said to the man, *"Heb is a preposition, I believe, sir, is it not?"* My countryman recovering some spirits upon the sudden question, cried out, *"So I humbly presume, sir,"* very comically.

Stories of humour do not tell well in books; and what made impression on the friends who heard a jest will seldom much delight the distant acquaintance or sullen critic who reads it. The cork model of Paris is not more despicable as a resemblance of a great city, than this book, levior cortice, as a specimen of Johnson's character. Yet everybody naturally likes to gather little specimens of the rarities found in a great country; and could I carry home from Italy square pieces of all the curious marbles which are the just glory of this surprising part of the world, I could scarcely contrive, perhaps, to arrange them so meanly as not to gain some attention from the respect due to the places they once belonged to. Such a piece of motley Mosaic work wills these anecdotes inevitably make. But let the reader remember that he was promised nothing better, and so be as contented as he can.

An Irish trader at our house one day heard Dr. Johnson launch out into very great and greatly deserved praises of Mr. Edmund Burke. Delighted to find his countryman stood so high in the opinion of a man he had been told so much of, "*Sir,*" said he, "*give me leave to tell something of Mr. Burke now.*" We were all silent, and the honest Hibernian began to relate how Mr. Burke went to see the collieries in a distant province; and he would go down into the bowels of the earth (in a bag), and he would examine everything. "*He went in a bag, sir, and ventured his health and his life for knowledge: but he took care of his clothes, that they should not be spoiled, for he went down in a bag.*" "*Well, sir,*" says Mr. Johnson, good-humouredly, "*if our friend Mund should die in any of these hazardous exploits, you and I would write his life and panegyric together; and your chapter of it should be entitled thus: 'Burke in a Bag.'*"

He had always a very great personal regard and particular affection for Mr. Edmund Burke, as well as an esteem difficult for me to repeat, though for him only easy to express. And when at the end of the year 1774 the General Election called us all different ways, and broke up the delightful society in which we had spent some time at Beaconsfield, Dr. Johnson shook the hospitable master of the house kindly by the hand, and said, "*Farewell, my dear sir, and remember that I wish you all the success which ought to be wished you, which can possibly be wished you, indeed—by an honest man.*"

I must here take leave to observe, that in giving little memoirs of Mr. Johnson's behaviour and conversation, such as I saw and heard it, my book lies under manifest disadvantages, compared with theirs, who having seen him in various situations, and observed his conduct in numberless cases, are able to throw stronger and more brilliant lights upon his character. Virtues are like shrubs, which yield their sweets in different manners according to the circumstances which surround them; and while generosity of soul scatters its fragrance like the honeysuckle, and delights the senses of many occasional passengers, who feel the pleasure, and half wonder how the breeze has blown it from so far, the more sullen but not less valuable myrtle waits like fortitude to discover its excellence, till the hand arrives that will crush it, and force out that perfume whose durability well compensates the difficulty of production.

I saw Mr. Johnson in none but a tranquil, uniform state, passing the evening of his life among friends, who loved, honoured, and admired him. I saw none of the things he did, except such acts of charity as have been often mentioned in this book, and such writings as are universally known. What he said is all I can relate; and from what he said, those who think it worth while to read these anecdotes must be contented to gather his character. Mine is a mere candle-light picture of his latter days, where everything falls in dark shadow except the face, the index of the mind; but even that is seen unfavourably, and with a paleness beyond what nature gave it.

When I have told how many follies Dr. Johnson knew of others, I must not omit to mention with how much fidelity he would always have kept them concealed, could they of whom he knew the absurdities have been contented, in the common phrase, to keep their own counsel. But returning home one day from dining at the chaplain's table, he told me that Dr. Goldsmith had given a very comical and unnecessarily exact recital there of his own feelings when his play was hissed: telling the company how he went, indeed, to the Literary Club at night, and chatted gaily among his friends, as if nothing had happened amiss; that to impress them still more forcibly with an idea of his magnanimity, he even sung his favourite song about an old woman tossed in a blanket seventeen times as high as the moon; "*but all this while I was suffering horrid tortures,*" said he, "*and verily believe that if I had put a bit in my mouth it would have strangled me on the spot, I was so excessively ill. But I made more noise than usual to cover all that, and so they never perceived my not eating, nor I believe at all imaged to themselves the anguish of my heart; but when all were gone except Johnson here, I burst out a-crying, and even swore by — that I would never write again.*"

"*All which, Doctor,*" says Mr. Johnson, amazed at his odd frankness, "*I thought had been a secret between you and me; and I am sure I would not have said anything about it for the world. Now see,*" repeated he, when he told the story, "*what a figure a man makes who thus unaccountably chooses to be the frigid narrator of his own disgrace. Il volto sciolto, ed i pensieri stretti, was a proverb made on purpose for such mortals, to keep people, if possible, from being thus the heralds of their own shame; for what compassion can they gain by such silly narratives? No man should be expected to sympathise with the sorrows of vanity. If, then, you are mortified by any ill-usage, whether real or supposed, keep at least the account of such mortifications to yourself, and forbear to proclaim how meanly you are thought on by others, unless you desire to be meanly thought of by all.*"

The little history of another friend's superfluous ingenuity will contribute to introduce a similar remark. He had a daughter of about fourteen years old, as I remember, fat and clumsy; and though the father adored, and desired others to adore her, yet being aware, perhaps, that she was not what the French call paitrie des graces, and thinking, I suppose, that the old maxim of beginning to laugh at yourself first when you have anything ridiculous about you was a good one, he comically enough called his girl trundle when he spoke of her; and many who bore neither of them any ill-will felt disposed to laugh at the happiness of the appellation.

"*See, now,*" says Dr. Johnson, "*what haste people are in to be hooted. Nobody ever thought of this fellow nor of his daughter, could he but have been quiet himself, and forborne to call the eyes of the world on his dowdy and her deformity. But it teaches one to see at least that if nobody else will nickname one's children, the parents will e'en do it themselves."*

All this held true in matters to Mr. Johnson of more serious consequence. When Sir Joshua Reynolds had painted his portrait looking into the slit of his pen, and holding it almost close to his eye, as was his general custom, he felt displeased, and told me *"he would not be known by posterity for his defects only, let Sir Joshua do his worst."* I said in reply that Reynolds had no such difficulties about himself, and that he might observe the picture which hung up in the room where we were talking represented Sir Joshua holding his ear in his hand to catch the sound. *"He may paint himself as deaf if he chooses,"* replied Johnson, *"but I will not be blinking Sam."*

It is chiefly for the sake of evincing the regularity and steadiness of Mr. Johnson's mind that I have given these trifling memoirs, to show that his soul was not different from that of another person, but, as it was, greater; and to give those who did not know him a just idea of his acquiescence in what we call vulgar prejudices, and of his extreme distance from those notions which the world has agreed, I know not very well why, to call romantic. It is indeed observable in his preface to Shakespeare, that while other critics expatiate on the creative powers and vivid imagination of that matchless poet, Dr. Johnson commends him for giving so just a representation of human manners, *"that from his scenes a hermit might estimate the value of society, and a confessor predict the progress of the passions."* I have not the book with me here, but am pretty sure that such is his expression.

The general and constant advice he gave, too, when consulted about the choice of a wife, a profession, or whatever influences a man's particular and immediate happiness, was always to reject no positive good from fears of its contrary consequences. *"Do not,"* said he, *"forbear to marry a beautiful woman if you can find such, out of a fancy that she will be less constant than an ugly one; or condemn yourself to the society of coarseness and vulgarity for fear of the expenses or other dangers of elegance and personal charms, which have been always acknowledged as a positive good, and for the want of which there should be always given some weighty compensation. I have, however,"* continued Mr. Johnson, *"seen some prudent fellows who forbore to connect themselves with beauty lest coquetry should be near, and with wit or birth lest insolence should lurk behind them, till they have been forced by their discretion to linger life away in tasteless stupidity, and choose to count the moments by remembrance of pain instead of enjoyment of pleasure."*

When professions were talked of, *"Scorn,"* said Mr. Johnson, *"to put your behaviour under the dominion of canters; never think it clever to call physic a mean study, or law a dry one; or ask a baby of seven years old which way his genius leads him, when we all know that a boy of seven years old has no genius for anything except a pegtop and an apple-pie; but fix on some business where much money may be got, and little virtue risked: follow that business steadily, and do not live as Roger Ascham says the wits do, 'men know not how; and at last die obscurely, men mark not where.'"*

Dr. Johnson had indeed a veneration for the voice of mankind beyond what most people will own; and as he liberally confessed that all his own disappointments proceeded from himself, he hated to hear others complain of general injustice. I remember when lamentation was made of the neglect showed to Jeremiah Markland, a great philologist, as some one ventured to call him. *"He is a scholar, undoubtedly, sir,"* replied Dr. Johnson, *"but remember that he would run from the world, and that it is not the world's business to run after him. I hate a fellow whom pride, or cowardice, or laziness drives into a corner, and does nothing when he is there but sit and growl; let him come out as I do, and bark. The world,"* added he, *"is chiefly unjust and ungenerous in this, that all are ready to encourage a man who once talks of leaving it, and few things do really provoke me more than to hear people prate of retirement, when they have neither skill to discern their own motives, or penetration to estimate the consequences. But while a fellow is active to gain either power or wealth,"* continued he, *"everybody produces some hindrance to his advancement, some sage remark, or some unfavourable prediction; but let him once say slightly, I have had enough of this troublesome, bustling world, 'tis time to leave it now: 'Ah, dear sir!' cries the first old acquaintance he meets, 'I am glad to find you in this happy disposition: yes, dear friend! DO retire and think of nothing but your own ease. There's Mr. William will find it a pleasure to settle all your accounts and relieve you from the fatigue; Miss Dolly makes the charmingest chicken-broth in the world, and the cheesecakes we ate of hers once, how good they were. I will be coming every two or three days myself to chat with you in a quiet way; so snug! and tell you how matters go upon 'Change, or in the House, or according to the blockhead's first pursuits, whether lucrative or politic, which thus he leaves; and lays himself down a voluntary prey to his own sensuality and sloth, while the ambition and avarice of the nephews and nieces, with their rascally adherents and coadjutors, reap the advantage, while they fatten their fool.'"*

As the votaries of retirement had little of Mr. Johnson's applause, unless that he knew that the motives were merely devotional, and unless he was convinced that their rituals were accompanied by a mortified state of the body, the sole proof of their sincerity which he would admit, as a compensation for such fatigue as a worldly life of care and activity requires; so of the various states and conditions of humanity, he despised none more, I think, than the man who marries for a maintenance. And of a friend who made his alliance on no higher principles, he said once, "*Now has that fellow (it was a nobleman of whom we were speaking) at length obtained a certainty of three meals a day, and for that certainty, like his brother dog in the fable, he will get his neck galled for life with a collar.*"

That poverty was an evil to be avoided by all honest means, however, no man was more ready to avow: concealed poverty particularly, which he said was the general corrosive that destroyed the peace of almost every family; to which no evening perhaps ever returned without some new project for hiding the sorrows and dangers of the next day. "*Want of money,*" says Dr. Johnson, "*is sometimes concealed under pretended avarice, and sly hints of aversion to part with it; sometimes under stormy anger, and affectation of boundless rage, but oftener still under a show of thoughtless extravagance and gay neglect, while to a penetrating eye none of these wretched veils suffice to keep the cruel truth from being seen.*

Poverty is hic et ubique," says he, "*and if you do shut the jade out of the door, she will always contrive in some manner to poke her pale, lean face in at the window."*

I have mentioned before that old age had very little of Mr. Johnson's reverence. *"A man commonly grew wickeder as he grew older,"* he said, *"at least he but changed the vices of youth; headstrong passion and wild temerity, for treacherous caution, and desire to circumvent. I am always,"* said he, *"on the young people's side, when there is a dispute between them and the old ones, for you have at least a chance for virtue till age has withered its very root."* While we were talking, my mother's spaniel, whom he never loved, stole our toast and butter; *"Fie, Belle!"* said I, *"you used to be upon honour."*

"Yes, madam," replies Johnson, *"but Belle grws old."* His reason for hating the dog was, *"because she was a professed favourite,"* he said, *"and because her lady ordered her from time to time to be washed and combed, a foolish trick,"* said he, *"and an assumption of superiority that every one's nature revolts at; so because one must not wish ill to the lady in such cases,"* continued he, *"one curses the cur."* The truth is, Belle was not well behaved, and being a large spaniel, was troublesome enough at dinner with frequent solicitations to be fed. *"This animal,"* said Dr. Johnson one day, *"would have been of extraordinary merit and value in the state of Lycurgus; for she condemns one to the exertion of perpetual vigilance."*

He had, indeed, that strong aversion felt by all the lower ranks of people towards four-footed companions very completely, notwithstanding he had for many years a cat which he called Hodge, that kept always in his room at Fleet Street; but so exact was he not to offend the human species by superfluous attention to brutes, that when the creature was grown sick and old, and could eat nothing but oysters, Mr. Johnson always went out himself to buy Hodge's dinner, that Francis the black's delicacy might not be hurt, at seeing himself employed for the convenience of a quadruped. No one was, indeed, so attentive not to offend in all such sort of things as Dr. Johnson; nor so careful to maintain the ceremonies of life: and though he told Mr. Thrale once that he had never sought to please till past thirty years old, considering the matter as hopeless, he had been always studious not to make enemies by apparent preference of himself.

It happened very comically that the moment this curious conversation passed, of which I was a silent auditress, was in the coach, in some distant province, either Shropshire or Derbyshire, I believe; and as soon as it was over, Mr. Johnson took out of his pocket a little book and read, while a gentleman of no small distinction for his birth and elegance suddenly rode up to the carriage, and paying us all his proper compliments, was desirous not to neglect Dr. Johnson; but observing that he did not see him, tapped him gently on the shoulder. "*'Tis Mr. Ch-lm—ley,*" says my husband. "*Well, sir! and what if it is Mr. Ch-lm—ley!*" says the other, sternly, just lifting his eyes a moment from his book, and returning to it again with renewed avidity.

He had sometimes fits of reading very violent; and when he was in earnest about getting through some particular pages, for I have heard him say he never read but one book, which he did not consider as obligatory, through in his whole life (and "Lady Mary Wortley's Letters," was the book); he would be quite lost to the company, and withdraw all his attention to what he was reading, without the smallest knowledge or care about the noise made round him. His deafness made such conduct less odd and less difficult to him than it would have been to another man: but his advising others to take the same method, and pull a little book out when they were not entertained with what was going forward in society, seemed more likely to advance the growth of science than of polished manners, for which he always pretended extreme veneration. Mr. Johnson, indeed, always measured other people's notions of everything by his own, and nothing could persuade him to believe that the books which he disliked were agreeable to thousands, or that air and exercise which he despised were beneficial to the health of other mortals.

When poor Smart, so well known for his wit and misfortunes, was first obliged to be put in private lodgings, a common friend of both lamented in tender terms the necessity which had torn so pleasing a companion from their acquaintance. "*A madman must be confined, sir,*" replies Dr. Johnson. "*But,*" says the other, "*I am now apprehensive for his general health, he will lose the benefit of exercise.*" "*Exercise!*" returns the Doctor, "*I never heard that he used any: he might, for aught I know, walk to the alehouse; but I believe he was always carried home again.*"

It was, however, unlucky for those who delighted to echo Johnson's sentiments, that he would not endure from them to-day what perhaps he had yesterday, by his own manner of treating the subject, made them fond of repeating; and I fancy Mr. B— — ['Mr. B— —' has since been identified as being James Boswell] has not forgotten that though his friend one evening in a gay humour talked in praise of wine as one of the blessings permitted by heaven, when used with moderation, to lighten the load of life, and give men strength to endure it; yet, when in consequence of such talk he thought fit to make a Bacchanalian discourse in its favour, Mr. Johnson contradicted him somewhat roughly, as I remember; and when, to assure himself of conquest, he added these words: "*You must allow me, sir, at least that it produces truth; in vino veritas, you know, sir.*" "*That,*" replied Mr. Johnson, "*would be useless to a man who knew he was not a liar when he was sobre.*"

When one talks of giving and taking the lie familiarly, it is impossible to forbear recollecting the transactions between the editor of "Ossian," and the author of the "Journey to the Hebrides." It was most observable to me, however, that Mr. Johnson never bore his antagonist the slightest degree of ill-will. He always kept those quarrels which belonged to him as a writer separate from those which he had to do with as a man; but I never did hear him say in private one malicious word of a public enemy; and of Mr. Macpherson I once heard him speak respectfully, though his reply to the friend who asked him if any man living could have written such a book, is well known, and has been often repeated—"*Yes, sir, many men, many women, and many children.*" I inquired of him myself if this story was authentic, and he said it was.

I made the same inquiry concerning his account of the state of literature in Scotland, which was repeated up and down at one time by everybody—"*How knowledge was divided among the Scots, like bread in a besieged town, to every man a mouthful, to no man a bellyful.*" This story he likewise acknowledged, and said, besides, "*that some officious friend had carried it to Lord Bute, who only answered, 'Well, well! never mind what he says, he will have the pension all one.'*" Another famous reply to a Scotsman who commended the beauty and dignity of Glasgow, till Mr. Johnson stopped him by observing, "*that he probably had never yet seen Brentford,*" was one of the jokes he owned; and said himself "*that when a gentleman of that country once mentioned the lovely prospects common in his nation, he could not help telling him that the view of the London road was the prospect in which every Scotsman most naturally and most rationally delighted.*"

Mrs. Brooke received an answer not unlike this, when expatiating on the accumulation of sublime and beautiful objects, which form the fine prospect up the River St. Lawrence, in North America. "*Come, madam,*" says Dr. Johnson, "*confess that nothing ever equalled your pleasure in seeing that sight reversed; and finding yourself looking at the happy prospect down the River St. Lawrence.*" The truth is, he hated to hear about prospects and views, and laying out ground and taste in gardening. "*That was the best garden,*" he said, "*which produced most roots and fruits; and that water was most to be prized which contained most fish.*"

He used to laugh at Shenstone most unmercifully for not caring whether there was anything good to eat in the streams he was so fond of, "*as if,*" says Johnson, "*one could fill one's belly with hearing soft murmurs, or looking at rough cascades!*" He loved the sight of fine forest trees, however, and detested Brighthelmstone Downs, "*because it was a country so truly desolate,*" he said, "*that if one had a mind to hang one's self for desperation at being obliged to live there, it would be difficult to find a tree on which to fasten the rope.*" Walking in a wood when it rained was, I think, the only rural image he pleased his fancy with; "*for,*" says he, "*after one has gathered the apples in an orchard, one wishes them well baked, and removed to a London eating-house for enjoyment.*" With such notions, who can wonder he passed his time uncomfortably enough with us, who he often complained of for living so much in the country, "*feeding the chickens,*" as he said I did, "*till I starved my own understanding. Get, however,*" said he, "*a book about gardening, and study it hard, since you will pass your life with birds and flowers, and learn to raise the largest turnips, and to breed the biggest fowls.*"

It was vain to assure him that the goodness of such dishes did not depend upon their size. He laughed at the people who covered their canals with foreign fowls, "*when,*" says he, "*our own geese and ganders are twice as large. If we fetched better animals from distant nations, there might be some sense in the preference; but to get cows from Alderney, or water-fowl from China, only to see nature degenerating round one, is a poor ambition indeed.*" Nor was Mr. Johnson more merciful with regard to the amusements people are contented to call such.

"*You hunt in the morning,*" says he, "*and crowd to the public rooms at night, and call it diversion, when your heart knows it is perishing with poverty of pleasures, and your wits get blunted for want of some other mind to sharpen them upon. There is in this world no real delight (excepting those of sensuality), but exchange of ideas in conversation; and whoever has once experienced the full flow of London talk, when he retires to country friendships, and rural sports, must either be contented to turn baby again and play with the rattle, or he will pine away like a great fish in a little pond, and die for want of his usual food.*"

"*Books without the knowledge of life are useless,*" I have heard him say; "*for what should books teach but the art of living? To study manners, however, only in coffee-houses, is more than equally imperfect; the minds of men who acquire no solid learning, and only exist on the daily forage that they pick up by running about, and snatching what drops from their neighbours as ignorant as themselves, will never ferment into any knowledge valuable or durable; but like the light wines we drink in hot countries, please for the moment, though incapable of keeping. In the study of mankind much will be found to swim as froth, and much must sink as feculence, before the wine can have its effect, and become that noblest liquor which rejoices the heart, and gives vigour to the imagination.*"

I am well aware that I do not and cannot give each

expression of Dr. Johnson with all its force or all its neatness; but I have done my best to record such of his maxims, and repeat such of his sentiments, as may give to those who know him not a just idea of his character and manner of thinking. To endeavour at adorning, or adding, or softening, or meliorating such anecdotes, by any tricks my inexperienced pen could play, would be weakness indeed; worse than the Frenchman who presides over the porcelain manufactory at Seve, to whom, when some Greek vases were given him as models, he lamented la tristesse de telles formes; and endeavoured to assist them by clusters of flowers, while flying Cupids served for the handles of urns originally intended to contain the ashes of the dead. The misery is, that I can recollect so few anecdotes, and that I have recorded no more axioms of a man whose every word merited attention, and whose every sentiment did honour to human nature.

Remote from affectation as from error or falsehood, the comfort a reader has in looking over these papers is the certainty that these were really the opinions of Johnson, which are related as such. Fear of what others may think is the great cause of affectation; and he was not likely to disguise his notions out of cowardice. He hated disguise, and nobody penetrated it so readily. I showed him a letter written to a common friend, who was at some loss for the explanation of it. "*Whoever wrote it,*" says our doctor, "*could, if he chose it, make himself understood; but 'tis the letter of an embarrassed man sir;*" and so the event proved it to be.

Mysteriousness in trifles offended him on every side. "*It commonly ended in guilt,*" he said; "*for those who begin by concealment of innocent things will soon have something to hide which they dare not bring to light.*" He therefore encouraged an openness of conduct, in women particularly, "*who,*" he observed, "*were often led away when children, by their delight and power of surprising.*" He recommended, on something like the same principle, that when one person meant to serve another, he should not go about it slily, or as we say, underhand, out of a false idea of delicacy, to surprise one's friend with an unexpected favour, "*which, ten to one,*" says he, "*fails to oblige your acquaintance, who had some reasons against such a mode of obligation, which you might have known but for that superfluous cunning which you think an elegance. Oh! never be seduced by such silly pretences,"* continued he; *"if a wench wants a good gown, do not give her a fine smelling-bottle, because that is more delicate: as I once knew a lady lend the key of her library to a poor scribbling dependant, as if she took the woman for an ostrich that could digest iron."*

He said, indeed, *"that women were very difficult to be taught the proper manner of conferring pecuniary favours; that they always gave too much money or too little; for that they had an idea of delicacy accompanying their gifts, so that they generally rendered them either useless or ridiculous."*

He did, indeed, say very contemptuous things of our sex, but was exceedingly angry when I told Miss Reynolds that he said *"It was well managed of some one to leave his affairs in the hands of his wife, because, in matters of business,"* said he, *"no woman stops at integrity."* This was, I think, the only sentence I ever observed him solicitous to explain away after he had uttered it. He was not at all displeased at the recollection of a sarcasm thrown on a whole profession at once; when a gentleman leaving the company, somebody who sat next Dr. Johnson asked him, who he was? *"I cannot exactly tell you, sir,"* replied he, *"and I would be loth to speak ill of any person who I do not know deserves it, but I am afraid he is an attorney."*

He did not, however, encourage general satire, and for the most part professed himself to feel directly contrary to Dr. Swift; *"who,"* says he, *"hates the world, though he loves John and Robert, and certain individuals."* Johnson said always, *"that the world was well constructed, but that the particular people disgraced the elegance and beauty of the general fabric."* In the same manner I was relating once to him how Dr. Collier observed that the love one bore to children was from the anticipation one's mind made while one contemplated them. *"We hope,"* says he, *"that they will sometime make wise men or amiable women; and we suffer 'em to take up our affection beforehand. One cannot love lumps of flesh, and little infants are nothing more."* *"On the contrary,"* says Johnson, *"one can scarcely help wishing, while one fondles a baby, that it may never live to become a man; for it is so probable that when he becomes a man, he should be sure to end in a scoundrel."*

Girls were less displeasing to him; *"for as their temptations were fewer,"* he said, *"their virtue in this life, and happiness in the next, were less improbable; and he loved,"* he said, *"to see a knot of little misses dearly."* Needlework had a strenuous approver in Dr. Johnson, who said *"that one of the great felicities of female life was the general consent of the world that they might amuse themselves with petty occupations, which contributed to the lengthening their lives, and preserving their minds in a state of sanity." "A man cannot hem a pocket-handkerchief,"* said a lady of quality to him one day, *"and so he runs mad, and torments his family and friends."* The expression struck him exceedingly, and when one acquaintance grew troublesome, and another unhealthy, he used to quote Lady Frances's observation, *"That a man cannot hem a pocket-handkerchief."*

The nice people found no mercy from Mr. Johnson; such, I mean, as can only dine at four o'clock, who cannot bear to be waked at an unusual hour, or miss a stated meal without inconvenience. He had no such prejudices himself, and with difficulty forgave them in another. *"Delicacy does not surely consist,"* says he, *"in impossibility to be pleased, and that is false dignity indeed which is content to depend upon others."* The saying of the old philosopher who observes, *"That he who wants least is most like the gods, who want nothing,"* was a favourite sentence with Dr. Johnson, who on his own part required less attendance, sick or well, than ever I saw any human creature.

Conversation was all he required to make him happy; and when he would have tea made at two o'clock in the morning, it was only that there might be a certainty of detaining his companions round him. On that principle it was that he preferred winter to summer, when the heat of the weather gave people an excuse to stroll about and walk for pleasure in the shade, while he wished to sit still on a chair and chat day after day, till somebody proposed a drive in the coach, and that was the most delicious moment of his life. *"But the carriage must stop some time,"* he said, *"and the people would come home at last,"* so his pleasure was of short duration. I asked him why he doated on a coach so? and received for answer, *"That in the first place the company were shut in with him there, and could not escape, as out of a room. In the next place, he heard all that was said in a carriage, where it was my turn to be deaf,"* and very impatient was he at my occasional difficulty of hearing. On this account he wished to travel all over the world, for the very act of going forward was delightful to him, and he gave himself no concern about accidents, which he said never happened. Nor did the running away of the horses on the edge of a precipice between Vernon and St. Denis, in France, convince him to the contrary, *"for nothing came of it,"* he said, *"except that Mr. Thrale leaped out of the carriage into a chalk-pit, and then came up again looking as white!"* When the truth was, all their lives were saved by the greatest Providence ever exerted in favour of three human creatures; and the part Mr. Thrale took from desperation was the likeliest thing in the world to produce broken limbs and death.

Fear was indeed a sensation to which Mr. Johnson was an utter stranger, excepting when some sudden apprehensions seized him that he was going to die, and even then he kept all his wits about him to express the most humble and pathetic petitions to the Almighty. And when the first paralytic stroke took his speech from him, he instantly set about composing a prayer in Latin, at once to deprecate God's mercy, to satisfy himself that his mental powers remained unimpaired, and to keep them in exercise, that they might not perish by permitted stagnation. This was after we parted; but he wrote me an account of it, and I intend to publish that letter, with many more. When one day he had at my house taken tincture of antimony instead of emetic wine, for a vomit, he was himself the person to direct us what to do for him, and managed with as much coolness and deliberation as if he had been prescribing for an indifferent person. Though on another occasion, when he had lamented in the most piercing terms his approaching dissolution, and conjured me solemnly to tell him what I thought, while Sir Richard Jebb was perpetually on the road to Streatham, and Mr. Johnson seemed to think himself neglected if the physician left him for an hour only, I made him a steady, but as I thought a very gentle harangue, in which I confirmed all that the doctor had been saying; how no present danger could be expected, but that his age and continued ill-health must naturally accelerate the arrival of that hour which can be escaped by none. "*And this,*" says Johnson, rising in great anger, "*is the voice of female friendship, I suppose, when the hand of the hangman would be softer.*"

Another day, when he was ill, and exceedingly low-spirited, and persuaded that death was not far distant, I appeared before him in a dark-coloured gown, which his bad sight, and worse apprehensions, made him mistake for an iron-grey. "*Why do you delight,*" said he, "*thus to thicken the gloom of misery that surrounds me? Is not here sufficient accumulation of horror without anticipated mourning?*" "*This is not mourning, sir,*" said I, drawing the curtain, that the light might fall upon the silk, and show it was a purple mixed with green. "*Well, well,*" replied he, changing his voice, "*you little creatures should never wear those sort of clothes, however; they are unsuitable in every way. What! have not all insects gay colours?*" I relate these instances chiefly to show that the fears of death itself could not suppress his wit, his sagacity, or his temptation to sudden resentment.

Mr. Johnson did not like that his friends should bring their manuscripts for him to read, and he liked still less to read them when they were brought. Sometimes, however, when he could not refuse, he would take the play or poem, or whatever it was, and give the people his opinion from some one page he had peeped into.

A gentleman carried him his tragedy, which, because he loved the author, Johnson took, and it lay about our rooms some time. "*What answer did you give your friend, sir?*" said I, after the book had been called for. "I told him," replied he, "*that there was too much tig and tirry in it!*" Seeing me laugh most violently, "*Why, what would'st have, child?*" said he. "*I looked at the dramatis, and there was TIGranes and TIRIdates, or Teribazus, or such stuff. A man can tell but what he knows, and I never got any farther than the first page. Alas, madam!*" continued he, "*how few books are there of which one ever can possibly arrive at the last page. Was there ever yet anything written by mere man that was wished longer by its readers, excepting 'Don Quixote,' 'Robinson Crusoe,' and the 'Pilgrim's Progress?'"*

After Homer's Iliad, Mr. Johnson confessed that the work of Cervantes was the greatest in the world, speaking of it I mean as a book of entertainment. And when we consider that every other author's admirers are confined to his countrymen, and perhaps to the literary classes among them, while "*Don Quixote*" is a sort of common property, an universal classic, equally tasted by the court and the cottage, equally applauded in France and England as in Spain, quoted by every servant, the amusement of every age from infancy to decrepitude; the first book you see on every shelf, in every shop, where books are sold, through all the states of Italy; who can refuse his consent to an avowal of the superiority of Cervantes to all other modern writers? Shakespeare himself has, till lately, been worshipped only at home, though his plays are now the favourite amusements of Vienna; and when I was at Padua some months ago, Romeo and Juliet was acted there under the name of Tragedia Veronese; while engravers and translators live by the hero of La Mancha in every nation, and the sides of miserable inns all over England and France, and I have heard Germany too, are adorned with the exploits of Don Quixote. May his celebrity procure my pardon for a digression in praise of a writer who, through four volumes of the most exquisite pleasantry and genuine humour, has never been seduced to overstep the limits of propriety, has never called in the wretched auxiliaries of obscenity or profaneness; who trusts to nature and sentiment alone, and never misses of that applause which Voltaire and Sterne labour to produce, while honest merriment bestows her unfading crown upon Cervantes.

Dr. Johnson was a great reader of French literature, and delighted exceedingly in Boileau's works. Moliere, I think, he had hardly sufficient taste of, and he used to condemn me for preferring La Bruyere to the Duc de Rochefoucault, who, he said, was the only gentleman writer who wrote like a professed author. The asperity of his harsh sentences, each of them a sentence of condemnation, used to disgust me, however;

though it must be owned that, among the necessaries of human life, a rasp is reckoned one as well as a razor. Mr. Johnson did not like any one who said they were happy, or who said any one else was so. "*It is all cant,*" he would cry; "*the dog knows he is miserable all the time.*"

A friend whom he loved exceedingly, told him on some occasion, notwithstanding, that his wife's sister was really happy, and called upon the lady to confirm his assertion, which she did somewhat roundly, as we say, and with an accent and manner capable of offending Mr. Johnson, if her position had not been sufficient, without anything more, to put him in very ill-humour. "*If your sister-in-law is really the contented being she professes herself, sir,*" said he, "*her life gives the lie to every research of humanity; for she is happy without health, without beauty, without money, and without understanding.*" This story he told me himself, and when I expressed something of the horror I felt, "*The same stupidity,*" said he, "*which prompted her to extol felicity she never felt, hindered her from feeling what shocks you on repetition. I tell you, the woman is ugly and sickly and foolish and poor; and would it not make a man hang himself to hear such a creature say it was happy? "The life of a sailor was also a continual scene of danger and exertion,*" he said; "*and the manner in which time was spent shipboard would make all who saw a cabin envy a gaol.*"

The roughness of the language used on board a man-of-war, where he passed a week on a visit to Captain Knight, disgusted him terribly. He asked an officer what some place was called, and received for answer, that it was where the loplolly man kept his loplolly, a reply he considered, not unjustly, as disrespectful, gross, and ignorant; for though in the course of these memoirs I have been led to mention Dr. Johnson's tenderness towards poor people, I do not wish to mislead my readers, and make them think he had any delight in mean manners or coarse expressions. Even dress itself, when it resembled that of the vulgar, offended him exceedingly; and when he had condemned me many times for not adorning my children with more show than I thought useful or elegant, I presented a little girl to him who came o'visiting one evening covered with shining ornaments, to see if he would approve of the appearance she made. When they were gone home, *"Well, sir,"* said I, *"how did you like little miss? I hope she was fine enough." "It was the finery of a beggar,"* said he, *"and you know it was; she looked like a native of Cow Lane dressed up to be carried to Bartholomew Fair."*

His reprimand to another lady for crossing her little child's handkerchief before, and by that operation dragging down its head oddly and unintentionally, was on the same principle. *"It is the beggar's fear of cold,"* said he, *"that prevails over such parents, and so they pull the poor thing's head down, and give it the look of a baby that plays about Westminster Bridge, while the mother sits shivering in a niche."* I commended a young lady for her beauty and pretty behaviour one day, however, to whom I thought no objection could have been made. *"I saw her,"* says Dr. Johnson, *"take a pair of scissors in her left hand, though; and for all her father is now become a nobleman, and as you say, excessively rich, I should, were I a youth of quality ten years hence, hesitate between a girl so neglected, and a negro."* It was indeed astonishing how he could remark such minutenesses with a sight so miserably imperfect; but no accidental position of a ribband escaped him, so nice was his observation, and so rigorous his demands of propriety.

When I went with him to Lichfield and came downstairs to breakfast at the inn, my dress did not please him, and he made me alter it entirely before he would stir a step with us about the town, saying most satirical things concerning the appearance I made in a riding-habit, and adding, *"'Tis very strange that such eyes as yours cannot discern propriety of dress. If I had a sight only half as good, I think I should see to the centre."* My compliances, however, were of little worth. What really surprised me was the victory he gained over a lady little accustomed to contradiction, who had dressed herself for church at Streatham one Sunday morning in a manner he did not approve, and to whom he said such sharp and pungent things concerning her hat, her gown, etc., that she hastened to change them, and returning quite another figure received his applause, and thanked him for his reproofs, much to the amazement of her husband, who could scarcely believe his own ears.

Another lady, whose accomplishments he never denied, came to our house one day covered with diamonds, feathers, etc., and he did not seem inclined to chat with her as usual. I asked him why, when the company was gone. "*Why, her head looked so like that of a woman who shows puppets,*" said he, "*and her voice so confirmed the fancy, that I could not bear her today. When she wears a large cap I can talk to her.*" When the ladies wore lace trimmings to their clothes he expressed his contempt of the reigning fashion in these terms: "*A Brussels trimming is like bread sauce,*" said he, "*it takes away the glow of colour from the gown, and gives you nothing instead of it. But sauce was invented to heighten the flavour of our food, and trimming is an ornament to the manteau or it is nothing. Learn,*" said he, "*that there is propriety or impropriety in everything how slight soever, and get at the general principles of dress and of behaviour; if you then transgress them you will at least know that they are not observed.*"

All these exactnesses in a man who was nothing less than exact himself made him extremely impracticable as an inmate, though most instructive as companion and useful as a friend. Mr. Thrale, too, could sometimes overrule his rigidity by saying coldly, "*There, there, now we have had enough for one lecture, Dr. Johnson. We will not be upon education any more till after dinner, if you please,*" or some such speech. But when there was nobody to restrain his dislikes it was extremely difficult to find anybody with whom he could converse without living always on the verge of a quarrel, or of something too like a quarrel to be pleasing.

I came into the room, for example, one evening where he and a gentleman, whose abilities we all respect exceedingly, were sitting. A lady who walked in two minutes before me had blown 'em both into a flame by whispering something to Mr. S—d, which he endeavoured to explain away so as not to affront the Doctor, whose suspicions were all alive. "*And have a care, sir,*" said he, just as I came in, "*the Old Lion will not bear to be tickled.*" The other was pale with rage, the lady wept at the confusion she had caused, and I could only say with Lady

Macbeth— *"Soh! you've displac'd the mirth, broke the good meeting With most admir'd disorder."*

Such accidents, however, occurred too often, and I was forced to take advantage of my lost lawsuit and plead inability of purse to remain longer in London or its vicinage. I had been crossed in my intentions of going abroad, and found it convenient, for every reason of health, peace, and pecuniary circumstances, to retire to Bath, where I knew Mr. Johnson would not follow me, and where I could for that reason command some little portion of time for my own use, a thing impossible while I remained at Streatham or at London, as my hours, carriage, and servants had long been at his command, who would not rise in the morning till twelve o'clock, perhaps, and oblige me to make breakfast for him till the bell rung for dinner, though much displeased if the toilet was neglected, and though much of the time we passed together was spent in blaming or deriding, very justly, my neglect of economy and waste of that money which might make many families happy.

The original reason of our connection, his particularly disordered health and spirits, had been long at an end, and he had no other ailments than old age and general infirmity, which every professor of medicine was ardently zealous and generally attentive to palliate, and to contribute all in their power for the prolongation of a life so valuable.

Veneration for his virtue, reverence for his talents, delight in his conversation, and habitual endurance of a yoke my husband first put upon me, and of which he contentedly bore his share for sixteen or seventeen years, made me go on so long with Mr. Johnson; but the perpetual confinement I will own to have been terrifying in the first years of our friendship and irksome in the last. Nor could I pretend to support it without help, when my coadjutor was no more. To the assistance we gave him, the shelter our house afforded to his uneasy fancies, and to the pains we took to soothe or repress them, the world perhaps is indebted for the three political pamphlets, the new edition and correction of his "Dictionary," and for the "Poets' Lives," which he would scarce have lived,

I think, and kept his faculties entire to have written, had not incessant care been exerted at the time of his first coming to be our constant guest in the country, and several times after that, when he found himself particularly oppressed with diseases incident to the most vivid and fervent imaginations. I shall for ever consider it as the greatest honour which could be conferred on any one to have been the confidential friend of Dr. Johnson's health, and to have in some measure, with Mr. Thrale's assistance, saved from distress at least, if not worse, a mind great beyond the comprehension of common mortals, and good beyond all hope of imitation from perishable beings.

Bibliography

The Works of Samuel Johnson, LL.D. Together with his Life, and Notes on his Lives of the Poets. By Hawkins, Sir John. II vols. 1787. Vols. XII and XIII (Debates [ed. Chalmers, George], printed for John Stockdale; *see* sec. B, *post*). 1787. Vol. XIV (Miscellaneous Pieces, printed for Stockdale.) 1788. Vol. XV (Miscellaneous Pieces, ed. Gleig, George). 1789.

——A new edition in twelve volumes. With an Essay on his Life and Genius. By Murphy, Arthur. 1792, 1796, 1801, etc.

——[edited by Chalmers, A.] 12 vols. 1806, etc.

——Works, 9 vols.; Debates, 2 vols. (Oxford English Classics.) Oxford, 1825.

——ed. Lynam, R. 6 vols. 1825.

——2 vols. 1850.

——16 vols. New York, 1903.

Miscellaneous and Fugitive Pieces. 3 vols. Ed. Davies, T. Vols. I and II n. d. [1774; ascribed by Boswell to 1773]. Vol. III. 1774.

The first volume consists wholly of pieces by Johnson. In the second by far the greater number are his. A few others are in the third.

The Poetical Works of Samuel Johnson, LL.D. Now first collected in one volume [ed. Kearsley, George]. 1785. New edn., considerably enlarged. 1789.

——Complete in one volume. A new edition. London and Gainsbrough. 1785.

——Dublin, 1785.

——with life by Blagdon, F. W. 1808.

——ed. Gilfillan, G. Edinburgh, 1855.

——ed. Ward, T. Methuen. [1905.]

——ed. Smith, D. Nichol. Oxford. (*In preparation.*)

The Works of Richard Savage, Esq.... with an Account of ... the Author, by Samuel Johnson, LL.D. Vol. I. 1775. Another edn. 1777. Rptd. in Works of the English Poets, 1781.

An Account of the Life of John Philip Barretier, who was Master of five Languages at the Age of nine Years. 1744. Rptd. from The Gentleman's Magazine.

Miscellaneous Observations on the Tragedy of Macbeth: With Remarks on Sir T. H[anmer]'s Edition of Shakespear. To which is affix'd, Proposals for a New Edition of Shakespear, with a Specimen. 1745.

Three Letters to The Idler. [1761.]

Mr. Johnson's Preface To his Edition of Shakespear's Plays. Tonson, etc. 1765.

[The preface to the edition issued separately, with a special title-page.]

Variorum editions of Shakespeare.

Eighteenth Century Essays on Shakespeare. Ed. Smith, D. Nichol. 1903.

Johnson on Shakespeare. Essays and Notes with an introduction by Walter Raleigh. 1908.

The False Alarm. 1770. 2nd edn. 1770.

Thoughts on the Late Transactions respecting Falkland's Islands. 1771. 2nd edn. 1771.

[Two issues of the 1st edn., with different readings on p. 68: *see* Boswell, ed. Hill, G. B., vol. II, p. 135.]

The Patriot. Addressed to the Electors of Great Britain. 1774.

Taxation no Tyranny; An Answer to the Resolutions and Address of the American Congress. 1775. 4th edn. 1775.

Political Tracts. Containing: The False Alarm. Falkland's Islands. The Patriot; and, Taxation no Tyranny. 1776.

[All Johnson's political pamphlets were anonymous.]

A Journey to the Western Islands of Scotland. 1775. Many other edns.: 1785, 1791, etc. French transl. in Nouveau Recueil de Voyages au nord de l'Europe, etc. Geneva, 1785.

The Works of the English Poets. With Prefaces,

Biographical and Critical. By Samuel Johnson. 68 vols. 1779–81. Enlarged edn. 75 vols. 1790. Ed. Chalmers, A. 21 vols. 1810

Johnson's Prefaces are in 10 vols. 1779 (I–IV)–1781 (V–X). [Each Preface is paged separately.] Revised and reissued, in different order, as—

The Six Chief Lives, with Macaulay's Life of Johnson. Ed., with a preface, by Arnold, Matthew. 1878.

The Patriot, A Tragedy. From a Manuscript of the Late Dr. Samuel Johnson, Corrected by Himself. 1785.

[By Joseph Simpson: *see* Boswell, ed. Hill, G. B., vol. III, p. 28.]
